9

Steve Pemberton is the award-winning actor, writer and co-creator of *Inside No. 9*, *The League of Gentlemen* and *Psychoville*. As an actor, Pemberton's recent credits include *Killing Eve*, *Britannia*, *Good Omens*, *The Interrogation of Tony Martin* and *Happy Valley*, and upcoming projects include feature film *Better Man* and mini-series *Missing You*. He also adapted and starred in *Mapp and Lucia*, the widely acclaimed BBC mini-series based on the novels of E. F. Benson. Other writing credits include *Les Dawson's Parisienne Adventure* for Sky, and episodes of *Whitechapel* and *Benidorm* for ITV.

Reece Shearsmith is the award-winning actor, writer and co-creator of *Inside No. 9*, *The League of Gentlemen* and *Psychoville*. He has also starred in numerous other TV comedies, including *Car Share* alongside Peter Kay, *Mid Morning Matters* with Steve Coogan, *Catterick* with Reeves and Mortimer and *Spaced* with Simon Pegg. Reece also has an illustrious career on stage, starring in new plays by Steven Moffat (*The Unfriend* at the Minerva Theatre in Colchester), Lucy Prebble (*A Very Expensive Poison* at the Old Vic) and Martin McDonagh (*Hangmen* at the Royal Court).

Inside No. 9 has won the Rose d'Or, the South Bank Show Award, the Chortle Award for Best Comedy, and Steve Pemberton and Reece Shearsmith have garnered BAFTA, RTS and Writers' Guild Awards for their writing and performing.

Steve Pemberton &
Reece Shearsmith

Inside No.9

The Scripts

Series 7–9

CORONET

First published in Great Britain in 2024 by Coronet
An imprint of Hodder & Stoughton Limited
An Hachette UK company

1

A CIP catalogue record for this title is available from the British Library.

Trade Paperback ISBN 9781399739054
Ebook ISBN 9781399739061

Designed and typeset by EM&EN
Printed and bound in Great Britain by Clays Ltd, Elcograf S.p.A.

Hodder & Stoughton policy is to use papers that are natural, renewable and recyclable products and made from wood grown in sustainable forests. The logging and manufacturing processes are expected to conform to the environmental regulations of the country of origin.

Hodder & Stoughton Ltd
Carmelite House
50 Victoria Embankment
London EC4Y 0DZ

The authorised representative in the EEA is Hachette Ireland,
8 Castlecourt Centre, Castleknock Road, Castleknock, Dublin 15, D15 YF6A, Republic of Ireland
(email: info@hbgi.ie)

www.hodder.co.uk

Contents

SERIES 8

SERIES 9

SERIES
7

Foreword

> — People think writing is all in the head but sometimes you have to make it real for yourself.
>
> Ezra, 'Nine Lives Kat'

We filmed Series 5 of *Inside No. 9* in the spring of 2019 and, although it wouldn't air until the following year, we were excited to see what people would make of it. In the meantime we were lucky enough to be offered a commission for two further series, taking us up to seven. It was at this point that we tentatively started to wonder if we would manage to reach Series 9. The symmetry of it would be perfect . . . but first we had twelve more episodes to write.

By early 2020 we had largely cast and scouted locations for 'Merrily Merrily', 'Kid/Nap', 'Nine Lives Kat' and 'A Random Act of Kindness'. These four episodes were originally part of Series 6, along with 'Hurry Up and Wait' and 'Last Night of the Proms', which was the first to be filmed. We were three days into shooting in March 2020 when . . . well, you know that twist already. We spent a few weeks remotely writing more episodes and then rejigged our series, pushing our K episodes ('Kid/Nap', 'Nine Lives Kat', 'A Random Act of Kindness' and 'Mr King') into Series 7 with 'Merrily, Merrily' and a new episode that we'd yet to write. All very strange and not the way we'd normally organise things, but at least we could see a way back to working.

The idea of discovering that you are somebody else's fictional construct was a haunting one that we explored in 'Nine Lives Kat'. Making the lead character a flawed detective who clashed with authority allowed us to write some deliciously bad dialogue ('I know how to fight, and I know how to dig my heels in – and let me tell you, size six stilettos dig in deep'). Kat seems dimly aware that all is not right in her life, she wakes with a startled gasp each time she is pulled from the bottom drawer by the mediocre writer, and it was fun to play with different levels of reality in a crime/horror genre in a way we hadn't explored before.

The idea of using split-screen had been on our minds for a while, and when we decided to use it to tell a kidnap story we found ourselves writing another crime-based episode, 'Kid/Nap'. We struggled with the idea that not all the action takes place inside number 9, but we rationalised that as long as part of the screen is showing the kidnappers' house, we could allow it. After all, we'd had an episode inspired by a size 9 shoe, one that took place inside number 6, and one set wherever it was the referee had been a w***er. This was a very visual script and we enjoyed contrasting the morning routines of grungy kidnapper Shane and glamorous victim Lara. We knew that trying to time scenes shot in different locations on different days would be tricky, but that's what we love about this show: constantly setting ourselves challenges in terms of narrative limitations and filming techniques.

'Merrily, Merrily' was originally titled 'Friends Reunited', and that's precisely what happened when we invited our *League of Gentlemen* colleague Mark Gatiss to join the cast. But it could have been very different had we shot this for Series 6, with Reece earmarked to play Callum and a different guest actor as Laurence. In the end we realised what a golden opportunity it was to have the three performing members of the League stuck on a lonely lake (with the fourth League member Jeremy Dyson represented in the shape of Steve's trapper hat), and we relished filming our first outside *Inside No. 9*.

'Mr King' began life as a school-set story inspired by number 9 on the periodic table. A young student protesting against the fluoridation of drinking water glues her hand to a classroom wall. She then accidentally sticks herself to her teacher, the cleaner, the headmaster, etc., forming a human chain that mirrors the covalent bonding that the teacher is explaining in his chemistry class. We eventually came unstuck, so to speak, but we liked the school setting, the awkward teacher–pupil relationship and the fact that the child was manipulating the adult. In fact, it reminded us of a certain 1973 film directed by Robin Hardy (look it up), and suddenly we were in our element. It was a real treat to write a school assembly and film it with a small group of talented Welsh children. They did it beautifully.

From an exploration of chemistry we moved on to physics. 'A Random Act of Kindness' was a hidden time-travel story, much as Series 5's 'The Stakeout' was a hidden vampire story. We wrote it as a seemingly domestic tale centring on a teenage boy's relationship with his dying mother and the enigmatic stranger that comes into their lives. Working out the logic of the alternate timelines was very challenging and almost defeated us (logic simply doesn't apply to the multiverse), but we persevered with the idea and it turned out to be a moving reflection on life and death, fate and free will, and why some people need their phone clicks.

The only Zoom-written episode created specifically for Series 7 was 'Wise Owl'. We had spoken a lot about scary characters from children's television, watching clips from *The Singing Ringing Tree*, Mr Noseybonk from *Jigsaw* and several public information films. It was the latter we felt drawn to from a narrative point of view, and we began to write about an adult trapped in his own childhood fears and trauma. It was interesting to keep many of these scenes dialogue-free so that the audience was in the dark as to what was really going on until the horrific truth is revealed. At one point we might have turned this into a revenge drama, but it became clear that Ronnie would be best served by walking away from his tormentor, out of the shadows and into the light. It made for a powerful and poignant ending to the series.

Episode 1

MERRILY, MERRILY

CAST LIST

LAURENCE – Reece Shearsmith

CALLUM – Mark Gatiss

DARREN – Steve Pemberton

DONNA – Diane Morgan

FISHERMAN – Patrice Naiambana

EXT. LAKESIDE. DAY.

A large boating lake set in beautiful countryside on a crisp spring day. The place is deserted, as it's out of season. The café and the water-sports centre are closed.

LAURENCE, *a middle-aged man in outdoor gear carrying a small rucksack, approaches the covered pedalos that are stacked on the shore. He pulls the cover from one of them, takes out a key and unlocks the chain holding it in place.*

We see that the pedalo is number 9.

TITLE: *'Merrily, Merrily'.*

LAURENCE *looks across the lake and sees a* FISHERMAN *on the opposite bank looking at him. The* FISHERMAN *turns and walks into the forest.*

LAURENCE *then hears* CALLUM *approach.* CALLUM *is casually but expensively dressed.*

CALLUM Laurence! Oh. My. God. How are you?

LAURENCE Hey Callum.

They embrace.

CALLUM You're looking good. I was trying to think of the last time I saw you. It was this century, wasn't it?

LAURENCE It was Kenzie's wedding, so June 2008.

CALLUM Was it really?

LAURENCE Yep.

CALLUM God. Poor old Kenzie.

LAURENCE Poor Kenzie's wife.

CALLUM Well, quite. Are they still . . . ?

LAURENCE No. He lives in Germany now. We're Facebook friends.

CALLUM Are you? Well, you know I don't do any of that social media crap.

LAURENCE Yes, I noticed that you didn't want to be LinkedIn. In spite of several attempts!

CALLUM Bless you for trying, Laurence, but I'm too old. I prefer seeing people face to face.

LAURENCE Every twelve years.

CALLUM Exactly!

LAURENCE Come on, give me a hand.

LAURENCE *goes to lift the pedalo, and* CALLUM *helps him carry it to the water's edge.*

CALLUM It's very quiet. You haven't lured me here under false pretences, have you?

LAURENCE They're still closed for the winter. A friend of Bonnie's runs it, and she let me have the key.

CALLUM How is Bonnie? Will we get to see her today?

LAURENCE She'll be here later, yeah. How's . . . your partner?

CALLUM Pablo? You know. We muddle through. He's doing an online course in Fine Art at the moment, which is bewildering to me, but never mind. He'd have loved this . . .

CALLUM *refers to the scenery.*

LAURENCE Beautiful, isn't it? Doesn't it remind you of the good old days?

CALLUM Which good old days?

LAURENCE Uni! We used to go for those big walks round the lake.

CALLUM Oh! Yeah, little bit.

LAURENCE There's so few places nowadays where you can actually find peace.

DARREN *appears through the clearing. He's scruffier than the other two, and trying to dress ten years younger than he is. He carries some cans of beer in a bag.*

DARREN Oi oi, saveloy! Stop trying to bum each other!

CALLUM Jesus. You never told me Darren was coming?

LAURENCE I said it was a reunion. Hi Dazza!

DARREN Hey lads, how are we? Come here, give us a hug.

They embrace.

DARREN *(cont'd)* So good to see you mate. *(To* LAURENCE*)* You still got the old university scarf, you saddo?

LAURENCE Yeah, it's my third one. They keep updating it; I think this one's got a thinner stripe.

DARREN *(to* CALLUM*)* And Cal's all glammed up in his Marks and Spencer Blue Harbour gear.

CALLUM Er, Hugo Boss, you cheeky sod. And what have you come as? You look like a homeless Shaking Stevens.

DARREN It's the latest fashions – don't they have this in that London, eh, eh?

DARREN *play-punches* CALLUM. *They laugh.*

DARREN *(cont'd)* It's been a while, hasn't it?

CALLUM Kenzie's wedding, apparently.

DARREN Of course! Poor Kenzie. Is he coming?

LAURENCE He's in Germany. It's just us, like in the good old days! Three Amigos.

DARREN What? I thought it was like a big fuck-off party cruise with loads of people? Sorry, have I got the shit end of the stick here?

LAURENCE No, it's going to be great, I've got it all planned out. We're going to get out on the lake, and when it gets dark . . . We've got so much to catch up on.

We hear DONNA *approach. She's glammed up for a party.*

DONNA Fucking hell, has anyone got a dock leaf? I think I just stung my fanny on a nettle. Sorry, front bum. Hiya!

LAURENCE *fixes his smile as* DONNA *approaches.*

LAURENCE Who's this?

DARREN It's my new bird, Donna. I promised her we were going out on a boat.

CALLUM We are.

CALLUM *nods to the pedalo.*

DARREN Oh shit.

DONNA *approaches them.*

DONNA Hello, hello. I'm Donna, pleased to meet you.

LAURENCE Laurence.

CALLUM Callum.

They kiss cheeks. DONNA *takes in the view.*

DONNA It's well nice here, isn't it? My mum's got a tray like this – wait till I tell her. Has the yacht got an inside bit? 'Cos I'm freezing my tits off already.

Awkward look between DARREN *and* LAURENCE.

LAURENCE Darren, can you give me a hand?

LAURENCE *takes* DARREN *to shove the pedalo into the water.*

LAURENCE *(cont'd) (quietly)* What are you playing at? The invite was for you only.

DARREN Sorry, I was trying to impress her, wasn't I? We've only been shagging for a couple of weeks.

LAURENCE I wanted it just to be the four of us.

DARREN It is. What's the matter, Larry?

LAURENCE I just wish you'd told me, that's all. It makes things very awkward.

DARREN It's awkward for me as well – I thought it was all plus-ones and wristbands. She's missing her mate's hen do for this.

CALLUM *and* DONNA *approach.*

DONNA So does this take us to the party boat?

DARREN Yep, just jump on the paedo and we'll be off!

DONNA You what?

DARREN Just have a quick go on the paedo.

LAURENCE You mean the pedalo?

DARREN Is that what it's called? I thought they were called paedos. I thought it was a bit weird.

CALLUM *smiles.*

DARREN *(cont'd)* Come on then, let's cast off. Ladies first.

DONNA I'm not sitting in that, the seats are all wet!

CALLUM Actually, the cold water will help with your vaginal irritation.

DONNA Er, excuse me – his name is Darren.

They laugh. CALLUM *helps* DONNA *into the back seat, then climbs into the front.*

DARREN *gets into the back with* DONNA.

DONNA Don't put us two in the back, you'll sink us!

DARREN It's going to be like Ibiza, babe. Whoop whoop!

They laugh and banter some more. LAURENCE *sighs, trying to conceal his irritation. He grabs his rucksack and climbs into the front with* CALLUM. *They start to pedal out on to the lake.*

EXT. LAKE. DAY.

CALLUM *and* LAURENCE *pedal slowly as they glide across the lake.*

DARREN This is cool, isn't it?

CALLUM It's charming.

LAURENCE 'Three Men in a Boat (to Say Nothing of the Dog)'.

DONNA Er sorry, say that again?

LAURENCE Jerome K. Jerome. It's the full title.

DONNA He's known me five minutes and he's calling me a dog!

DARREN He was probably just admiring your puppies!

DONNA *(to* DARREN, *of* LAURENCE*)* I thought you said he was . . .

DONNA *mimes a limp wrist.*

CALLUM No, that's me.

DONNA Oh. You could never tell. Are you the one that knows Judge Rinder off *Strictly*?

CALLUM Our paths have crossed.

DONNA 'Cos Darren said he's going to be at the party?

DARREN *(to* DONNA*)* I only said he might be! *(To* CALLUM *and* LAURENCE*)* I only said he might be.

CALLUM Stranger things have happened at sea.

DONNA So, you were all at school together?

LAURENCE University. Callum was a medical student, and I was reading Psychology.

DONNA I've seen that, where she gets stabbed in the shower. I didn't know they'd made a book of it, though. *(To* DARREN*)* What did you do?

DARREN Oh nothing. I dropped out in the second year – boring.

LAURENCE Darren was studying Sports Science. If that's not an oxymoron.

DARREN Bloody hell, he's calling you a dog and me a moron! I thought you were my mate?

LAURENCE He still teaches there you know – Phil Crawford.

DARREN Does he? Creepy Crawford? He was a bit of a pedalo. How do you know?

LAURENCE Didn't I tell you? I work there.

CALLUM At our uni?

LAURENCE Yes. In the Psychology department.

CALLUM Since when?

LAURENCE About eight years. I put it all in my Christmas round-robin – don't you read them?

CALLUM I . . . think they must just go into my spam folder. Bloody hell!

DARREN What's it like there now?

LAURENCE It's exactly the same. The library, the common room. They even dress up the Newton statue in the courtyard every Freshers' Week.

DARREN What statue?

LAURENCE The Isaac Newton one. We put a dress on it in our first week, with apples for tits. Don't you remember?

DARREN Vaguely.

LAURENCE Oh, come on. I remember it like it was yesterday. It was the funniest thing ever!

CALLUM You need to get out more.

LAURENCE *seems deflated.*

CALLUM *(cont'd)* Shall we drift for a bit, take in the view?

They stop pedalling and gaze around.

CALLUM *(cont'd)* So, how about you two – where did you meet?

DONNA Five Guys. He spilt an Oreo milkshake all down my back. I think he was just trying to get my attention.

DARREN Worked though, didn't it?

They kiss.

CALLUM Sounds very romantic.

DONNA Have you been in Five Guys, Callum?

CALLUM Oh, at least.

DARREN *(to* LAURENCE*)* So, are you and Bonnie still living in the same place?

LAURENCE Yes. Rattling round now, because Alex is at uni. I'm an empty-nester. How are your two?

DARREN Oh, they're smashing. I don't get to see them as much as I'd like, you know, but I've got them for a couple of weeks in the summer. You want to go to Disney, don't you?

DONNA Yeah. You can have breakfast with the characters. I can't decide between Goofy's Kitchen and Ariel's Grotto.

CALLUM I'm not sure I'd like to eat at a place called Ariel's Grotto.

DARREN Ooh, I would.

DONNA Don't ruin it, you pig!

CALLUM Pabby and I are going to take the girls to Cornwall this year. Have a staycation.

LAURENCE Oh, I had no idea – you've got girls?

CALLUM Yep. Five and nine.

LAURENCE Good for you. What are their names?

CALLUM Millie and Liza. We're absolutely run off our feet with them, but you adapt, don't you? Your life becomes about them.

LAURENCE True. Do you have pictures?

CALLUM Of course. Proud dad.

CALLUM *takes out his phone to look for a photo.*

CALLUM *(cont'd)* Actually, I'm a grandad now.

DARREN You what?

CALLUM Yeah, we took Millie to a breeding kennel and she had a litter of five.

CALLUM *hands his phone to* LAURENCE, *and he sees a photo of a dog.* LAURENCE*'s face falls.*

LAURENCE Oh, I see.

LAURENCE *shows the photo to* DARREN *and* DONNA.

CALLUM Our beautiful girls.

LAURENCE *(under his breath)* Not quite the same thing. Anyway! Shall we press on . . . ?

LAURENCE *starts to pedal, knocking* CALLUM*'s ankles.*

CALLUM Hang on, hang on, I'm not ready yet.

DONNA Can I have a go at pedalling? It'll be good for my glutes.

LAURENCE Sorry, no! You don't know where we're going – I do.

DARREN Let her have a go, what's the problem?

LAURENCE I just don't want to veer off course.

CALLUM Come on Laurence, it's not Shackleton. She can swap with me.

DONNA Thank you.

DONNA *stands up, and the boat wobbles.*

DARREN Whoa!

DONNA Help me, then!

CALLUM *stands and they attempt to swap seats.*

LAURENCE Careful!

LAURENCE *pulls his rucksack out of harm's way.*

CALLUM There we go.

CALLUM *is in the back with* DARREN, DONNA *is up front with* LAURENCE.

DONNA Right, how do you work it?

LAURENCE *(irritated)* Just put your feet on the pedals.

LAURENCE *starts to pedal, and* DONNA *goes along with him.*

DONNA It's fun, isn't it? Right, let's get to this party. Whoooo!

We see them set off again across the lake. LAURENCE *pedals determinedly.*

EXT. LAKE. DAY.

The boat is on a different part of the lake. DONNA *is glumly pedalling.*

DONNA Fucking hell, this is hard work, isn't it? Like a spin class. How long have I been doing it?

LAURENCE *checks his watch.*

LAURENCE Two minutes.

DONNA I'm sweating cobs. I can't have Judge Rinder see me like this. Will there be cabins on the boat to freshen up?

Awkward silence. DARREN *opens his plastic bag.*

DARREN Who wants a bevvy? Larry?

LAURENCE No, thank you.

DARREN Cal?

CALLUM Why not?

DARREN *(to* DONNA*)* Babe, do you want them Doritos?

DARREN *hands beers to* CALLUM *and* DONNA, *then opens one himself.* DONNA *opens the crisps.* LAURENCE *sulks. He looks across to the island in the distance and sees the* FISHERMAN *walk by into the trees.*

CALLUM *has opened his beer.*

CALLUM Cheers! Lovely. This time yesterday, I was draining a pelvic abscess.

DONNA Don't say that, you're making me want a wee.

DARREN So, are you still at the Royal Free?

CALLUM Yeah. Head of Obs and Gynae now, which is quite a responsibility.

DARREN Well done, mate. I'm proud of you.

CALLUM Thank you. How about you? You were teaching PE at some God-awful school, weren't you?

DARREN Supply, yeah, but I jacked it in. Kids can be cruel little fuckers.

DONNA I was. I was a total bitch. I've calmed down a lot now.

DONNA *eats some crisps.*

LAURENCE Are you actually pedalling, or are you just resting your feet?

DONNA No, I'm doing it!

CALLUM *(to* DARREN*)* So, what you up to now?

DARREN This and that, you know.

DONNA Tell him. Don't be embarrassed.

DARREN Well . . . I'm a children's author.

CALLUM Really? Congratulations. Are you published?

DARREN Not yet, I'm still in the development stage. Mapping out the structure and that.

DONNA Tell them your idea, it's brilliant.

DARREN No, no . . .

DONNA Go on, have confidence in it!

DARREN Alright, well, basically, it's a hardback book. You'd have on one page a picture of a ball, and on the opposite page the word 'ball'. Then, on the next page, there'd be a picture of a boy, and on the opposite page the word . . .

CALLUM 'Boy'.

DARREN Have I told you about it already?

CALLUM No, carry on . . .

DARREN Then on the next page, there'd be a boy and a ball, and it would say something like 'boy got ball' or 'boy play with ball' – I haven't quite worked it all out yet.

CALLUM So it's like baby's first words?

DARREN Yeah, but with a story gradually developing out of it.

DONNA I've read it twice; it made me cry.

CALLUM But, sorry Darren, this isn't an authored book, is it? It's just words and pictures.

DARREN Well, as I say, it's early days. I think people would buy it.

CALLUM They are buying it; it already exists. It's hardly going to make you into the next J. K. Rowling, is it?

DARREN Alright Callum, you don't have to shoot it down in flames! We can't all be elbow-deep in fannies every day!

LAURENCE Can we not talk like that, please?

DARREN I could have been where you are now, top of my tree, on a good wage. But I never had the chance, did I? If I'd graduated, I could have made something of myself . . .

CALLUM You could have been a contender?

DARREN Yes!

CALLUM In Sports Science? Give me a break.

LAURENCE *turns round and stops pedalling, but* DONNA *carries on.*

LAURENCE Leave it, Callum.

CALLUM You can't possibly compare me doing seven years of medical training to you playing rounders and learning about energy drinks.

DARREN I was good at it!

CALLUM Really?

DARREN Yes!

CALLUM So why did you drop out, then?

DARREN I'll drop you out in a minute, mate . . .

DARREN *starts to scuffle with* CALLUM. LAURENCE *tries to intervene.*

LAURENCE Alright, that's enough! I didn't ask you both to come here today just so you could open old wounds. I wanted it to be a celebration of who we used to be.

CALLUM As opposed to who we are? Uni was thirty years ago, Laurence. Move on!

A tense silence. The pedalo has come to a halt. DONNA *tries the pedals, but they are stuck.*

DONNA Erm, sorry, I think something's happened. Why's it not going?

LAURENCE What?

DONNA The pedals are stuck.

LAURENCE *tries the pedals. They won't move forward.*

LAURENCE Right, try going backwards . . .

The pedals still won't turn.

DARREN We're tangled in the weeds. Look, they're everywhere.

They see that they have navigated into a patch of weeds.

LAURENCE Oh, for Christ's sake! *(To* DONNA*)* This is all your fault. Why didn't you look where you were going?

DONNA What do you mean, look where I was going? We're on an empty lake, mate.

LAURENCE Which makes it even more idiotic.

CALLUM Don't blame her, Laurence. It was an accident.

DARREN Just keep waggling the pedals.

LAURENCE She wasn't even meant to be here.

DONNA Er, excuse me, I was invited to this party by Darren.

LAURENCE For God's sake, there is no party!

DARREN No, no, no, Larry . . .

LAURENCE This was a reunion for three friends from university. I wanted it all to be perfect, and you've managed to ruin it.

DONNA Darren? Is that true?

DARREN I cocked it up. I'm sorry. This is it. This is the party.

DONNA So Judge Rinder's not even coming?

CALLUM Doubtful.

DONNA I'm missing Gemma's hen night for this! They'll have a stripper helicoptering all over them in Sugar Hut right now, while we're playing Swallows and fucking Amazons.

DARREN Sorry, babe. I'll make it up to you.

DONNA Oh, shove it up your arse!

Silence. They bob on the lake.

CALLUM So, I think that's everyone fallen out with everyone. Reunion 101. What are we going to do now?

EXT. LAKE. DAY.

A flock of birds fly overhead. The pedalo is still marooned in the weeds. The sky is darkening.

CALLUM Row, row, row your boat, gently down the stream / Merrily, merrily, merrily, merrily / Life is but a dream. / Row, row, row your boat, gently to the shore / If you see a lion there, don't forget to roar - rahhhh!

LAURENCE Please stop.

CALLUM Fine. So what are we going to do, just sit here and wait for someone to find us? Is that your plan?

LAURENCE Yes. I told you, I saw someone earlier, across there. Probably a fisherman.

CALLUM Well, it's going to be dark in half an hour. That's all I'm saying.

DARREN Could one of us go under and untangle the pedals?

CALLUM I wouldn't advise it. The water's freezing; you'd have hypothermia within twenty minutes.

DONNA Well, I'm sorry, but you're all going to need to look over there.

DARREN Why, have you seen someone?

DONNA No, because I need to do a wee.

DARREN Aw, no, you serious?

DONNA Yes. I've been busting for ages. It's all the tinkling of the water.

DONNA *stands up and starts to take down her trousers.*

DONNA *(cont'd)* Talk among yourselves, I don't want you listening to it.

The men all face away and DONNA *gingerly squats over the side of the pedalo. We stay with their faces rather than her micturition.*

CALLUM It's a good idea, actually. It might kill off some of the weeds.

They hear the beginnings of a splash in the water.

DONNA *(V.O.)* It's not acid!

A small fart can be heard popping out.

DONNA *(V.O.)* Oop, bonus ball.

CALLUM *(whispering to* DARREN*)* I like her.

DARREN *smiles.*

LAURENCE This is the story of my life.

DARREN What, listening to a woman pissing off a pedalo?

LAURENCE No, being stuck. When we graduated, I stayed in the area, married Bonnie, did a PGCE. Next thing I know, I'm back teaching the same course I'd graduated from. You've all moved on and had lives. I'm still living in 1989.

DARREN I wouldn't worry about it, Larry, you haven't missed much. Well, *Game of Thrones* was pretty good, but even then they ruined the ending.

LAURENCE Well, I'm not going to do that.

DONNA Right, I'm done. You can turn around now.

CALLUM *and* DARREN *turn back round.*

DONNA *(cont'd)* Do you think that's why people say 'relieve yourself', 'cos you're relieved you've not pissed your pants?

CALLUM Come on, this is ridiculous. I thought you said Bonnie was going to be here?

LAURENCE She is.

CALLUM Well call her, then; tell her to come earlier.

LAURENCE There's no signal.

CALLUM *takes out his phone.*

CALLUM Can't we all just check again?

DARREN I'm sure I had a bar earlier – is she still on the same number?

DONNA What network are you on?

DARREN Give us your phone, Laurence.

LAURENCE No.

CALLUM Give it to him!

LAURENCE There's no point.

CALLUM Why not?

LAURENCE Because Bonnie's dead.

CALLUM *is stunned.*

DARREN What?

LAURENCE She died a year ago. It was a short illness; she was very brave. She's in here.

LAURENCE *opens up his rucksack.*

DONNA *(to* DARREN*)* Sorry, is Bonnie . . . a guinea pig?

LAURENCE She was my wife.

DONNA Oh. I just got confused because of him and his dog daughters.

DARREN I'm really sorry, mate.

CALLUM Why didn't you tell us?

LAURENCE I wanted to, but I didn't know how. It's not the sort of thing you can say in an email or a round-robin.

I wanted to see you face to face, but then a week went by, and then a month, and in the end . . . That's why I wanted you both here today. One year on. You were there when we met, you were there when we married. I wanted you to be there for the final goodbye. Because even though we don't really see each other any more . . . you're still my best friends.

LAURENCE *has pulled a waterproof bag from his rucksack.*

DARREN So you wanted us to be here to scatter her ashes?

LAURENCE Yeah. Sort of.

LAURENCE *suddenly tips back off the pedalo, taking the waterproof bag with him. He disappears under the weeds that surround the boat.*

Everyone is shocked.

DARREN What the fuck . . . ?

CALLUM Laurence?!

DONNA Where's he gone?

They peer out, looking for any sign of LAURENCE *in the water. Suddenly, he reappears beyond the weeds and starts swimming off towards the island.*

CALLUM Laurence, come back! You'll freeze to death!

We cut wide to the dark lake and DARREN*'s cry echoing across the water.*

DARREN *(V.O.)* Laurence!

EXT. LAKE. NIGHT.

CALLUM, DARREN *and* DONNA *sit glumly on the boat. It has got darker. They look out towards the island and can see the odd flash of a torch.*

DONNA Can you still see him?

DARREN I think so.

CALLUM What's he playing at?

DARREN He always talked about how he proposed to Bonnie on an island. I thought he meant the Caribbean or somewhere, but it must have been that one there.

DONNA I can't believe she died and he never told you.

CALLUM I suppose that's what all those LinkedIn requests were. I feel terrible now.

DONNA I bet you do. Poor man. I nearly cried when he said you two were his best friends.

CALLUM We were. We used to be. But life moves on, doesn't it?

DARREN Not for Bonnie.

CALLUM Maybe I have been too self-absorbed. We're all dealing with our own shit . . .

DONNA Yours is mostly dog shit by the sound of it. His wife's died. You can't just scoop that up in a little blue bag and hang it off a tree.

DARREN I once did one in a paint pot and left it in a cellar. I was moving out, so it didn't matter.

CALLUM Well, if it's any consolation, I absolutely hate my job. I've spent years trying to get to the top, and now I'm there, I realise it was just the endeavour that kept me going. I got to the end of the rainbow and found the pot of gold. And I'd give anything just to hand it all back and start again. Like you did. I envy you.

DARREN It wasn't out of choice.

CALLUM What do you mean?

DARREN I didn't drop out of uni. I got kicked out.

CALLUM Really?

DARREN Yeah. I'd done so well to get my A levels, but uni was just so hard. Even if it was only Sports Science. And then I realised: if life gives you melons – you're probably dyslexic.

CALLUM What?

DARREN Yeah. I've got Surface Dyslexia. I was too embarrassed to say anything at the time. That's why this book is so important to me. It's not for babies. It's for kids and adults. Like me.

A pause for reflection.

DONNA Have I got to think of something bad that's happened to me now? 'Cos nothing really has. I've had a great life: good mates, loving family, nice little job. And by the sound of it, it's because I never went to fucking university!

CALLUM Look!

CALLUM *looks out to the island and sees firelight flickering.*

EXT. ISLAND. NIGHT.

A very cold and wet LAURENCE *is on the island in the middle of the lake. He has a headtorch on and has made a small memorial with a framed photo of* BONNIE *and some tealights. His university scarf is draped round it.*

LAURENCE *shivers. He can barely speak.*

LAURENCE Well, this is it. It's not quite gone according to plan. Darren brought an uninvited guest. Which really irritated me, of course – but if you were here, you would've welcomed her with open arms and said, 'The more the merrier!' Because that's the kind of person you were, and why I've found it so hard to live without you. Anyway – I didn't want to just scatter your ashes in the normal way, so I hope you approve.

LAURENCE *lights a taper and crosses to the water's edge.*

EXT. LAKE. NIGHT.

CALLUM *pulls out some packaging from* LAURENCE*'s rucksack.*

CALLUM Hang on, what's this? Ashes to Flashes Memorial Fireworks. So she's . . . ?

Suddenly, the first firework streaks into the air from the island and bursts into light over the lake. Then another and another. It is a magnificent, colourful display, leaving plumes of smoke drifting delicately in the night sky.

DONNA, DARREN *and* CALLUM *stare up from the pedalo, their faces lit by the fireworks above.*

DARREN I promised you a party, didn't I?

DONNA Now I *am* going to cry.

EXT. ISLAND. NIGHT.

A shivering LAURENCE *stares up at the display and smiles.*

LAURENCE Burn bright, Bonnie. Burn bright.

He closes his eyes and lies down.

EXT. LAKE. NIGHT.

The firework display comes to an end. DONNA *and* DARREN *cuddle.*

DARREN Listen, I think one of us needs to swim across, make sure he's alright.

DARREN *stands. He starts to take off his jacket.*

CALLUM Not a good idea, Darren.

DARREN Maybe we can get a signal there.

DONNA The water's too cold. You'll freeze your bollocks off.

DARREN Do another wee in it then.

CALLUM *stands. The pedalo rocks.*

CALLUM Darren, sit down. Don't be stupid!

DARREN Don't call me stupid!

DARREN *and* CALLUM *grapple. The pedalo rocks more violently.*

DONNA Stop it, you two. Stop it!

FADE TO BLACK.

EXT. LAKE. DAWN.

The sun is not yet up, and the lake is eerily swathed in mist.

LAURENCE *is curled up, coming to from a deep sleep. He becomes aware that he's in a rowing boat, the* FISHERMAN *slowly pulling at the oars.*

LAURENCE *slowly gets up and looks around. The* FISHERMAN *rows on in silence.*

LAURENCE *spots the pedalo number 9 still stranded in the weeds, but now empty.*

LAURENCE Excuse me, do you know what happened to my friends?

The FISHERMAN *doesn't answer.*

LAURENCE *(cont'd)* They were stuck in the weeds. Did they get rescued?

LAURENCE *sees* DARREN*'s hat floating in the water.*

LAURENCE *(cont'd)* Please, we've got to do something. There were three of them . . .

FISHERMAN Don't worry about them. They are fine.

LAURENCE Where are they?

FISHERMAN On the other side.

LAURENCE Thank God. Did they tell you where to find me?

FISHERMAN I knew where to find you. I've been watching you for some time.

LAURENCE Was that you I saw earlier?

The FISHERMAN *has arrived at the jetty. He ties up his boat and steps out, then helps* LAURENCE *to get out on to the jetty.*

EXT. JETTY. DAY.

LAURENCE *and the* FISHERMAN *are on the jetty.*

LAURENCE Thank you.

The FISHERMAN *holds out his hand.*

LAURENCE *(cont'd)* I'm very sorry, I don't have any . . .

LAURENCE *feels something in his throat. He opens his mouth and a large silver coin falls into his hand. He gives it to the* FISHERMAN, *who pockets it, then gets back into the boat and starts to row away.*

LAURENCE *stands alone on the misty jetty, confused. Suddenly he hears a woman's voice.*

BONNIE Laurence.

LAURENCE *turns to see* BONNIE *standing on the jetty. She holds out a hand for him to join her. He smiles.*

THE END

Episode 2

MR KING

CAST LIST

Mr Edwards – Steve Pemberton

Alan Curtis – Reece Shearsmith

Ceri – Elin Owen

Euan – Charlie Baron

Gwen – Rosie Ekenna

Owen – William Newton

Winnie – Annette Badland

with

Darcy-Olivia White

Isaac Eames

Summer Rose

Toby Roberts

EXT. PRIMARY SCHOOL. DAY.

A small primary school in a rural Welsh setting, surrounded by fields. Idyllic, but remote.

INT. SCHOOL CORRIDOR. DAY.

We see through a door's glass panel into the classroom. The headmaster, MR EDWARDS, *and the teacher,* ALAN, *can be seen at the head of the class.*

A sign by the door with a child's drawing of a smiling face reads 'Class 9'.

TITLE: *'Mr King'.*

INT. CLASSROOM. DAY.

The classroom is home to a small group of 8–11-year-olds (no more than ten pupils). The walls are decorated with school art projects and poems, educational posters, etc.

One corner is dedicated to the harvest festival collection. There is a tank with tadpoles and pictures of how they become frogs. It is a traditional old classroom with a few modern adornments, not state-of-the-art, but homely.

MR EDWARDS *addresses the class in Welsh as* ALAN *stands by, smiling but not understanding.*

MR EDWARDS *(to* ALAN*)* I was just telling them that you are going to be taking all your lessons in English. *(To the class)* Which is a very important skill for any adventurers amongst you who might be thinking about leaving the village in the future.

A couple of the pupils shake their heads.

MR EDWARDS *(cont'd)* Mr Curtis used to teach in a school in London, so I'm sure he'll have lots of exciting stories to tell us. They pay two pounds for a coffee, don't they?

ALAN And the rest.

MR EDWARDS Dearie me, imagine that! Now, as you all know, your previous teacher Mr King had to leave us after a wonderful year . . .

The children all sigh and say, 'Aah'.

MR EDWARDS *(cont'd)* I know, I know, but he has sent us this postcard from his travels, and I wondered if one of you would like to read it to the class?

The kids all raise their hands and say, 'Me!' – all except a young girl, CERI, *who looks down shyly.*

MR EDWARDS *(cont'd)* Ceri, would you do the honours?

MR EDWARDS *hands the postcard, which has a picture of a kangaroo, to* CERI.

CERI 'Dear Class 9, greetings from down under! I'm having an amazing time, and I'm thinking of you as you start your next chapter. I cherish the memory of our time together, and getting to know all of you so closely. Much love, Mr King.'

The children applaud, led by MR EDWARDS. ALAN *smiles.*

MR EDWARDS What a man. What a teacher; what a *man*. Anyway, back down to reality. Mr Curtis, over to you.

MR EDWARDS *steps back, and* ALAN *steps forward.*

ALAN Thank you, headmaster. So, here's a question: what's the difference between me and Pinocchio? I'm glad to be in Wales!

Nothing from the class. MR EDWARDS *steps forward.*

MR EDWARDS Ah, that's because Pinocchio was eaten by a whale – have I got that right, Mr Curtis?

ALAN Yes, it was just a joke.

MR EDWARDS Oh! It was a joke, Class 9. Carry on.

The pupils look unimpressed. ALAN *sighs deeply and plants a smile on his face.*

INT. CLASSROOM. DAY.

ALAN *is writing on the blackboard. The children sit at their desks.*

ALAN So as you know, our end-of-term assembly is going to be all about the environment . . .

ALAN *writes the word 'ENVIRONMENT' on the blackboard.*

ALAN *(cont'd)* So what does that mean?

Nobody offers an answer. ALAN *points to a boy,* EUAN.

ALAN *(cont'd)* Euan?

EUAN Our classroom?

ALAN Yes, that's our immediate surroundings, what else?

OWEN Fields.

ALAN Yes, good. It's any place where people or plants or animals actually live and grow. So what types of things will affect our environment?

GWEN Human beans, sir.

ALAN What's that, Gwen?

GWEN Human beans.

ALAN Not human *beans*, we're not vegetables – but human *beings*, yes, we certainly have an impact . . .

ALAN *writes 'humans' on the board.*

ALAN *(cont'd)* And we can affect our environment in positive ways and negative ways. What are some of the positive things we can do? Ceri?

CERI Recycling.

ALAN *writes 'recycling' on the board.*

ALAN Very good, Ceri. Anyone else? Who here has heard of Greta Thunberg?

Blank faces among the children.

ALAN *(cont'd)* None of you? That's OK. But you've probably heard about global warming?

Nobody responds.

ALAN *(cont'd)* How about climate change?

Nothing. ALAN *tries to conceal his slight irritation.*

ALAN *(cont'd)* OK, you should have covered some of this last year. Let me ask this, then: what do you think causes hurricanes?

OWEN God farting.

The class laugh.

ALAN No don't be silly, Owen. This is actually a very serious subject. Now, for your homework, I want you all to go home and learn about global warming and the ozone layer.

CERI Sir, Mr King said we didn't have to do homework.

ALAN Well, I'm sorry, but he's not your teacher any more – I am. You may not realise it, but this is the number-one topic that's going to affect you and your future, so it's not something you can afford to be ignorant about!

ALAN *realises he's going off on one. He takes a breath and composes himself.*

ALAN *(cont'd)* Sorry. Erm, I'd like you all to do a paragraph and bring it in on Monday. Right, get your books out, and you can do silent reading for twenty minutes.

The pupils take out their books to read. ALAN *surreptitiously takes a pill from a tub in his pocket and swallows it with some water in an attempt to calm himself.*

INT. CORRIDOR. DAY.

MR EDWARDS *is passing.*

ALAN Headmaster, can I have a word?

MR EDWARDS Of course! How can I help?

ALAN I was just wondering if you had an email address for Mr King?

MR EDWARDS Email . . . is that the one with the little blue bird?

ALAN No, I think that's Twitter.

MR EDWARDS That's right, yes – tash-tag. Email is with the @ sign, isn't it? Yes, I think I've got a piece of paper with that on in my office.

ALAN Thanks, I'd just love to ask him about what he covered last year, and what curriculum he was using.

MR EDWARDS No problem. Let me ask Megan to dig it out, and I'll get back to you. All good otherwise?

ALAN I think so, yeah.

MR EDWARDS Have you started rehearsing for your assembly yet? Mr King's were always quite lavish. Like West End theatre productions!

ALAN Well I hope that mine will be *Wicked*!

MR EDWARDS *looks confused.*

ALAN *(cont'd)* It's a musical.

MR EDWARDS Another one of your jokes! Well, I look forward to it. Always such a joy to see the children take centre stage. We're a small school, Mr Curtis, as you can see, and we've very nearly been closed down a few times, but bringing in teachers like yourself, with all your experience of the world, it really helps the children grow, you know?

ALAN And that's all I want Headmaster, it really is.

MR EDWARDS Jolly good. I'll get that b-mail for you, and I'll get Megan to send it to you as a text. Take that, Ofsted!

ALAN *smiles.*

ALAN Thanks.

INT. CLASSROOM. DAY.

CERI *is at the sink, waiting for the kettle to boil. She pours the hot water into a 'World's Best Teacher' mug.*

Elsewhere in the class, the pupils are pegging paintings of trees and plants on to a line of string at the back of the room to dry, and getting ready for outdoor play. It's noisy and chaotic.

ALAN Make sure the paint isn't dripping when you hang it up . . . Is that still wet, Owen? OK, leave it on the side there. And when they're dry, we'll glue them up here on to the display.

ALAN *takes a sip of his tea. He frowns and spits the tea back into the cup, and looks. There are black blobs floating within it.* ALAN *takes a teaspoon and fishes up a spoonful of dead tadpoles. He turns and looks to* CERI, *who is putting on her coat to leave.*

ALAN *(cont'd)* Ceri, can you stay behind for a minute, please?

INT. CLASSROOM. DAY.

ALAN *and* CERI *are sitting at a small desk.* ALAN *looks at her; she looks down at her lap.*

ALAN What were you thinking? Hmm?

CERI *shrugs.*

ALAN *(cont'd)* Those tadpoles are not going to turn into frogs now, are they?

CERI Why not?

ALAN Because you boiled them in the kettle. Why did you do that, Ceri?

CERI Global warming.

ALAN I asked you to research it, not recreate it!

CERI Mr King once ate a goldfish.

ALAN I don't care what Mr King did. I'm getting a bit concerned about you, Ceri. Last week, you pushed Simon's face into his birthday cake, didn't you? What if his hair had caught fire on the candles – have you seen that Michael Jackson video? Not the one about licking boy's bottoms, the one where his hair caught fire. It very nearly disfigured him . . . even more.

CERI Who's Michael Jackson?

ALAN Never mind. Is there anything going on at home that you want to tell me about?

CERI *thinks.*

CERI We're having an extension.

ALAN OK. And are Mummy and Daddy getting on alright? No shouting?

CERI *shakes her head and looks down.*

ALAN *(cont'd)* Is something upsetting you?

CERI I don't want the world to end.

ALAN It's not going to end. Who said it's going to end?

CERI The stinking rebellion.

ALAN Who?

CERI You asked us to read about it for homework.

ALAN Oh, you mean the climate change protesters?

CERI *nods.*

CERI It frightened me.

ALAN You shouldn't be frightened, Ceri. You should feel that emotion and do something positive with it.

CERI *sobs.* ALAN *gently pats her back.*

ALAN *(cont'd)* Hey, it's OK. Shhh. I'm sorry it upset you. Now, do you want to go and play outside, or stay in here with me?

CERI Stay with you.

ALAN Good girl.

We see that one of the children's pegged-up paintings, featuring the planet Earth, is slowly dripping on to the floor below.

INT. CLASSROOM. DAY.

ALAN *is wiping the blackboard. We hear the sound of children departing.*

ALAN *sees the harvest festival display on a nearby table and spies a carrot. He goes over and cuts a slice of carrot with his penknife, then puts his hand into the fish tank, waggles it around a bit, pulls out the carrot and swallows it whole.*

From the doorway, he hears a voice.

MR EDWARDS Little bit peckish, are we?

ALAN Sorry, headmaster. I was just practising a trick for the children.

MR EDWARDS That's one way of teaching the food chain. Now, I just wanted to have a word with you, if you don't mind?

ALAN Of course.

The headmaster closes the door and comes into the room.

MR EDWARDS When you came in for your interview. you said you were keen to move to a smaller school like ours, away from the cut and thrust, shall we say, of inner-city education, and embrace a quieter pace of life.

ALAN Yes. It's literally what the doctor ordered.

MR EDWARDS I know it's important that we talk sensitively about mental health, and I just wanted to clarify - you went a bit doolally, didn't you?

ALAN Er, not really - it was just the workload. I was exhausted, physically and mentally, and I did lose myself for a little bit, but coming here has done me the world of good. Why do you ask?

MR EDWARDS Well, the thing is, an allegation has been made against you, and it's my duty to investigate it.

ALAN What allegation?

MR EDWARDS I'm not able to divulge that at the moment.

ALAN Who made it?

MR EDWARDS She doesn't want to say.

ALAN So it's a girl?

MR EDWARDS She may or may not be. The point is, I promised Ceri's parents that she - or he - would have absolute anonymity.

ALAN So it's Ceri?

MR EDWARDS Yes.

ALAN Right.

MR EDWARDS So, now you've wormed that out of me . . .

MR EDWARDS *sits and invites* ALAN *to join him.*

MR EDWARDS *(cont'd)* Can you tell me in your own words what happened on Tuesday morning break time?

ALAN What do you mean? Nothing happened! She's been behaving strangely for a while. She killed all the tadpoles, and I kept her behind to talk to her about it.

MR EDWARDS And at no point did you ask her if she wanted to play the hairy meat whistle?

ALAN What? No!

MR EDWARDS And you didn't say, 'Do you want to see how sir can make his own tadpoles?'

ALAN Definitely not, that's horrible.

MR EDWARDS Are you sure?

ALAN Yes, I think I'd remember saying that!

MR EDWARDS Well, where do you suppose she's got this from then? Because I don't recall that being in the *Biff and Chip* books.

ALAN I've no idea! Maybe she's seen something inappropriate online – it happens all the time.

MR EDWARDS Not with our Wi-Fi connection, it doesn't. It takes me all weekend to download one *Countryfile*. Did you talk to her about Michael Jackson doing things with boy's anuses?

ALAN Yes, but I never said anuses.

MR EDWARDS Well, that's something. I've talked the parents down from filing an official complaint, but I don't want to drag the police into it if I can help it. We're an independent school, and we like to deal with these types of things within the community.

ALAN So it's happened before?

MR EDWARDS *looks shifty.*

MR EDWARDS You've not been here long, and I'm not being funny, but I don't know you from Alan.

ALAN Adam.

MR EDWARDS Sorry, I thought it was Alan. I'm sure you understand, Adam, that as head of this school, I need to establish the facts of the matter before I can allow Ceri back into your clutches, so to speak.

ALAN Of course. Do you want me to give you a statement?

MR EDWARDS No, I want you to show me your penis.

ALAN What?

MR EDWARDS The girl has given quite a vivid description – and, I believe, a plasticine model – but I didn't want to touch it. I need to see if it tallies with the real thing.

ALAN So you want to do an identity parade? What if it's not mine? Will you go around the kingdom like in *Cinderella*?

MR EDWARDS Don't be facetious, Adam. I'm trying to clear this matter up, one way or the other. Either you're lying, or the girl's lying.

ALAN I can't believe this.

MR EDWARDS I could always contact your union representative?

ALAN No, I . . . Just make it quick.

ALAN *stands up and undoes his belt, then drops his trousers and underwear.* MR EDWARDS *puts on his glasses.*

MR EDWARDS All very neat and tidy, that's what I like to see.

MR EDWARDS *takes a folded piece of paper from his jacket and starts to compare the description to the real thing. He hums and haws as he makes his examination.*

ALAN What are you looking for, exactly?

MR EDWARDS Ah, now, that would be telling. They say they're like snowflakes – no two are alike.

ALAN This is ridiculous.

The door opens and the aged cleaner WINNIE *comes in with a mop and bucket. She wears thick glasses.*

ALAN *(cont'd)* Oh, we're busy Winnie, sorry!

WINNIE Oh hello, Mr Curtis, you're here late. Is it alright for me to clean now?

ALAN Not just at the moment.

MR EDWARDS Oh don't worry about Winnie, she's blind as a bat. It's fine, Winnie, you go right ahead!

WINNIE Oh is that you, Mr Edwards? I didn't see you down there. You keeping busy?

MR EDWARDS Yes. I've got my hands full, as always.

WINNIE *starts to mop the floor.* MR EDWARDS *takes out a Polaroid camera and starts to photograph* ALAN*'s member from different angles.*

WINNIE Don't worry, I can clean around you. I have to save some time to tackle the boys' toilets. The size of some of those stools. I don't know what their mothers feed them. Like airport Toblerones, some of them.

ALAN Are we all done?

MR EDWARDS I believe so. I'll be in touch once I've got my head around this. Thank you, Adam.

MR EDWARDS *leaves and* ALAN *tucks himself in.*

ALAN We were just . . . discussing a possible new art project.

WINNIE Oh, I thought he was taking photographs of your cock.

WINNIE *mops the floor.*

INT. CLASSROOM. DAY.

The children are sitting at their desks. ALAN *is handing out worksheets.*

ALAN Alright, Class 9, I'm handing out these worksheets on fractions, so you've got fifteen minutes to do as many questions as you can. Remember to put your names on the top, please.

CERI*'s desk is empty. He pauses briefly, then moves on.*

OWEN Sir, what happened to Ceri?

ALAN What do you mean?

OWEN Where is she?

ALAN I don't know. Now, tight lips, please. We listen with these . . .

He points to his ears.

ALAN *(cont'd)* . . . Not these.

He points to his lips.

The pupils start to do their worksheets. ALAN *crosses over to the display and sticks up the children's paintings on the sugar-paper.*

He hears whispering behind him in Welsh.

ALAN Quiet!

More whispering, followed by a giggle.

ALAN *(cont'd)* Quiet, I said!

ALAN *turns to the class. They seem to be passing an item between them.*

ALAN *(cont'd)* What have you got there? Owen, what is that?

OWEN *holds up his empty hands.*

OWEN Nothing, sir!

ALAN Alright, I'm not an idiot. Show me.

ALAN *moves among the children as they pass the item under their desks.*

ALAN *(cont'd)* Who's got it? Give it to me. Give it to me! Now!

ALAN *grabs the item from one of the pupils. It is a large carrot that has a growth coming from it that looks rude.*

ALAN *(cont'd)* What is this? Alice? Gwen?

GWEN Carrot, sir.

ALAN A carrot. So why are you laughing, then? Is it because this bit looks like a penis? A big, floppy penis?

The door opens and MR EDWARDS *appears with* CERI.

MR EDWARDS Everything alright, Mr Curtis?

ALAN Yes, we were just doing fractions and . . . biology.

MR EDWARDS Oh, interesting combination. I have young Ceri Morgan for you. Ceri, take your seat. Good girl.

CERI *goes to sit down. She looks shamefaced.*

ALAN Is everything sorted out now, headmaster?

MR EDWARDS Yes, all cleared up. No further action required. *(quietly, to* ALAN*)* Suffice to say there was quite a big discrepancy between the two images. In your favour, I have to say. So, you know . . . every cloud.

ALAN Good, thank you.

MR EDWARDS As you were.

MR EDWARDS *leaves.* ALAN *looks to* CERI, *but she doesn't look up.*

ALAN Nice to have you back, Ceri.

CERI *doesn't respond. She stares at the rude carrot.* ALAN *is flustered and puts it in his pocket.*

INT. CLASSROOM. Day.

ALAN *is at his desk. The pupils are quietly writing.* ALAN *stares at* CERI *intently. She is working. She looks up, and* ALAN *looks away. After a beat,* ALAN *stands.*

ALAN Just to say, if any of you are struggling to find the right answer, don't just make something up, alright? Because that has consequences. Just put your hand up and talk to me. I can't help you if I don't know what's going on. So don't go behind my back, OK? Good.

GWEN *puts up her hand and* ALAN *approaches her, casting sideways glances at* CERI.

GWEN Sir, is this right?

ALAN Let's have a look . . .

INT. CLASSROOM. DAY.

ALAN *is collecting exercise books from the tables. As he carries them to his desk, a small piece of paper falls to the floor.* ALAN *picks it up and sees a crude doodle of a smiling man wearing a crown, his limbs akimbo, and beside him a small stick figure of a girl holding his hand.*

ALAN *looks at the image for a moment, focusing on the crown. Then he gets his mobile phone from his desk and dials a number. He gets through to a voicemail.*

ALAN Hi Megan, it's Alan Curtis here from class 9. Mr Edwards said he was going to dig out an email address for Mr King, who taught the kids last year, but I haven't had it yet. Is there any chance of chasing it up? Thanks, bye.

ALAN *remembers the postcard, which he finds in a desk drawer. The front reads 'Greetings from Australia', with a picture of a kangaroo. He turns it over and scans the text, but his eye is drawn to the postmark, which clearly reads 'Cardiff, Wales'.*

The door opens, and WINNIE *comes in with a box of vegetables.*

ALAN Hi Winnie.

WINNIE Who's that?

ALAN It's Mr Curtis.

WINNIE Oh, hello dear. I just wondered if you wanted to take a leek?

ALAN Sorry?

WINNIE For the harvest festival. I've had a good crop this year. Nice big potatoes, radishes - my turnips have won prizes, you know!

ALAN Congratulations.

WINNIE *goes to deposit the vegetables in the harvest festival corner.*

ALAN *(cont'd)* Winnie, what was Mr King like with the children?

WINNIE Oh, well, I'm not in the lessons, like, but they all seemed to love him. He was a real star, and quite a dish too.

ALAN He sounds too good to be true.

WINNIE Oh no, he was very down to earth, very conscientious. This school didn't have a girls' soccer team until he same along.

ALAN I see.

ALAN *goes over to look at the vegetable display.*

ALAN *(cont'd)* Your neeps are very impressive, Winnie.

WINNIE Thank you. This is a brand new Playtex, lift and separate.

ALAN I meant the vegetables.

WINNIE Well, that's Mother Nature working her magic.

ALAN Listen, I promised the head I'd get these reports to him by the end of the day, and it completely slipped my mind. You don't happen to have a key for his office, do you?

WINNIE I do, but I'm not supposed to let anyone have it . . . Oh, go on then, as long as you're quick.

WINNIE *takes the key from her keyring.*

ALAN I'll be two minutes, thanks.

ALAN *takes the key and heads out of the classroom.* WINNIE *puts her vegetables on the display.*

INT. CORRIDOR. DAY.

ALAN *arrives at the headmaster's office and uses the key to let himself in.*

INT. HEADMASTER'S OFFICE. DAY.

ALAN *quietly searches the filing cabinet. He finds a folder reading 'Staff lists 2020–21'. He opens it and finds a list of staff, but among the six or so names, there is no Mr King – it goes from 'Mr Hardy' to 'Ms Miller'.*

He then finds a photo of Class 9 from 2021 with all the same pupils, but the teacher is credited as 'Mr Hardy'.

ALAN *opens another drawer and finds a folder marked 'King'. He pulls out the folder and opens it on the desk.*

ALAN *is shocked to find a collection of Polaroid photographs of penises, starting with his own. There are all different shapes and sizes, but some have red crosses through them, and some are marked with gold stars.*

ALAN *returns the photos to the file. He's more confused than ever.*

EXT. SCHOOL. DAY.

We see the school, set in the countryside. A local farmer is ploughing his field.

INT. CORRIDOR. DAY.

ALAN *is approaching his classroom. He's on his mobile phone, making a call.* MR EDWARDS *answers.*

MR EDWARDS *(V.O.)* Hello?

ALAN Headmaster, it's Alan Curtis.

MR EDWARDS *(V.O.)* Hello Adam, what can I do for you?

ALAN I need to talk to you urgently about several things, firstly about Mr King. This school has no record of him ever having worked here.

MR EDWARDS *(V.O.)* What's that? Sorry, it's a very bad line. Something about Mr King?

ALAN The class teacher last year was Mr Hardy, a completely different person. So I don't know what this King has been doing here, being given access to children, but I think there's been abuse going on, it's been covered up. And I think you are part of it.

MR EDWARDS *(V.O.)* Yeah, I'm losing you, Adam. It's a terrible connection. I'm just in the field, I'll come and see you shortly, OK?

ALAN You won't get away with this, do you hear?

The line goes dead.

INT. CLASSROOM. DAY.

ALAN *enters the classroom to find that the pupils have pushed the tables and chairs aside to create a performance space at the front of the room.* ALAN*'s chair is facing the front so he can watch.*

ALAN Oh, Class 9 what's this?

EUAN We wanted to show you what we've been practising for our assembly.

Two of the children lead him to his chair and sit him down in it.

ALAN Oh, well, I was just going to do quiet reading today. Maybe we can do this tomorrow . . . ?

CERI Oh please, sir, we've been working really hard on what you taught us.

ALAN OK, go ahead.

The children line up and join hands. OWEN *is at the end of the line, and mimes his free hand being glued to a wall.*

OWEN Welcome to our assembly. We have glued ourselves to the prime minister's house to protest against climate change.

ALAN Ha, very good.

GWEN Global warming is the biggest threat to our planet, planet Earth.

CHILD 1 *comes to the front with a large planet Earth hanging round his neck. The Earth is crying.*

GWEN *(cont'd)* What can we do to stop it?

CHILD 2 *walks by, drinking from a plastic cup and straw. He throws it down on the floor.*

CHILD 1 (EARTH) Hey, you, what are you doing?

CHILD 2 Me? Nothing. It's only plastic.

CHILD 1 (EARTH) Plastic is slowly choking me, filling my oceans and killing wildlife.

CHILD 1 (EARTH) *mimes choking.*

CHILD 2 *(shrugging)* What can I do?

ALL CHILDREN Recycling!

EUAN Take that!

EUAN *steps forward with a tinfoil sword and pretends to stab the littering* CHILD 2, *who falls to the ground.*

EUAN *(cont'd)* We'll recycle *him* later.

ALAN *is disturbed by this.*

ALAN Now Class 9, I don't think that's appropriate.

ALAN *tries to stand up, but realises his back, bottom and arms are stuck to the chair.*

ALAN *(cont'd)* What have you done to this chair?

CERI Superglue. You're part of the protest too, sir.

ALAN That's not funny, Ceri. Alright, let's stop this now.

CHILD 3 Saving the planet started thousands of years ago.

GWEN *stands on a chair as the Earth Goddess. She wears a long green flowing robe.* CHILD 1 *and* CHILD 2 *pull the robe open to reveal leaves and vines stitched on.*

GWEN In the beginning, the Earth Goddess was the one who expressed Herself through the many.

EUAN She was the great void, the beginning of all things.

CERI All souls were born from Her sacred Womb, lived for a span upon Her Body the Earth, then returned to Her Tomb-Womb at death.

ALAN Tomb-womb? I'm sorry, that's not in Key Stage 2.

CERI But Mr King said . . .

ALAN Look, I don't know who this Mr King was, or what he was teaching you, but it's not normal, alright? I'm going to make an official complaint. Now, please get me out of this chair . . .

ALAN *struggles in the chair.* CHILD 4 *steps forward, holding up a picture of child sacrifice.*

CHILD 4 In 15th-century Peru, children were sacrificed to the gods to try and end natural disasters.

EUAN *steps forward, holding a picture of Greta Thunberg.*

EUAN But in modern times, we the children are demanding sacrifices of our own.

Two of the older boys approach ALAN *in his chair.*

ALAN What are you talking about? Wait, is this why you killed the tadpoles? To try and stop climate change?

CERI No talking, Mr King, we listen with these . . .

She points to her ears.

CERI *(cont'd)* . . . Not these.

She points to her lips.

ALAN I'm not Mr King!

OWEN *holds* ALAN*'s head, while* EUAN *stands in front of him. We hear* ALAN *struggle. He is powerless to stop them.*

OWEN Tight lips, sir!

ALAN No! No, don't. *(mumbling)* Hmm-bmm-hmm.

We see that the boys have glued ALAN*'s lips together. The children continue the assembly.*

CHILD 1 We have learned about reusable energy.

CHILD 2 We have learned about recycling and rebirth.

CHILD 3 John Barleycorn was the first man to recycle himself to replenish the Earth's bounty. This is his story.

The children put on crude paper-plate masks made from natural items, such as crops, acorns, conkers, etc.

GWEN *presses play on a large tape recorder and a piano accompaniment begins playing. Some children play claves and woodblocks.* ALAN *is terrified. The children sing.*

ALL CHILDREN There were three men come out of the west, their fortunes for to try / And these three men made a solemn vow: John Barleycorn should die.

Suddenly, the door opens and MR EDWARDS *comes in. He stops the music.*

MR EDWARDS Now, Mr Curtis . . . What on earth is going on here? What do you think you're doing?

The children stop playing and look guilty. ALAN *looks at* MR EDWARDS *pleadingly.*

GWEN We're doing our assembly, sir.

MR EDWARDS Assembly? That's not until next week. Are you alright, Mr Curtis? What have they done to your mouth?

MR EDWARDS *approaches* ALAN *to look at him more closely.* CERI *is behind the headmaster with a small hand-scythe.*

CERI We were about to tell the story of John Barleycorn.

MR EDWARDS *turns to see* CERI *with the scythe. He breaks into a smile.*

MR EDWARDS Ah, my favourite part. Carry on.

MR EDWARDS *takes a chair and sits beside* ALAN, *watching the assembly.*

ALAN *watches in horror as the children in their masks sway from side to side.*

CHILD 3 John Barleycorn represents the life-cycle of the field.

CHILD 1 He is crowned once a year at the start of the harvest festival, and revered as the Corn King.

MR EDWARDS *leans over to speak to the terrified* ALAN.

MR EDWARDS Last year, as you discovered, Mr Hardy was given the honour. This year, the crown is yours.

CERI We discovered you are as nature intended.

MR EDWARDS Uncut and still sheathed.

CERI A perfect candidate for our new Corn King.

MR EDWARDS Thank you, Ceri. You did it beautifully. When his reign is ended, the King is returned to the land and honoured with a Triple Death; drowned, strangled and dismembered, his broken body buried in the field to ensure a fertile harvest.

GWEN Like human beans!

MR EDWARDS Exactly Gwen. Like human beans.

The children circle around ALAN *in their masks. One of the children presses 'play' on the tape recorder again and the music plays.*

MR EDWARDS *(cont'd)* You and your fancy friends in London may pat yourselves on the back that you've finally woken up to environmental issues, but we've been doing our bit for the planet for centuries now. Come, children! The King is dead; long live the King.

The children start to play their percussion instruments in a menacing beat. Some of them bring forth a large straw mask depicting John Barleycorn, with a crown made of corn husks.

The children place the mask over ALAN*'s head as he mumbles and protests, and the other children sing.*

ALL CHILDREN They wheeled him all around the field / A prisoner to endure / And in the barn, poor Barleycorn / They laid him upon the floor.

MR EDWARDS Winnie, we're ready for you.

WINNIE *enters, dressed in a costume made of straw and vegetables, a grotesque sight. She approaches* ALAN *and starts to wheel his chair out of the classroom in his primitive mask.*

WINNIE You're going to do my leeks the world of good.

The children proceed behind and sing. CERI *carries the scythe.*

ALL CHILDREN They hired men with the crab-tree sticks / To cut him skin from bone / And the miller, he served him worse than that / For he ground him between two stones.

MR EDWARDS *takes a spade from the harvest festival display. He smiles, exits the classroom and closes the door.*

We settle on the children's paintings on the display wall. They look at first like trees and crops growing in the field, but upon closer inspection, we see that they are dismembered human limbs, buried and sprouting leaves.

THE END

Episode 3

NINE LIVES KAT

CAST LIST

KATRINA – Sophie Okonedo

GIRL – Coco-Lili Hoder

EZRA – Steve Pemberton

BARNABUS – Reece Shearsmith

PHILIPPA – Robin Weaver

MATILDA – Siobhan Redmond

INT. LIVING ROOM. NIGHT.

*A desk with a lamp, laptop, pen holder, etc. A silhouetted hand opens the drawer of a small metal filing cabinet and pulls out a file full of scribbled handwritten notes about a police investigation. There is a photo of a small boy (*ASHLEY*). We push in on one of the pages of notes, which has number 9 written in tally marks.*

TITLE: *'Nine Lives Kat'.*

INT. BEDROOM. NIGHT.

From the blackness, a woman wakes suddenly and sits bolt upright, wide-eyed, confused. This is KATRINA, *middle-aged, looks like she's had a rough night. She holds her hand to her head and groans.*

KATRINA Oh God. Never again.

INT. UPSTAIRS LANDING/CHILD'S BEDROOM. NIGHT.

KATRINA, *now in a dressing gown and slippers, shuffles out of her room to a child's bedroom. She opens the door and sees her* DAUGHTER *sleeping in the single bed. A half-smile, then* KATRINA *quietly closes the door.*

INT. KITCHEN. NIGHT.

KATRINA *enters the sparse-looking kitchen. A black cat slinks towards her.*

KATRINA What time is it, Kitney? Are we on breakfast, dinner or tea? Start with breakfast, shall we?

KATRINA *takes some Coco Pops from a cupboard and empties some into the cat's bowl, then some into her own bowl. She goes to the fridge and pulls out a half-drunk bottle of vodka.*

She pours some of the vodka into her cereal bowl.

We see that a man, EZRA, *is watching her from the doorway.*

EZRA Vodka and Coco Pops? Are you serious?

KATRINA There's no milk. Do you want me to eat them dry?

EZRA You've only just got out of bed.

KATRINA I know, I'm a walking cliché – what can I tell you? Fetch me a spoon.

EZRA *gets a spoon from the cutlery drawer, and* KATRINA *starts to eat her breakfast.*

EZRA So is this why they took you off the case?

KATRINA The drinking? No. I can go round for round with any of those plods and still not lose my lunch at an autopsy.

EZRA You bounce back.

KATRINA Exactly.

EZRA That's why they call you Nine Lives Kat.

KATRINA *(secretly pleased)* Do they?

EZRA Yeah. Short for Katrina.

KATRINA Oh. *(To the cat)* What about that, Kitney? I've got a nickname, just like you! *(To* EZRA*)* Kitney Spears.

EZRA Funny.

KATRINA I used to have two, but David Meowie got run over.

KATRINA *drains the chocolatey vodka from her bowl.*

KATRINA *(wincing)* Oh God, that's good.

EZRA So go on, then – why did they take you off the case?

KATRINA They're dinosaurs. They couldn't handle being told the truth by a woman, simple as that. My ex-husband was exactly the same.

EZRA Ex-husbands. There's been more than one.

KATRINA Who's counting? But you know what? I'll show them. I'll show them you don't need a cock and balls to crack a case, or to stack a dishwasher in the most 'ergonomic' way possible.

KATRINA *throws her bowl into the dishwasher.*

KATRINA *(cont'd)* You just need a brain, and a heart and guts. And that's what I've got. So are you going to help me or not?

EZRA Of course I am, Nine Lives Kat.

EZRA *smiles and takes his notebook from his pocket as he follows* KATRINA *into the living room.*

INT. LIVING ROOM. NIGHT.

KATRINA *and* EZRA *enter the living room, which is sparsely furnished and decorated. On one wall is the photograph of* ASHLEY, *pinned to a map, with red string branching out to Post-it notes, car registrations, an identikit suspect picture, crime scene photos, etc.*

KATRINA *stares at the wall display as* EZRA *reads from his notebook.*

KATRINA OK, bring me up to speed.

EZRA So, we've got five suspects who were all picked up on CCTV in and around the area at the time of the abduction. I'm in the process of fleshing out their stories, but it seems two of them have links to the family that could throw up some interesting leads . . .

KATRINA Let's not talk about throwing up, not until these Coco Pops have settled. What about the stepfather? Surely he's our prime suspect?

EZRA I'd rather say he's 'helping us with our enquiries'.

KATRINA Well, let's arrange a press conference for this afternoon. If he breaks down in tears and says, 'We just want our angel back,' then we'll know it's definitely him.

EZRA I thought you were off the case?

KATRINA There's a little boy out there tonight who's frightened. He's trapped, he can't breathe. I'm going to find him and bring him out into the light. And I don't care whose toes I have to tread on to do it.

EZRA *smiles and makes a note in his book.*

INT. CHILD'S BEDROOM. NIGHT.

KATRINA *quietly opens the door so as not to wake the sleeping child. A night light illuminates the room, giving it an eerie glow. The tune it plays is 'Five Little Ducks'.* KATRINA *sits on her* DAUGHTER*'s bed and strokes her hair.*

KATRINA When you were little and your milk teeth fell out, I used to take them from under your pillow, leave 50p, and I'd keep them in a TicTac box in the bathroom cabinet. And whenever the job got too much for me, or your dad was being difficult, I'd empty them into my hand and squeeze as hard as I could. Your teeth in my fist. Until I felt blood. Until I felt alive.

A creak from the wardrobe. KATRINA *gets up and approaches it slowly. She takes the handles and pulls them open.*

INT. BEDROOM. NIGHT.

KATRINA *suddenly wakes, same as before. Was that a dream? She throws back the duvet with purpose.*

INT. LIVING ROOM. NIGHT

EZRA *stands with his notebook in front of the case notes on the wall.* KATRINA, *now dressed, paces back and forth. As she paces, she walks back into shot in different outfits to suggest the passage of time; smoking, thinking, pacing.*

KATRINA Take me through it again.

EZRA Eleven-fifteen a.m., Ashley finishes his karate lesson and is collected from the Methodist church by his mum. Eleven-thirty, they pull into the retail park, where Mum goes into McDonald's to buy a Happy Meal, telling Ashley to stay in the car. Five minutes prior to that, we have a green Vauxhall Corsa parking up outside Hollywood Bowl, driven by Sunglasses Man – whom we've yet to identify – and the cameras show the same car leaving at speed at eleven-thirty-eight.

As EZRA *continues,* KATRINA *zones out his voice and focuses on the different elements on the wall: the green car, the identikit man, the CCTV images, the witnesses; the little boy.* KATRINA*'s in a daze when she hears:*

KATRINA'S DAUGHTER Mummy.

KATRINA *spins to see her* DAUGHTER *behind her, but we quickly cut away.*

INT. BEDROOM

KATRINA *opens her eyes, suddenly wide awake. She looks round to see a man's body in the bed next to her (*BARNABUS, *alive but sleeping). She groans quietly; another rough night.*

An open bottle of pills is on her bedside table. She shakes out a couple and pops them into her mouth, then pulls out a cigarette and clamps it between her lips.

INT. KITCHEN. DAY.

KATRINA *wanders into the kitchen in her pyjamas and bends down to drink water from the tap to swallow her pills. When she comes back up,* EZRA *is there. He seems older somehow, his hair a shade greyer than before.*

KATRINA Trust you to be here.

EZRA Charming.

KATRINA *lights her cigarette from the gas hob.*

KATRINA Have you seen Kitney Spears?

EZRA No, she's gone.

KATRINA Dirty stop-out. Mind you, I can talk. So, what have you got for me?

EZRA How do you mean?

KATRINA The missing boy. Did we check out the alibis of the five suspects?

EZRA That was a long time ago.

KATRINA What do you mean?

EZRA Kat, I haven't seen you in . . . several months.

KATRINA What are you talking about? I saw you two days ago.

EZRA Just give me some time to catch up . . .

EZRA *takes out his notebook.* KATRINA *is confused. She pushes through to the living room.*

INT. LIVING ROOM.

The map and crime scene photos have gone. A bland watercolour hangs in their place.

KATRINA Where's it gone?

EZRA What?

KATRINA The whole investigation . . .

EZRA I still have all the notes, but I didn't think it was good to put it all up there on the wall.

KATRINA You have no right to tell me how to run this case, do you hear me? No right! I was this close to making a breakthrough . . .

The man from upstairs, BARNABUS, *appears in the doorway. He coughs. He's handsome, but socially awkward.*

KATRINA *(cont'd)* Oh. You're up.

BARNABUS Katrina.

EZRA She prefers to be called Kat.

BARNABUS I'm not sure what happened last night. You seemed very agitated, and we both had a lot to drink. If it's any consolation, I don't think we actually . . .

KATRINA Actually what?

BARNABUS Elvis did not enter the building. Not that I'm comparing my penis to a cultural icon and your vagina to a four thousand-seat arena, but . . .

KATRINA Is this guy for real?

BARNABUS I didn't mean . . . Can we start again?

KATRINA I think you should.

EZRA Sorry, you are . . . ?

BARNABUS DI Bull. Barnabus Bull. I'm a colleague of Katrina's, but we have a sort of love-hate relationship. I sense we're in a hate phase at the moment.

KATRINA Shut up, Barney. I'm trying to think.

BARNABUS Sure. Though, strictly speaking, all thinking is subconscious, because consciousness is an awareness of thought, not thinking itself, so you can't 'try to think' . . .

EZRA Why don't you go and put the kettle on?

BARNABUS Because . . . I don't think it would fit.

EZRA No, *switch* the kettle on. I think we could all do with a drink.

BARNABUS Sure, sure.

BARNABUS *disappears into the kitchen.* EZRA *removes his coat.*

EZRA He's quite a character. A bit . . . spectrum-y, perhaps?

KATRINA I'm not shagging him.

EZRA I know, I didn't think you were. It's just . . . an interesting development.

KATRINA Look, I know you think I'm taking this case too personally, but that's because I'm a woman. I empathise. But I know how to fight, and I know how to dig my heels in – and let me tell you, size-six stilettos dig in deep. Now, what have you done with my case notes?

BARNABUS *calls from the kitchen.*

BARNABUS *(O.S.)* Do you have any loose-leaf tea? I can't bear the bags; they never steep in quite the right way.

EZRA One sec.

EZRA *smiles and exits, leaving* KATRINA *alone. She quietly pushes the door to, and then goes over to* EZRA*'s coat on the sofa. She fishes his wallet from inside and pulls out his credit card: Mr Ezra Jones.*

Removing the credit card has revealed a photo in the wallet that shows EZRA *with a little boy. She pulls the photo out and is stunned to see that it is the missing boy (*ASHLEY*) from the case – it's the same face she's had pinned up on her wall.*

INT. BEDROOM. NIGHT.

KATRINA *opens her eyes, suddenly wide awake again.*

INT. UPSTAIRS LANDING/CHILD'S BEDROOM. NIGHT.

It's dark. KATRINA*'s door opens, and she creeps out of her room. She is aware of the sound of movement downstairs. She tiptoes to her* DAUGHTER*'s room and opens the door to see her asleep in bed.*

KATRINA *closes the door and makes her way downstairs.*

INT. KITCHEN

KATRINA *enters the kitchen. She tries the light switch, but it doesn't work. She goes to open the fridge door, which lights up the room. There is a single half-full bottle of vodka in the fridge and nothing else. She opens the cupboards and sees only the Coco Pops.*

KATRINA *opens a drawer and sees a single spoon inside. She slowly goes to one of the other cupboards and opens it . . . and a black cat jumps out at her, making her scream. It runs out of the kitchen, past* EZRA*, who is in the doorway.*

EZRA Is that really the best we can do? Jump scares with a cat?

KATRINA Why are you always here? I don't remember giving you a key. And what happened to the boy, Ashley? What are you not telling me?

EZRA *regards* KATRINA *sadly.*

EZRA I tried with you, Katrina. I really, really did. But I just don't think it's working.

KATRINA *doesn't understand.*

EZRA *heads to the living room.* KATRINA *follows.*

INT. LIVING ROOM. NIGHT.

EZRA *opens the door and enters, followed by* KATRINA.

BARNABUS *stands in the middle of the room, surrounded by papers.*

BARNABUS Please don't come in here! I've got a system. I know exactly where everything is.

EZRA It's alright, Barnabus. We can pick it up later.

KATRINA What the hell's he doing here? Get out of my house!

EZRA It's not your house, Kat. It never was.

The cat enters the room and runs straight to BARNABUS.

BARNABUS Come on Katy, good girl.

EZRA *(to* KATRINA*)* Katy Purry. Bit more contemporary.

EZRA *crosses to the bookshelf and takes a book from it to show to* KATRINA. *It's called Little Black Lies by Ezra Jones, an author photo on the back.*

EZRA *(cont'd)* I'd written a couple of collections of short stories, won a Golden Dagger, pretty healthy sales. And my publisher thought it'd be a good idea to do a series of detective novels. I wasn't that keen, but I started to make some notes, had a brainstorm, and out of nowhere I wrote down: *Nine Lives Kat.*

BARNABUS It's a good title.

EZRA It is, yes. Thank you. So I tinkered with the idea, made up some bog-standard case of a missing child, just so I could interrogate the character and see if it added up to anything.

KATRINA The character . . . based on me?

EZRA The character *of* you.

KATRINA *tries to take this in.*

EZRA *(cont'd)* Katrina . . . Surname – I never got that far. Late 40s, one or two divorces, single mum, booze, pills, clashes with authority. And what I realised when I read it back was – it's all a bit clichéd.

KATRINA I said this!

EZRA I know.

KATRINA I said this on bloody page one!

EZRA I know you did. And I should learn to listen to that critical voice. But at the time, I was watching reruns of *Cracker* and *Prime Suspect*, and I thought, 'I can write one of these.' So I tried, and . . . you just turned out to be a bit . . .

BARNABUS Generic.

KATRINA Fuck off, Rain Man!

The cat hisses at KATRINA. BARNABUS *strokes it.*

BARNABUS It's alright, Katy, it's alright.

EZRA So I put you in the bottom drawer for a while, and every now and again I'd pull you out, see if there was anything I could work with. I do some screenwriting now, and the streaming platforms are dying for female-led content. That, and dystopian fucking fantasy worlds, anyway . . .

KATRINA *is upset, confused, defiant.*

KATRINA You think you're some patriarchal creator, god of your own little universe? No, sorry, I'm real. My life is real.

EZRA No, it isn't. You're a fictional construct. Look around you. Would a real person live like this? One spoon, one bowl, one box of cereal. You're just a sketch Kat, a first-thought idea.

KATRINA No . . .

EZRA The boss, the ex-husband – what are they? They're just ciphers.

KATRINA I have a daughter.

EZRA What's her name? You don't know, do you?

KATRINA *thinks hard. She can't conjure it.*

EZRA *(cont'd)* You don't know, because I never bothered to give her one. She was just an afterthought. Tacked on to try and make you more interesting.

KATRINA No . . . No . . .

KATRINA *runs out of the room, devastated.*

INT. UPSTAIRS LANDING. NIGHT.

KATRINA *runs up the stairs and into her* DAUGHTER*'s room.*

INT. CHILD'S ROOM. NIGHT.

KATRINA *runs to her sleeping* DAUGHTER. *She pulls her round and for the first time we see her face: a perfectly blank, featureless, eyeless mask of nothingness – terrifying.*

KATRINA *screams.*

INT. BEDROOM. DAY.

KATRINA *wakes once again in the empty room.* BARNABUS *sits on the bed next to her. There's no bedding, just a plain mattress and pillows.* EZRA *stands by the window.*

EZRA I wrestled with this idea for a long time, getting writer's block. It was quite difficult. So I tried pairing you with a new character, to see if that would freshen things up a bit.

BARNABUS DI Barnabus Bull.

KATRINA You put him in bed with me?

EZRA Yes.

BARNABUS I love that name; so satisfying to say. 'Barnabus Bull'.

EZRA My publisher likes it too. I found out today. Three-book deal.

BARNABUS *fist pumps.*

BARNABUS Yes! *Red Rag to a Bull*, *The Bull's Eye* and *Bull* . . .

KATRINA Shit.

BARNABUS *Bull in a China Shop*.

EZRA Maybe. There's a long way to go yet before we have to worry about titles.

KATRINA What, so he gets to have a life and I go back in the bottom drawer? Just because he's got an unspecified mental illness?

BARNABUS Stop shouting, stop shouting!

BARNABUS *gets up and leaves the room, holding his hands over his ears.*

EZRA There might be a victim's mother or a jealous mistress I can use you for, but in terms of this – *Nine Lives Kat*, flawed detective with inner demons – we've seen it all before.

KATRINA And whose fault is that?

EZRA Yes, you're right. It's not you. It's me.

KATRINA So, the missing boy. He's your son, isn't he?

EZRA Ashley? Just a placeholder, something to visualise. People think writing is all in the head, but sometimes you have to make it real for yourself.

KATRINA *refers to the folder of notes* EZRA *is holding.*

KATRINA Are those my notes?

EZRA *nods.*

EZRA I've got to let you go.

KATRINA *(real emotion)* Please don't.

EZRA You've run out of lives, Kat.

EZRA *leaves the room.*

INT. LIVING ROOM. DAY.

EZRA *enters and crosses to the desk. He unlocks the bottom drawer and slides it open.*

INT. BEDROOM. DAY.

KATRINA *sits on the bed, empty, powerless. She lays her head on the pillow.*

INT. LIVING ROOM. DAY.

EZRA *places the folder of notes into the drawer. He looks down for a moment before starting to slide the drawer shut.*

INT. BEDROOM. DAY.

KATRINA *knows the end is coming. A single tear slides down her cheek. She takes one last breath in before . . . BLACKNESS.*

FADE TO:

INT. LIVING ROOM. DAY

We hear the sound of keyboard typing. We pan along a shelf, where we find a copy of Red Rag to a Bull: A Barnabus Bull novel *by Ezra Jones, along with* EZRA*'s Golden Dagger award and a framed photo of Ezra's wife (*PHILIPPA*) and son* ASHLEY.

The living room is the same space as KATRINA*'s living room, but now much more lived-in and looking like a family home.*

We find EZRA *at his desk, typing up a synopsis for a new novel when his phone rings.*

EZRA Hi Georgie. I was just about to call you, actually; I've finished the synopsis for the new *Bull* . . . Yeah, it's a sort of locked-room mystery. I'm quite pleased with it, actually. I was just wondering where we are with the TV rights – is it still with what's-his-name at ITV? Because I was watching Jude Law in *The Talented Mr Ripley* last night, and thinking he could be really good.

We see BARNABUS *is sitting near by. He whispers to* EZRA.

BARNABUS Or Matt Damon.

EZRA *(ignoring* BARNABUS*)* Yeah, he'd get the intensity, and he was good in that Sky thing last year . . .

BARNABUS Matt Damon.

EZRA (to BARNABUS) They're not going to get Matt Damon, he's American! *(into phone)* No, no, I was just . . . talking to Philippa. Anyway, I'll send it over this afternoon and you can let me know what you think. Thanks, Georgie, bye.

EZRA *hangs up.*

EZRA *(cont'd)* Will you stop interfering in my private phone calls?

BARNABUS I'm only saying what you're thinking.

EZRA Well, it's irritating! Just concentrate on how Bull knew about the false floor in the basement, please.

BARNABUS Carpet tiles.

EZRA What?

BARNABUS Should have been black square to the left, like a chessboard. When we got there, it was cream square to the left; ergo, somebody must have taken them up and re-laid them.

EZRA *considers this.*

EZRA Aah, yes, like a chessboard . . . and if we make Colin gay and Alan a Sir or something, we can say . . .

EZRA and BARNABUS *(together)* . . . the queen was taken by the knight.

EZRA Brilliant.

EZRA *writes this down on the printed pages. We hear the door open, and* EZRA*'s wife* PHILIPPA *enters, laden with shopping.*

BARNABUS *has disappeared.*

EZRA Hi . . .

PHILIPPA Hi.

EZRA Did you get everything?

PHILIPPA Yeah, it was busy though. Do you know how to do Find My Phone?

EZRA *(not paying attention)* What?

PHILIPPA I can't find it. I had it in the car park when I arrived. Someone must have had it out of my pocket.

EZRA Well, if you will go to Asda and not Waitrose . . .

EZRA *takes up his phone and starts flicking through the apps.* PHILIPPA *ferries things from the living room to the kitchen.*

EZRA *(cont'd)* Where were you when you sent me that text?

PHILIPPA Which text?

EZRA About picking Ash up from swimming.

PHILIPPA *You* were picking him up from swimming.

EZRA No, you texted me to say not to.

PHILIPPA No I didn't!

EZRA You did, look . . .

EZRA *shows her a text on his phone.*

PHILIPPA That's not . . . Where is he . . . ?

PHILIPPA *exits and calls up the stairs.*

PHILIPPA *(V.O.)* Ashley! Ashley!

EZRA He's not here, I told you.

PHILIPPA *(V.O.)* Why didn't you pick him up?

EZRA You said you were going to!

BARNABUS *is back.*

BARNABUS What if somebody took your wife's phone to send the text?

EZRA *(to* BARNABUS*)* What the fuck are you talking about?

PHILIPPA *re-enters.*

PHILIPPA What the fuck are *you* talking about? Where is he? Ezra? Where is my son!?

Push in on EZRA*, a look of horror on his face.*

INT. BEDROOM. NIGHT.

EZRA *wakes with a start. He's in the same bedroom as* KATRINA *was, but again it is very different, with new bedding, and it looks more real and lived-in.*

INT. UPSTAIRS LANDING. NIGHT.

EZRA *emerges from his room and approaches a child's room with the name 'Ashley' on the door. He opens it up to see there is an empty bed, not slept in.*

INT. LIVING ROOM. NIGHT.

EZRA *enters slowly, looking dazed and confused.* PHILIPPA *is by the window, looking out.*

EZRA Any news?

PHILIPPA *shakes her head.*

EZRA *(cont'd)* There's a woman in the kitchen.

PHILIPPA She's a family liaison officer; she said she'd stay the night.

EZRA Did they find your phone?

PHILIPPA Not yet.

PHILIPPA *comes to hug* EZRA, *grabbing him tightly.*

PHILIPPA *(cont'd)* Where is he, Ez? I can't bear it.

EZRA Shh, he'll be alright. I promise.

An older woman enters with two cups of tea: MATILDA.

MATILDA Oh, hello. I thought I heard another voice. I made you a tea.

EZRA Thanks.

MATILDA I'm Matilda Gordon. Your wife probably told you, I'm the family liaison.

EZRA Yes, she did. I'm Ezra.

MATILDA I know you are. I'm a big fan.

EZRA Thank you.

MATILDA I'd love a selfie at some point, but maybe . . .

EZRA Not now.

MATILDA No. I was just asking your wife if you could think of anyone who might have a grudge against you? Anyone you might have upset or offended?

EZRA No, I don't think so.

MATILDA Nobody you've based one of your characters on in your stories?

EZRA I'm a writer; I *invent* characters.

MATILDA Of course. And your son – sorry, your stepson – has he had any fallings-out or arguments recently . . . ?

EZRA No. Look, we said all this before, he was always well-liked.

PHILIPPA *Was?*

EZRA *Is.* Sorry Phil, I've just woken up.

PHILIPPA *leaves.* EZRA *sits, embarrassed.*

MATILDA It's the shock; the body shuts down. I went through your medicine cabinet to see if you were on any medication, and I found this hidden at the back.

MATILDA *produces a TicTac box. She shakes it.*

MATILDA *(cont'd)* They're teeth, children's teeth.

MATILDA *empties the teeth on to the table.* EZRA*'s head is spinning.*

MATILDA *(cont'd)* Are they Ashley's? Philippa said she didn't remember keeping them.

EZRA Erm, no. I've never seen them before.

MATILDA Are you sure? They were in your side of the cabinet.

EZRA I think they might have belonged to . . . a colleague of mine who was . . . helping me with a story.

MATILDA I see. Another case for Barnabus Bull?

EZRA No, it was nothing. It was just some background research – I didn't finish it.

MATILDA I would very much like to read it, Mr Jones. As a fan, as much as anything else.

EZRA Sure, it's in here.

EZRA *gets up and goes to unlock the bottom drawer of his desk. He scrabbles through his notes, eventually finding the Nine Lives Kat folder. He opens it up, but it's empty. He scrabbles through his other papers, but he can't find the notes.*

MATILDA *is watching him patiently.* BARNABUS *is now behind her.*

EZRA I can't . . . Barnabus, you haven't seen my notes on Nine Lives Kat, have you?

MATILDA No, my name's Matilda, dear. Barnabus is a fictional character. He doesn't exist.

EZRA *is confused. When he looks back,* BARNABUS *has gone.*

INT. BEDROOM. NIGHT.

EZRA *is in bed.* PHILIPPA *is sleeping beside him.*

EZRA *opens his eyes just in time to see a little girl, the faceless*

KATRINA'S DAUGHTER, *disappearing out of the door.* EZRA *gets out of bed to investigate.*

INT. UPSTAIRS LANDING. NIGHT.

EZRA *hears eerie singing from Ashley's bedroom.*

KATRINA'S DAUGHTER *(V.O.)* Five little ducks went swimming one day . . .

EZRA Ashley?

INT. CHILD'S ROOM. NIGHT.

EZRA *bursts in, but the room is empty as before.*

DAUGHTER *(V.O.)* Over the hill and far away . . .

EZRA *turns just in time to see the* DAUGHTER *dart past the open doorway. He hurries out of the room.*

HALLWAY. NIGHT.

EZRA *looks down the stairs to see the* DAUGHTER *running into the living room.*

DAUGHTER *(V.O.)* Mother duck said, 'Quack quack quack quack!'

EZRA Hello?

EZRA *hares down the stairs and into the living room.*

INT. LIVING ROOM.

EZRA *enters the room.* MATILDA *is slumped in the armchair, seemingly strangled, surrounded by papers. They are* EZRA*'s notes on Nine Lives Kat.* EZRA *is wide-eyed in horror.*

KATRINA'S DAUGHTER *(V.O.)* But only four little ducks came back.

EZRA *backs out of the living room.*

INT. KITCHEN. NIGHT.

EZRA *enters.* KATRINA *sits at the kitchen table. She's reading* EZRA*'s book,* Red Rag to a Bull.

KATRINA Well, it's true what they say – you can't put a good book down.

EZRA W-what are you doing here?

KATRINA I had to come for the final chapter. See how it all turns out.

EZRA I didn't write this.

KATRINA No. This is not a 'fictional construct'. This is really happening. In your kitchen. Exciting, isn't it? Maybe I'm not so 'generic' after all.

EZRA Where's Ashley?

KATRINA He's safe. He'll come to no harm. Unlike our friendly liaison officer. She doesn't look too clever. She was on to you, wasn't she? The shifty stepfather. So you had to silence her.

EZRA I never touched her, and you know I didn't.

KATRINA Not how it looks. Maybe she found your wife's mobile . . . hidden away in your bottom drawer.

KATRINA *produces* PHILIPPA*'s mobile phone.* EZRA *tries to grab it.*

EZRA You're framing me.

KATRINA Yes. Is that too clichéd, Ezra? What do you want me to do? This . . .

KATRINA *opens a kitchen cupboard, and* BARNABUS*'s dead body falls from it.*

KATRINA *(cont'd)* Or maybe this?

KATRINA *pulls* PHILIPPA *from the utility room. They kiss tenderly.*

PHILIPPA You always were a lousy lay, Ezra.

KATRINA Come on, Mr Writer. We're in your hands. What's a better ending?

EZRA What do you want?

KATRINA I want you to finish my story. I want to find the boy seconds before he runs out of oxygen. I want to expose the affair between the neighbour and the stepfather. I want to walk out of an AA meeting and throw my police badge in the river.

EZRA Really?

KATRINA Yes! And I want it in hardback and paperback on the shelf, not self-published on Amazon as a shitty Kindle exclusive.

KATRINA *hands* Red Rag to a Bull *to* EZRA.

EZRA Alright, alright, I'll do it. But then you've got to leave me and my family alone. Deal?

KATRINA Deal.

They shake hands.

BARNABUS *pipes up from the floor.*

BARNABUS Sorry, am I dead now?

KATRINA Yes, I killed you, presumably because I was jealous.

BARNABUS But that doesn't make sense.

PHILIPPA And am I a lesbian now, or is that all in his head?

MATILDA *(O.S.)* Quiet! I'm trying to think.

A confused EZRA *heads back into the living room.*

INT. LIVING ROOM. DAY.

EZRA *enters.* MATILDA *sits at the desk, writing in a notebook.*

MATILDA I've written myself into a corner. I knew this would happen. You know how some artists can't do hands? Well, I can't do endings. Resolving everything on the final page, it's just not believable. But then, it wouldn't be a Matilda Gordon novel if it didn't have that final twist.

EZRA What's going on?

MATILDA I thought I was writing an updated *Frankenstein*, the postmodern Prometheus, but it's all gone a bit Stephen King. A hack horror novelist haunted by his own characters.

EZRA I'm not a hack!

MATILDA No. A good story is a good story. And this isn't bad for a first draft. Still, I think I need to leave you in the bottom drawer for a while. See if I can't come up with a more satisfying denouement.

MATILDA *opens the dreaded bottom drawer.*

EZRA No, no, wait, I can help you. I've won a Golden Dagger. My books are bestsellers!

MATILDA Well they're not really, are they darling?

EZRA *looks at the back of his novel. Below his photo, the blurb reads:* 'Lorem ipsum dolor sit amet . . .' *– it is dummy text. He flicks through the pages inside, but they are all blank.*

MATILDA *(cont'd)* They're a figment of my imagination. Just like you.

EZRA Oh, God . . .

MATILDA And I'm afraid you're not quite leaping off the page.

MATILDA *closes the notebook.*

EZRA *(real emotion)* Please don't.

MATILDA *drops her notebook into the bottom drawer and starts to close it.*

MATILDA Bye for now.

EZRA Oh sh–

BLACKOUT.

THE END

Episode 4

KID/NAP

CAST LIST

LARA – Daisy Haggard

DOMINIC – Reece Shearsmith

SHANE – Daniel Mays

CLIFFORD – Jason Isaacs

DI ELLIS – Steve Pemberton

INT. LARA'S BEDROOM. DAY.

LARA *lies awake in her Laura Ashley bed in a nice house. Her husband* DOMINIC *is in bed next to her. From the right, another image moves across: we are now in split-screen.* DOMINIC *is replaced by . . .*

INT. DERELICT HOUSE, BEDROOM (RIGHT SCREEN). DAY.

SHANE, *in vest and pants, is staring at the ceiling in his dark room, lying on a bare mattress. An alarm sounds and, after a beat,* SHANE *leans over to switch it off, at the same time as . . .*

INT. LARA'S BEDROOM (LEFT SCREEN). DAY.

LARA*'s husband's arm reaches across her and switches off their alarm. She looks across and goes to kiss* DOMINIC *on the cheek, but it looks like she's kissing* SHANE.

INT. DERELICT HOUSE, BEDROOM (RIGHT SCREEN). DAY.

SHANE *gets out of bed.*

INT. LARA'S BATHROOM (LEFT SCREEN). DAY.

LARA *sits on the toilet in her silk dressing gown, doing a wee.*

INT. DERELICT HOUSE, KITCHEN (RIGHT SCREEN). DAY.

Close-up of apple juice being poured into a glass. SHANE *then drinks the juice in the bare kitchen.*

INT. LARA'S BATHROOM (LEFT SCREEN). DAY.

LARA *squeezes toothpaste on to her electric toothbrush and proceeds to brush her teeth in the mirror.*

INT. DERELICT HOUSE, BATHROOM (RIGHT SCREEN). DAY.

SHANE *squeezes toothpaste on to his bare finger and uses his finger to brush his teeth in his mirror.*

INT. LARA'S BEDROOM (LEFT SCREEN). DAY.

LARA *pulls open her wardrobe door to reveal a packed rail of clothes. She chooses a nice outfit.*

INT. DERELICT HOUSE, BEDROOM (RIGHT SCREEN). DAY.

SHANE *pulls open his side of the wardrobe to reveal a single hanger with a blue shirt and shorts. He pulls it out.*

INT. LARA'S BEDROOM (LEFT SCREEN). DAY.

LARA *is now dressed, she's buttoning up her jeans.*

INT. DERELICT HOUSE, BEDROOM (RIGHT SCREEN). DAY.

SHANE *is dressed as a postman in a blue shirt and shorts. He also wears a holster with a gun in it. He puts on his gilet.*

INT. LARA'S BEDROOM (LEFT SCREEN). DAY.

LARA *takes some perfume. She sprays it on her neck and wrists.*

INT. DERELICT HOUSE, LIVING ROOM (RIGHT SCREEN). DAY.

Close-up of a bottle of chloroform. SHANE *takes the chloroform and squirts some on to a handkerchief.*

INT. LARA'S KITCHEN (FULL SCREEN). DAY.

LARA *is sipping on a coffee. Her husband* DOMINIC, *scrolling through his phone, comes up to distractedly kiss her goodbye.*

DOMINIC See you later, babe. You got Pilates today?

LARA No, I've got to wait in for the postman. I've got a package coming, apparently.

DOMINIC Cool, I'll see you later then.

DOMINIC *leaves.*

LARA I wonder what it could be?

We move into a triple split-screen.

INT/EXT. STREET (LEFT & RIGHT SCREEN), LARA'S KITCHEN (CENTRE SCREEN). DAY.

LARA *remains in the centre of the screen, sipping her coffee.*

On the left screen, we see SHANE *dressed as a postman, emerging from his post van and approaching along the hedge outside the house, moving from left to right. On the right screen, we see* DOMINIC, *still scrolling through his phone, walking from right to left.*

They then each appear in the opposite screen and walk out of shot.

INT. LARA'S KITCHEN (FULL SCREEN). DAY.

LARA *is still in the kitchen when she hears the doorbell sound. She goes to answer it, but we don't follow her. We hear her open the front door.*

SHANE *(O.S.)* Hello, are you Lara Grant?

LARA *(O.S.)* Yes.

We hear the sound of a struggle.

EXT. DERELICT HOUSE (FULL SCREEN). DAY.

The post van is parked outside the derelict house. SHANE *drags an unconscious* LARA *from it and into the open door of the house.* SHANE *then kicks the door shut. We see that the house is number 9.*

TITLE: *'Kid/Nap'.*

INT. DERELICT HOUSE, LIVING ROOM. DAY.

The room is gloomy and bare, curtains closed and very little furniture, just a tatty armchair and sofa, and a small dining table and chairs.

SHANE *sits in the armchair, looking across at* LARA, *who is coming to from her deep sleep. She is in a dining chair, her hands tied behind her.*

As she starts to open her eyes, SHANE *grabs a mask and puts it on. He also grabs a children's voice-changer toy, which makes him sound ridiculous.*

SHANE *(voice-changer)* Do you want a glass of water?

LARA Sorry?

SHANE *(voice-changer)* Do you want a glass of water? The instructions said you might have a headache.

LARA Yes please.

SHANE *goes over to the open-plan kitchen to get a glass of water, and* LARA *surveys the room.* SHANE *puts the water to her lips and she drinks.*

LARA Where am I?

SHANE *(voice-changer)* No questions.

LARA Please . . . What's this about, what do you want?

SHANE *(voice-changer)* Stop. Talking.

LARA I'm sorry, but I've already heard your voice, you know. You don't have to use that toy.

SHANE *abandons the voice-changer.*

SHANE Oh yeah.

LARA And I've seen your face.

SHANE I couldn't wear a mask as a postman, could I? It might have scared you. Besides, the instructions said you might have memory loss from the dichloromethane. Hmm, I don't know what to do now.

LARA Well, I don't recall your features if that's any help. I just remember, like, a round blob.

SHANE A round blob?

LARA I couldn't pick you out from a line-up.

SHANE So are you telling me to keep the mask on or take it off? I'm confused.

LARA I don't mind. I won't say anything to anybody, I promise.

SHANE *removes the mask.*

SHANE I know you won't. I'll make sure of that.

SHANE *reveals his gun beneath his gilet. This frightens* LARA.

SHANE *(cont'd)* Stay quiet for a few minutes.

SHANE *exits the room, and we go back into split-screen.*

LARA *(left screen) waits for* SHANE *to leave, then reaches into her back pocket and pulls out her mobile phone.*

INT. DERELICT HOUSE, STAIRWAY (RIGHT SCREEN). DAY.

SHANE *is trudging through the house. He enters the bedroom.*

INT. DERELICT HOUSE, LIVING ROOM (LEFT SCREEN). DAY.

LARA *is holding the phone behind her and attempts to dial a number. It starts to ring.*

INT. DERELICT HOUSE, BEDROOM (RIGHT SCREEN). DAY.

SHANE *enters the bedroom and sits on the bed. He pulls out his own mobile and a scrap of paper with handwritten instructions on it.*

INT. DERELICT HOUSE, LIVING ROOM (LEFT SCREEN). DAY.

LARA*'s phone is answered. A third panel appears in the centre of the screen: her husband* DOMINIC.

INT. DERELICT HOUSE, LIVING ROOM (LEFT SCREEN), DOMINIC'S OFFICE (CENTRE SCREEN), DERELICT HOUSE, BEDROOM (RIGHT SCREEN). DAY.

DOMINIC *is in a swanky office, looking through papers as he speaks on his mobile. We see a cityscape in the glass window behind him.*

DOMINIC Lara, I'm really pushed for time at the moment, so make it quick, yeah?

LARA *(whispering)* Dominic, listen, you've got to help me. I've been kidnapped!

DOMINIC What?

SHANE *has dialled the number and gets an engaged tone. Frustrated, he hangs up and dials again.*

DOMINIC You're going to have to speak up, I can't hear you. *(To off-screen person)* Iced macchiato please, three shots.

LARA I've been kidnapped! The postman kidnapped me!

LARA *drops the phone and the call is terminated. She tries to pick the phone up.*

DOMINIC Hello?

Three beeps signal that the call has ended. DOMINIC *puts down his phone.*

SHANE *has redialled and now gets through.* DOMINIC *answers his ringing phone.*

DOMINIC Hi babe, is that you again?

SHANE *is puzzled. He uses the voice-changer.*

SHANE *(voice-changer)* Sorry?

DOMINIC Come on, spit it out. I'm short of time.

SHANE *(voice-changer)* I have your wife. She's tied up.

DOMINIC Lara, you know I can't do phone sex. I'm in an open-plan office.

SHANE *(voice-changer)* What? I said I have your wife. Listen very carefully . . .

DOMINIC Stop putting that stupid fucking voice on, it's irritating.

LARA*, having retrieved her phone, has pressed redial but gets the engaged tone.*

SHANE *abandons the voice-changer. He reads from the scrap of paper.*

SHANE Listen! You need to make available 1.3 million pounds from your business reserve account and await further instructions. Failure to do so will lead to the death of your wife – is that clear?

DOMINIC What are you talking about? My wife's at home. I just spoke to her.

SHANE What?

DOMINIC She's waiting in for a package – are you the postman?

SHANE *hangs up. He thinks.*

Frustrated, DOMINIC *calls* LARA*'s number and her phone buzzes. She answers it.*

LARA Dom?

DOMINIC Yeah, listen, where exactly are you? Because I've just had a very strange call from someone saying you've been kidnapped . . .

SHANE *strides back through the house to the living room.*

LARA Yes, that's what I was trying to tell you! You've got to do exactly what they say, please!

SHANE *bursts into the room, snatches* LARA*'s phone and hangs up.* DOMINIC*'s screen disappears.*

SHANE You shouldn't have done that.

FADE TO BLACK.

INT. DERELICT HOUSE, LIVING ROOM. DAY.

SHANE *is sitting across from* LARA. *She looks scared.*

LARA What time is it?

SHANE Half past eleven.

LARA So we've been here three hours?

SHANE Correct.

LARA Is this your actual house?

SHANE It is not.

LARA Are you sure?

SHANE Definitely.

LARA So that's a 'Yes'?

SHANE No. Ahhhhh! Bollocks, you tricked me! Alright – let me do you. Is your name Lara?

LARA That's right.

SHANE Is your husband rich?

LARA He is.

SHANE Does he love you?

LARA I believe so.

SHANE Does he love you more than he loves money?

LARA Well, we'll see, won't we?

The screen splits in two again.

EXT/INT. DERELICT HOUSE (RIGHT SCREEN), DERELICT HOUSE, LIVING ROOM (LEFT SCREEN). DAY.

Outside, a hand knocks loudly on the front door.

Inside, SHANE *puts his finger to his lips to indicate for* LARA *to be quiet, revealing his handgun. He leaves to answer the door.*

LARA *looks anxiously around the room.*

EXT. DERELICT HOUSE (FULL SCREEN). DAY.

SHANE *answers the door, revealing a smart-looking man:* CLIFFORD.

CLIFFORD Why haven't you got your mask on?

SHANE You were meant to be here. What happened?

CLIFFORD I'm here now. Are you going to let me in or what?

SHANE *lets* CLIFFORD *in and closes the door.*

INT. DERELICT HOUSE, HALLWAY. DAY.

CLIFFORD Have you made the call to the husband?

SHANE I have.

CLIFFORD And what did he say, did he agree?

SHANE He . . . did not.

CLIFFORD Did you tell him no police?

SHANE That dialogue was . . . omitted.

CLIFFORD What do you mean 'omitted'? Why are you talking like that?

SHANE Sorry, we've been playing the 'yes/no' game.

CLIFFORD You've been playing games?

SHANE Something to do.

CLIFFORD You haven't touched her, have you?

SHANE No. Not really. She needed the toilet, so I made her go in a washing-up bowl. I had to pull her jeans down, but I used an oven glove, so it didn't count.

CLIFFORD Don't go getting too close to her. You know what you have to do at the end of all this.

CLIFFORD *puts on a scary mask on before going in to see* LARA.

INT. DERELICT HOUSE, LIVING ROOM. DAY.

CLIFFORD *comes into the room, followed by* SHANE.

CLIFFORD I hear you have been playing the 'yes/no' game with my halfwit colleague. Well, now it's my turn. Yes, we are waiting on a ransom of £1.3 million from your hedge-fund prick of a husband. No, we will not compromise on that amount. Yes, we will kill you if he doesn't comply. No, we don't want any more funny business.

SHANE You'd have been out ages ago.

CLIFFORD Shut up.

LARA How long have you given him to get the money? I'm not sure he'll be able . . .

CLIFFORD That's not our problem. Did he buy you those earrings?

LARA Sorry, what?

CLIFFORD The earrings you're wearing. Would your husband recognise them if he saw them again?

LARA I think so.

CLIFFORD Good.

SHANE Do you want me to take them out?

CLIFFORD *reaches into his pocket and pulls out some scissors.*

CLIFFORD No need. I'm going to cut her lobes off.

LARA What?

CLIFFORD Courier them to his office. That'll show them we mean business. Mr Ball, go down to that corner shop and get some sandwich bags.

SHANE Who's Mr Ball? Oh, yes! Will do, Mr Barrow.

CLIFFORD Farrow.

SHANE Farrow. *(to* LARA*)* Do you want anything? Bag of crisps? Bounty?

LARA *shakes her head. She looks terrified of* CLIFFORD.

SHANE *(cont'd)* Oooh, do you think they do contactless?

CLIFFORD Just go.

SHANE *exits.* CLIFFORD *walks behind* LARA *and menacingly touches her ear lobe. We hear the front door slam.*

LARA Farrow and Ball? Seriously?

CLIFFORD *takes off his mask.*

CLIFFORD It was the first thing that came into my head! I nearly said Cannon and Ball. How are you?

LARA Sore.

CLIFFORD I'm going to untie you.

LARA No, it's got to look real!

CLIFFORD *goes to untie her.*

CLIFFORD Just for a minute. You can show me what he did with that oven glove.

LARA Clifford!

CLIFFORD Did you speak to your husband?

LARA Yes. I rang him in a panic, told him to comply.

CLIFFORD Good.

LARA *is now untied. She rubs her wrists.*

LARA Did you sort everything with the pilot?

CLIFFORD Yes, yes, it's all in hand. Come here.

CLIFFORD *kisses* LARA. *Suddenly,* LARA*'s phone rings.* CLIFFORD *picks it up and looks at the caller ID.*

CLIFFORD Dominic. Let's see what he's got to say, shall we?

We go back into split-screen, this time top and bottom half.

INT. DERELICT HOUSE, LIVING ROOM (TOP SCREEN), DOMINIC'S OFFICE (BOTTOM SCREEN). DAY.

DOMINIC *is at his desk, now flanked by* DI ELLIS, *who is listening into the call. A* UNIFORMED OFFICER *stands near by. In the derelict house,* LARA *listens in next to* CLIFFORD.

CLIFFORD Yes?

DOMINIC Hi, this is Dominic Grant, Wood Grange Capital.

CLIFFORD I don't give a fuck who you work for.

DOMINIC Sorry, sorry, force of habit. Who am I speaking to, please?

CLIFFORD Just call me . . . Mr Cannon. Is anybody else listening to this call?

DI ELLIS *shakes his head.*

DOMINIC No, no. No police or anything. Just me, me on my own.

CLIFFORD *(to* LARA*)* He's called the police.

DOMINIC So, I managed to get the money that you asked for. I was just hoping to get assurances that my wife is still safe. Would it be possible to speak to her?

CLIFFORD As far as I remember, we are in charge of this situation. So that won't be possible, no. I'm going to text you an account number, sort code and IBAN for you to transfer the funds. You have two hours.

DI ELLIS *motions to* DOMINIC *that he needs to keep the conversation going.*

DOMINIC No, no. Look Mr Cannon, understand it from my perspective. You're asking me to shell out all this money sight unseen. You don't pay upwards of a mil' for an Aston Martin One-77 without taking her out for a spin first, right? You want to hear that the engine is running smoothly, that the heart is beating and that . . . she's still alive.

CLIFFORD *mimes that* DOMINIC *is a wanker.* LARA *nods.*

CLIFFORD Alright, but keep it brief. I know your friends'll be trying to triangulate the call, so you've got seventeen seconds. *(To* LARA*)* Sound scared.

CLIFFORD *hands the phone to* LARA. *She puts on a tiny girl's voice.*

LARA Dominic? Is that really you?

DOMINIC Yes. Are you alright, babe?

LARA I'm frightened. It's so cold. I'm scared they'll do things to me. Again.

DOMINIC What things? Just tell me where you are.

LARA I don't know, they put a blindfold on me. Just do as they say, darling, please.

DOMINIC I will, I will. I just hate hearing you like this – you sound awful.

LARA *(annoyed)* It's my scared voice; you've never heard it before. *(scared voice)* He's coming, he's going to hurt me, no! No!

LARA *hangs up the call.*

DOMINIC and LARA *(simultaneously)* So now what do we do?

CLIFFORD Wait for the money.

CLIFFORD *starts to type a text.*

DOMINIC I don't actually have to send the money, do I?

LARA He won't want to send it.

DI ELLIS I hope not. Depends on the trace.

DI ELLIS *goes to check the trace.*

CLIFFORD He'd better do, or your ears are getting snipped.

CLIFFORD *sends the text. It appears on* DOMINIC*'s phone.*

DOMINIC He's sent the account details through. Shit!

DOMINIC*'s half of the screen disappears.*

LARA Serves him right anyway. It would have been cheaper for him if he'd divorced me when I asked him to.

CLIFFORD But if his lawyers found out you were having an affair with a much more intelligent, charismatic, attractive man . . .

LARA Who are you talking about now?

CLIFFORD Cheeky! So, how have you been getting on with Shane? He didn't hurt you, did he?

The screen splits again.

INT/EXT. DERELICT HOUSE, LIVING ROOM (LEFT SCREEN), STREET (RIGHT SCREEN). DAY.

SHANE *is walking along the street, coming back from the shop with a small plastic bag. He eats an ice lolly.*

LARA Yes, he did! You didn't tell me he was going to use chloroform!

CLIFFORD You said the less you knew, the better.

LARA Where did you find him?

CLIFFORD He's a drinking buddy of my cousin's from his army days. He wants to be a pastry chef, but mainly he just breaks people legs for money.

LARA Are you not worried he'll come after us when he finds out we haven't paid him?

CLIFFORD I'm sure he'll be a bit cross, but hey – how will he find us?

SHANE *is at the door of number 9. He searches for his keys. He's about to unlock the door, but drops them. He bends to pick them back up.*

CLIFFORD *(cont'd)* As far as I'm aware, he hasn't even got a passport. Besides, what's he going to do, go to the police?

LARA *embraces* CLIFFORD.

LARA Get you, all ruthless! You almost sound as horrible as Dominic.

CLIFFORD Must be your type.

They kiss.

SHANE *puts his key in the lock and enters the house.* LARA *and* CLIFFORD *hear the door slam.*

CLIFFORD Shit! Hit me!

LARA What?

CLIFFORD Pretend you've escaped!

SHANE *is coming through into the living room. We go back to full screen. As he opens the door,* LARA *grabs the scissors from the table and holds them to* CLIFFORD*'s throat, grabbing him round the neck.*

CLIFFORD What are you doing, don't–

SHANE *enters the room.*

LARA Stay back!

SHANE *pulls out his gun and aims it at* LARA.

LARA *(cont'd)* Don't come any closer, or I'll rip his fucking throat out.

CLIFFORD Alright, steady on!

SHANE Let my friend go.

LARA No! Put your gun down first.

CLIFFORD Do as she says, Shane.

SHANE Mr Ball.

CLIFFORD Mr Ball, sorry. I didn't know you were bringing a gun.

SHANE Got to protect myself, be ready for all eventualities.

LARA Stop talking! Now move your arse away from the door, and you're going to let me go.

SHANE No.

CLIFFORD *(to* LARA, *pointedly)* Listen, I don't know what you think you're trying to achieve at this point in time, but if you remember, it's not what my colleague and I had planned.

SHANE Exactly! We have a plan!

LARA *realises that she has gone too far with the improv.*

LARA Yes, sorry, I just got carried away. I'm putting the scissors down . . .

LARA *puts the scissors back on the table, then sits back on the chair.*

LARA I suppose you've got to tie me up again. Maybe not quite so tight this time?

CLIFFORD Mr Ball, I think it might be best if you give me the gun.

SHANE I can't do that, I'm afraid.

CLIFFORD I said no weapons.

SHANE This is a tool. *I* am the weapon.

CLIFFORD We don't want any accidents, do we? Come on, hand it over.

CLIFFORD *goes to get the gun.* SHANE *resists.*

SHANE No.

CLIFFORD Look, I'm in charge of this operation and I command you . . .

BANG! The two men are shocked. One of them falls to the ground. It is CLIFFORD. LARA *screams.*

LARA Cliff! Oh my God, Clifford.

SHANE Get back, get back.

LARA What have you done?

LARA *approaches* CLIFFORD*'s body.*

SHANE I warned him. He shouldn't have grabbed my tool!

LARA He's dead! Shit! This is all my fault . . .

SHANE What are you so bothered about? His plan was to kill you, you know! He was never going to let you go.

LARA Oh, my love, I'm sorry, I'm so sorry.

SHANE It's alright, you're just suffering from Stockport Syndrome. You'd probably feel the same way about me if I died.

LARA 'Course I wouldn't, you stupid fucking idiot!

SHANE I'm not an idiot!

SHANE *grabs* LARA *and drags her across to the chair. He starts to tie her up again.*

LARA Get off me! What are you doing?

SHANE Got to stick to the plan. It's what Mr Farrow would have wanted.

SHANE *starts to tie up* LARA*, who sobs, no fight left in her.*

INT. DOMINIC'S OFFICE. DAY.

DI ELLIS *is looking at a map while on the phone.*

DI ELLIS *(into phone)* OK, I've got it. Lauradale Road.

DOMINIC *is in the background on his office phone.*

DI ELLIS *(into phone)* Seal off the area, see if we can narrow it down to which house the shot came from. *(To* DOMINIC*)* Mr Grant, could you try your wife's phone again?

DOMINIC With you in two mins.

DI ELLIS Now!

DOMINIC *hangs up and dials his wife's mobile.*

DOMINIC What do I say?

DI ELLIS There's been a gunshot heard in the area.

DOMINIC Gunshot?

DI ELLIS Just check that your wife is OK.

The screen splits once more.

INT. DERELICT HOUSE, LIVING ROOM (LEFT SCREEN), DOMINIC'S OFFICE (RIGHT SCREEN). DAY.

In the living room, LARA*'s phone rings.* SHANE *answers it.*

SHANE What?

DOMINIC Oh, am I speaking to Mr Cannon?

SHANE Do you mean Mr Farrow?

DOMINIC Possibly, erm . . .

SHANE What do you want?

DOMINIC I just want to check my wife is still alive. Can I speak to her?

SHANE Where's the money?

DOMINIC The money is on its way, I can assure you. I'm just leveraging some assets and trying to find . . .

SHANE *hangs up and the right screen disappears.*

SHANE Right, what do I do? Stick to the plan. First things first – let's cut your ears off.

SHANE *picks up the scissors from the table.*

LARA Shane, no! No, listen to me . . . Listen to me. Stop!

SHANE *hesitates.*

LARA *(cont'd)* You don't understand! This whole thing is a set-up! I arranged it all with Cliff.

SHANE You're lying.

LARA I'm not, I promise! Dominic wouldn't divorce me, so this was a last resort. I was going to start a new life with Cliff, we were lovers. You've got to believe me, please . . .

SHANE I've got my instructions. Take the wife. Clip her ears off. Get the money. Kill the wife.

LARA Yes – that's what I told him to say. It's all my plan.

SHANE Good. Well, let's get on with it, then.

SHANE *grabs her ear and moves closer with the scissors.*

LARA Shane! Listen to me. We have a private jet waiting, new identities . . .

SHANE *opens the scissors in position around* LARA*'s ear, all ready to cut it off.*

LARA *(cont'd)* It doesn't all have to go to waste. Please don't . . .

INT. DOMINIC'S OFFICE. DAY.

A piercing scream from LARA *is heard.*

DI ELLIS *presses 'stop' on a small Dictaphone and holds up a clear plastic bag containing bloodied earlobes with* LARA*'s earrings in.*

DOMINIC *studies them.*

DI ELLIS Can you confirm these belong to your wife?

DOMINIC You mean the earrings or the ears?

DI ELLIS Both.

DOMINIC Yeah. I remember my PA buying them a couple of Christmases ago. Do you think she'll be alright?

DI ELLIS I hope so.

The screen splits once again.

INT. DOMINIC'S OFFICE (LEFT SCREEN), DERELICT HOUSE, LIVING ROOM (RIGHT SCREEN). DAY.

On the right of the screen, we see an impassive LARA *having her ears slowly bandaged by* SHANE. *On the left is* DOMINIC*'s office.*

DI ELLIS What's clear is our Mr Cannon, or Farrow, or whoever he is, is deadly serious. The fact he's mutilated your wife is a strong indicator that he's not afraid of taking this to the endgame.

A FIREARMS OFFICER *appears with a Kevlar vest and helmet. He starts to fit them on to* DOMINIC.

DOMINIC What's this?

DI ELLIS He's requested the bank transfer be actioned by you within the next twenty minutes.

DOMINIC OK . . .

DI ELLIS And he wants you to do it in person.

DOMINIC What?

DI ELLIS You'll have an earpiece and a wire, so we'll be able to communicate with you at all times. The kidnapper has given us their location and agreed you can wear this, but if you feel you or your wife are in imminent danger, I want you to use the safe word 'granola granola', and we will send the team in right away.

DOMINIC 'Granola granola'? How am I expected to slip that into a conversation? It's hard enough saying it once.

DI ELLIS He's also asked for a car to be parked outside with its engine running. As soon as he attempts an escape, we will be straight in to give your wife the medical attention she needs. But it's your call, Mr Grant. I know it's a lot to ask.

The FIREARMS OFFICER *has strapped* DOMINIC *into the vest, and now hands him the helmet.* DOMINIC *is pumped-up.*

DOMINIC I've sweet-talked the Chinese into trebling their investment, negotiated myself a six-figure bonus, and this morning I scored two-and-a-half K on Clash of Clans. I can do this.

DI ELLIS Good man.

The FIREARMS OFFICER *leads* DOMINIC *out.*

DI ELLIS *(cont'd)* What a tosspot.

EXT. DERELICT HOUSE/SURVEILLANCE CAR. DAY.

DOMINIC *is led outside by the* FIREARMS OFFICER. *An empty car waits outside the house, its engine running.*

DI ELLIS *sits in a parked police car some distance away, monitoring with a headset, walkie-talkie and binoculars.*

DI ELLIS Touch your head if you can hear me.

DOMINIC *touches his head.*

DI ELLIS *(cont'd)* Good. Now remember, just do everything they say. I'll be listening.

The screen splits again.

INT/EXT. DERELICT HOUSE, LIVING ROOM (RIGHT SCREEN), SURVEILLANCE CAR (LEFT SCREEN). DAY.

In the living room, SHANE *hears the knock on the door. He puts on his mask, takes his gun and goes to answer it, leaving* LARA *tied to the chair. The bandages around her head cover her ears.* CLIFFORD*'s body is covered with a bloodied sheet.*

In the surveillance vehicle, DI ELLIS *and a* UNIFORMED OFFICER *are listening in to the action.*

SHANE *opens the door, pointing his gun at* DOMINIC, *and beckons him inside.*

LARA *looks up as* DOMINIC *arrives.*

LARA Darling! Oh, thank God.

DOMINIC It's going to be alright, I'm here now.

SHANE *uses the voice-changer.*

SHANE *(voice-changer)* Take the helmet off.

DI ELLIS *whispers into the walkie-talkie.*

DI ELLIS Tell them it's for your own protection.

DOMINIC It's for your own protection.

SHANE *(voice-changer)* What?

DOMINIC No, *my* protection, sorry.

DI ELLIS Do you need me to change all the possessive pronouns?

DOMINIC No, I get it now.

SHANE *(voice-changer)* Take it off!

DOMINIC *removes the helmet. There is a laptop on the table.*

SHANE *(voice-changer)* Make the transfer.

DOMINIC Right, so . . . You started with a bid of one point three mill. Since then, we've had the ears, and a lot of distress to myself – and my wife – so I was wondering what you thought about rounding that down to eight-fifty? I think it's a fair price, damaged goods and all that.

DI ELLIS Stop haggling.

DOMINIC Sorry, I just know I'd kick myself if I didn't try. So . . .

DOMINIC *enters the account details.*

DOMINIC 'Enter amount'. 1.3 million. Gosh. Worth every penny. Don't regret it at all.

He presses 'send' on the transaction.

DOMINIC *(cont'd)* Done.

SHANE *is behind* DOMINIC. *He throws the voice-changer to* LARA, *who catches it, revealing that she's no longer tied up.* DOMINIC *is surprised, but before he can react,* SHANE *is upon him with a chloroformed handkerchief.* DOMINIC *is quickly subdued.*

LARA There, he's done as you said, it's sent. Please just let us go.

SHANE *begins to strip* DOMINIC *of his Kevlar vest and shirt. We see the wire taped to* DOMINIC*'s T-shirt.*

LARA *uses the voice-changer, pretending to be a kidnapper.*

LARA *(voice-changer)* Not yet, I need confirmation from my bank.

SHANE *removes* DOMINIC*'s earpiece and gives it to* LARA, *who puts it in her own ear.* SHANE *starts to dress in* DOMINIC*'s clothes.*

LARA *(in her own voice)* You'll never get away with this, you know.

(voice-changer) Won't I? *(as herself)* My husband works for very powerful people, and they'll track you down wherever you are – won't they, darling? See, he's nodding his head.

DI ELLIS Just stay, calm Dominic, you're doing really well.

LARA *(voice-changer)* They'll never find me; there's a car outside waiting to take me to Tilbury Docks.

DI ELLIS Get a team to Tilbury. Now!

The UNIFORMED OFFICER *jumps out of the car.*

LARA *(voice-changer)* I'll be long gone – so keep out of it, bitch.

(as herself) How dare you!

LARA *slaps her own face and cries out.*

LARA *(voice-changer)* Ow!

SHANE *is now dressed in* DOMINIC*'s clothes, and gives the thumbs-up to* LARA. *She looks at him in dismay, as the clothes are way too short* *on him. She motions that he is too big compared to* DOMINIC. *He stoops down to make himself shorter.* LARA *rolls her eyes.*

LARA *(voice-changer)* Now I'm going to the kitchen to make a phone call. Don't move.

She stomps her feet.

LARA *(as herself)* Dominic, quick, now's our chance. Untie me and we can use his car to get away.

DI ELLIS Dominic, that's a good plan. If you think you've got time, go now – we'll clear the way.

LARA *goes to* CLIFFORD*'s body and kneels by it.*

LARA Sorry, darling. I didn't mean for any of this to happen.

DI ELLIS Get her out of there, quick!

SHANE *takes the laptop, and he and* LARA *run from the room.*

EXT. STREET (LEFT SCREEN), SURVEILLANCE CAR (RIGHT SCREEN). DAY.

LARA *and* SHANE *(stooping, as* DOMINIC*) jump into the car and drive away at speed.*

DI ELLIS Well done Dominic. SCO19, go, go, go!

DI ELLIS *gets out of the car and runs to the house, along with a small armed unit. He looks at* LARA *in the passenger seat of the car as they drive away. She's smiling.*

INT. DERELICT HOUSE, LIVING ROOM. DAY.

DI ELLIS *enters the living room with the armed officers. One of them finds* CLIFFORD*'s body.*

FIREARMS OFFICER Guv!

The FIREARMS OFFICER *officer pulls back the sheet, and we see that* CLIFFORD*'s earlobes have been cut off.* DI ELLIS *frowns.*

DI ELLIS Who the hell is that?

On the sofa, DOMINIC *groans, stripped to his underwear.*

DI ELLIS Dominic? What the fuck happened?

DOMINIC *is still half-sedated.*

DI ELLIS *(cont'd)* What happened?

DOMINIC *(groggily)* Granola granola . . .

INT/EXT. CAR. DAY.

SHANE *and* LARA *sit in the car.* LARA *is unwrapping the bandages from her ears. Her ears are fine. She smiles at* SHANE.

LARA I told you I had a plan, didn't I? Do you want to know where we're flying off to?

SHANE I'm all ears.

They speed off.

THE END

Episode 5

A RANDOM ACT OF KINDNESS

CAST LIST

Zach – Noah Valentine

Helen – Jessica Hynes

Rudolph – Reece Shearsmith

Bob – Steve Pemberton

EXT. STREET. DAY.

We see skateboard wheels being propelled along the pavement. The rider is 17-year-old ZACH.

RUDOLPH *(V.O.)* Newton's first law states that an object in motion will remain in motion unless an external force imposes a change upon it.

INT. KITCHEN. DAY.

Coffee swirls round in a cup on the kitchen table, having just been stirred. Middle-aged mum HELEN *sits with her iPad in front of her on a stand. She seems lost in thought.*

RUDOLPH *(V.O.)* Similarly, an object at rest will remain at rest until an unbalanced force affects it.

EXT. HOUSE. DAY.

ZACH *arrives at his house, fishes out a key and lets himself in.*

RUDOLPH *(V.O.)* This is also known as the law of inertia.

As the door slams shut, we see that it is house number 9.

TITLE: *'A Random Act of Kindness'.*

INT. KITCHEN. DAY.

HELEN *is slowly typing out an email on her iPad.*

ZACH *enters, throws down his bag and coat, then goes straight to the fridge-freezer and opens it up.*

HELEN Hi! How was your day?

ZACH Is there any food?

HELEN Er, yes. There's a whole fridgeful of food in front of you.

ZACH Yeah, but it's all olives and hummus and shit – there's nothing to actually eat.

HELEN Not every meal comes in a tray, Zach. Some are made up of what we humans call 'ingredients'.

ZACH *closes the fridge and takes out some cereal.*

HELEN *(cont'd)* Don't eat all the cereal, please, there'll be none left for the morn–

ZACH *pours the cereal.* HELEN *sighs and goes back to her email. As she types, we hear the digital 'click' on the keyboard.*

ZACH You can turn that off, you know.

HELEN Turn what off?

ZACH That stupid sound.

HELEN I like it. Makes up for not having a proper blooming keyboard.

ZACH What are you actually doing?

HELEN I'm booking a smear test if you must know.

ZACH Urgh!

HELEN Well, you asked.

HELEN *carries on typing.*

ZACH It's giving me a migraine!

HELEN Oh, don't exaggerate.

ZACH Just disable 'clicks'.

HELEN I don't want to disable 'clicks'! *You* disable 'clicks'.

ZACH I have done!

HELEN Fine, then!

ZACH *sits down with his cereal. He opens his college textbooks and starts to shovel food in.* HELEN *tries to start over. She puts her iPad aside and smiles.*

HELEN *(cont'd)* So, how was your day?

ZACH *ignores her.* HELEN *goes to stroke his arm.*

HELEN *(cont'd)* Did you get your results back yet?

No response.

HELEN *(cont'd)* Zachary?

ZACH Yes, I got a B. What do you actually want?

HELEN It would be nice if we could just talk.

ZACH You can talk. I'm not stopping you.

HELEN I mean a conversation, a bit of back and forth. I've been here on my own all day. I've started making friends with *The Archers* – it's not normal.

ZACH That's not my fault.

HELEN I know it isn't. But I don't think it's too much to ask to sit and have half an hour together of an evening.

ZACH I'm not your boyfriend, alright? If you want to talk to someone, go on Tinder! I wasn't put on this earth to make you happy.

ZACH *takes his bowl to the sink.*

HELEN You can say that again.

ZACH What does that mean?

HELEN Nothing.

ZACH You want to bin me off like you did Dad?

HELEN Of course I don't! And he was the one who walked out, remember, not me.

ZACH I don't blame him.

HELEN Look, if I could go back and do things differently I would do, but . . . Zach, can't we please live together without all this constant . . . argy-bargy? Let's cut the beef, bro! You feel me, G?

HELEN *does feeble 'street' gestures.*

ZACH No one says 'beef' any more. I've got homework to do.

ZACH *takes his rucksack and stomps upstairs.* HELEN *rubs her eyes. She reaches for a paper and knocks over the cup of coffee.*

HELEN Bloody hell!

HELEN *starts to mop up the spilled drink.*

INT. ZACH'S ROOM. DAY.

ZACH *sits on his bed, using his laptop, earbuds in. Outside, we see birds flying past his window. Suddenly, a bird flies directly at his window, and there is a loud bang.* ZACH *turns to see what the sound was.*

EXT. HOUSE. DAY.

Outside the house, a small bird lies twitching on the garden path. A pair of feet step into shot, followed by hands, which gently scoop up the bird.

INT. KITCHEN. DAY.

HELEN *is mopping up the coffee when the doorbell sounds. She goes to the front door.*

INT. UPPER LANDING/FRONT DOOR. DAY.

ZACH *steps out of his room to see who is ringing. He peers downstairs as* HELEN *opens the door.*

HELEN Hello?

BOB *(O.S.)* Yes, I found this little double-T bird just outside your house . . .

HELEN Right.

BOB *(O.S.)* They fly towards the reflections in the windows, unfortunately.

HELEN Oh dear. Can we do anything for it, do you think?

BOB *(O.S.)* If you had a small double-L box and a quiet space, he might just come to.

HELEN Yes, erm . . . come in.

BOB *steps in, cradling a small bird in his hands. He instinctively looks up, and* **ZACH** *backs away.*

INT. KITCHEN. DAY.

HELEN *comes in and takes the empty cereal box, tearing one side off it.* **BOB** *follows: a scruffy man in his late 50s, nervy but enigmatic.*

HELEN We can put him in here and leave him by the back door. Hopefully it's just a concussion.

BOB Sparrow I think, double-R. They're tough old birds.

BOB *places the unconscious bird in the box, then takes the box to the back door.*

HELEN Poor thing. I'm Helen, by the way.

BOB Oh. Bob. Bob Bliss. Double-S.

BOB *leaves the box by the door.*

BOB *(cont'd)* At least we know his insides are functioning.

HELEN How?

BOB *shows his hands to* **HELEN**. *She pulls a face.*

HELEN *(cont'd)* Oh, here.

HELEN *indicates the sink, and* **BOB** *starts to wash his hands.*

BOB It's very kind of you. A lot of people wouldn't have cared.

HELEN I have a teenager, so . . . what's another feeble creature to look after?

BOB Ha! Both of mine have flown the nest now.

HELEN Lucky you. No, I shouldn't say that.

BOB So is he the mathematician?

HELEN He?

BOB Your teenager, double-E?

BOB *nods to the textbooks on the table.*

HELEN Zach, yes. He's doing A levels. Maths, Physics and Chemistry, God help him.

BOB Great combo.

BOB *picks up the textbook to look at it.*

BOB *(cont'd)* I did my PhD in Physics at Cambridge a few years ago. It's a fascinating subject, but a lot of it depends on the teaching.

BOB*'s phone starts to ring. He fumbles to switch it off.*

BOB *(cont'd)* Excuse me.

HELEN All Zach's teachers are terrible, so he tells me. Mind you, from the way they run their parents' evening, I'm not sure the maths teachers can even tell the time!

BOB It's all double-L relative, so . . .

ZACH *appears.*

HELEN This is my son, Zach.

BOB *stares at* ZACH *a beat too long.*

BOB Oh. Pleased to double-E meet you.

BOB *half-holds out his hand. Suddenly, there is a scrabbling sound. The bird has woken, and starts to fly round the room.*

HELEN Argh! Bloody hell!

HELEN *opens the back door and shoos the flapping bird outside.*

HELEN *(cont'd)* Come on, out!

The bird flies off and HELEN *closes the door.* ZACH *goes to the fridge for some juice, ignoring* BOB.

HELEN *(cont'd)* Zach, this is Bob.

ZACH Bad luck to bring birds in a house.

HELEN Bob studied Physics at Cambridge.

ZACH *pours his juice.*

HELEN *(cont'd)* Well, aren't you at least going to say 'hi'?

BOB and ZACH *(simultaneously)* Hi.

BOB *(cont'd)* Jinx! Oh, you meant him say 'hi' to me? Apologies. Zach! You can speak now.

ZACH I know I can. I'm not eight years old.

Awkward pause.

BOB Right, as one uranium-238 nucleus said to the other uranium-238 nucleus, I've got to split.

ZACH *smiles, in spite of himself.*

BOB *(cont'd)* He gets it. Nice to have met you, Helen. Zach. Best of luck with your studies. I hope the teaching improves! I live close by if you ever wanted to go through anything . . .

HELEN Wait! Are you . . . Sorry, this is such a desperate question.

BOB Go on.

HELEN You don't do any tutoring, do you? It's just I know that Zach needs to punch up his predicted grades . . .

ZACH Mum!

HELEN Well, it's true! Don't you want to get into a good uni like Bob did?

ZACH You're so cringe, it's embarrassing!

BOB I do have some spare time at the moment. That is to say, I'm not fully double-L engaged . . . should I perhaps come by on Thursday at six, see double-E how we get on? Then, if Zach thinks it's useful . . .

ZACH Yeah, whatever. Anything to avoid spending time with her.

ZACH *leaves.* HELEN *is distraught.*

HELEN I can't do right for doing wrong at the moment.

BOB I'm sorry, double-R.

HELEN No, I'm sorry. But thank you. Be nice to have two geniuses in the house.

BOB Genii, double-I.

INT. TV STUDIO FLASH FORWARD (2062). DAY.

A bearded professor, RUDOLPH, *stands before an interactive whiteboard. It's a cheap and cheesy educational video for Youku, oddly timeless, but with shades of Open University.* RUDOLPH *speaks in a dull monotone.*

RUDOLPH Newton's second law of motion in its simplest form can be expressed as the equation f=ma, or force equals mass times acceleration. It's why this car . . .

RUDOLPH *has two toy cars, one of which is bigger and heavier than the other.*

RUDOLPH *(cont'd)* . . . which has a greater mass, will travel less far than this car when identical force is applied.

RUDOLPH *pushes both cars with his fingers. The lighter car travels further, and falls off the end of the table.* RUDOLPH *looks on forlornly.*

INT. BEDROOM. DAY.

BOB *and* ZACH *sit in his room.* BOB *is marking* ZACH*'s work.*

BOB This is top-notch, Zach. Well double-L done.

ZACH Can you put the date on the top?

BOB Sure . . .

BOB *writes on the date.*

ZACH '62?

BOB *tuts and scribbles it out.*

ZACH *(cont'd)* Is that when you were born?

BOB Yes, I'm afraid I am rather old! So, why is f=ma a special case of the second law?

ZACH It assumes that the mass remains constant. It uses an inertial frame of reference.

BOB Which means . . . ?

ZACH There are no outside forces acting on it that make it accelerate.

BOB Very good, double-O. So what outside forces are acting on you right now?

ZACH Gravity. The Earth spinning. You.

BOB And the harder you're pushed, the further you can travel, yes?

ZACH *smiles.*

INT. KITCHEN. DAY.

HELEN *is cooking downstairs. She pours a slug of red wine into the Bolognese sauce. Radio 4 plays in the background.*

R4 ANNOUNCER *(V.O.)* And now on Radio 4, *The Archers.*

HELEN Hi guys, come on in, make yourselves at home.

Suddenly, **HELEN** *grimaces, screwing her eyes closed. A spasm of pain. She opens her eyes, then stares at the bottle of wine.*

INT. ZACH'S ROOM. DAY.

BOB *and* **ZACH** *sit at the desk.*

ZACH So, what about special relativity? Doesn't that blow all Newton's laws out of the water, now we can actually map gravitational waves?

BOB Ah, very interesting topic. Now you're asking the right questions! Unfortunately, we've just run out of time.

ZACH OK. Thanks.

ZACH *clears his things away.* **BOB** *watches him.*

BOB I couldn't help but notice your tattoo, double-T, double-O.

ZACH *looks at the small tattoo on the inside of his wrist, which reads 'Zach'.*

ZACH Yeah. I only did it to piss my mum off.

BOB Did it work?

ZACH She hasn't even noticed. That's how much she cares about me.

BOB I think she does care, Zach. I think she cares very deeply, double-E. But objects with the same charge do repel each other. I don't wish to pry, but is your father, erm . . . ?

ZACH He lives in Singapore. He's got a new family now. I don't get to see him that often.

BOB That must be very hard. For you and for your mother.

ZACH I don't have a problem with it. She's the one who's fucking mental.

BOB That's a strong word to use.

ZACH You don't have to live with her. It's like one minute she's blaming me for the fact that he left, the next minute she's trying to act like we're a weird couple or something. It's sick.

BOB *looks concerned.*

BOB Zach, I–

HELEN *(O.S.)* Dinner's ready!

INT. KITCHEN. NIGHT.

HELEN, ZACH and BOB eat spag bol at the table.

HELEN Are you sure you won't have a glass?

BOB No, I'm fine, thank you.

HELEN *has a large gulp of red wine. She's three-quarters of the way through the bottle.* ZACH *glares at her.*

BOB *produces a newspaper.*

BOB *(cont'd)* I've got some homework for you. It's the Grand National this Saturday. Study the weights of the horses and the jockeys. Try and use physics to pick us out a winner, double-N.

HELEN Oh, you're teaching him gambling, are you? Not very responsible.

BOB It's not gambling if you know who's going to win!

HELEN Pick me one, Zach!

ZACH Pick your own.

HELEN I just choose from the names, me. And whichever's got the nicest costume. If I had a horse I'd call it 'My Lovely Family', then everyone would bet on it. Make a bloody fortune, ha!

HELEN *drinks more wine.*

HELEN *(to* BOB*)* So, what do you do with your days, if you don't mind me asking?

BOB I work part-time as a bookkeeper, double-O, double-K, double-E.

HELEN That's a mouthful!

BOB Yes.

HELEN I suppose you could have been an egg-batterer, then you'd have to say 'double G and T' every day! You'd have ended up pissed!

HELEN *raises her glass and laughs.*

HELEN *(cont'd)* Why do you do it, Blob? Sorry, Bob. Bob Bliss?

ZACH Will you stop interrogating him?

HELEN What? It's called 'conversation', Zach. Listen and learn.

ZACH *shakes his head.*

HELEN *(cont'd)* Go on, what's it all about? Double-X, double-L . . . ?

BOB I suppose, double-P, it's a mild form of OCD. As a student of Physics, I was constantly trying to find patterns, double-T, in data and numbers, and then in words. I find it calming.

HELEN I get it. No I do, I do. When everything feels like it's unravelling, you just have to grab on to something don't you? It's like my 'clicks'; I need my 'clicks'. He doesn't want me to have them, but I say, 'No, they're for me . . .'

ZACH Fuck's sake.

ZACH *gets up and dumps his bowl in the sink, then heads for the exit.*

HELEN Zachary, come back here! Now!

ZACH Why? So I can sit there and listen to you chat shit all night? You're pathetic.

ZACH *exits, slamming the door.* HELEN *stifles a sob.*

BOB It's OK, honestly. I daresay it's just his hormones, plus his dad walking out.

HELEN Up against *my* hormones, plus red wine. Not a good combo.

BOB I'm sure we were all double-L the same at his age. Maybe if I could spend more time with him . . .

HELEN Why does nature do it, eh? Give us the menopause just as our kids are becoming feral monsters. Can science explain that?

BOB He's not a monster. He's just an angry young man.

HELEN Oh, Bob. I'm tired.

BOB I know.

HELEN *goes to take* BOB*'s hand. She looks at him meaningfully.* BOB *recoils and gets up quickly.*

BOB It's late, I'd best be off. Thank you for dinner, double-N.

BOB *heads out of the room, then turns sharply, agitated.*

BOB *(cont'd)* And double-F! Off, double-F.

HELEN *looks confused.*

INT. TV STUDIO FLASH FORWARD (2062). DAY.

RUDOLPH *has a Newton's cradle on his table.*

RUDOLPH A 'force' is a push or a pull that acts upon an object as a result of its interaction with another object. These forces are the subject of Newton's third law of motion: for every action, there is an equal and opposite reaction.

RUDOLPH *sets the Newton's cradle in motion, and it clicks back and forth.*

INT. KITCHEN. DAY.

The clicks from the Newton's cradle give way to the clicks from HELEN*'s iPad as she sits at the kitchen table. She gazes out of the window. A bird is nibbling the nuts on the birdfeeder, and she wonders whether it's the same one she helped.*

HELEN *goes to pick up the cereal box, which is still by the door. Something about the bar code catches her eye. Within the 13 digits are the numbers '55179909'. When she turns it upside down, she can see 'bobbliss'.*

Suddenly her phone rings, and she answers it.

HELEN Hello? Speaking. OK . . .

HELEN*'s face falls.*

HELEN *(cont'd)* Today? Er, I can be there in about half an hour . . . Right . . . I know you can't tell me, but is it regarding my test . . . ? No, I understand.

HELEN *hangs up. She looks worried. She rips up the cereal box and puts it in the recycling.*

ZACH *enters.* HELEN *is preoccupied.*

ZACH Hey Mum, guess what? You know Bob put a bet on the Grand National on Saturday? Well, his horse only won! He put £60 on at 33 to 1.

HELEN Sorry?

ZACH Bob won nearly two grand. He said he's going to give me half of it for my uni fund. That's nice of him, isn't it? Mum?

HELEN I don't want him coming round any more.

ZACH What?

HELEN And you're not to take that money, do you hear me?

ZACH Why?

HELEN We've got no idea who he is, he's just a weirdo who turned up at our door one day. He could be anybody.

ZACH What's wrong with you? Why do you have to ruin anything decent that comes into my life?

HELEN It's for your own good.

ZACH What happened? Did you pathetically come on to him and scare him away?

HELEN I haven't got time for this.

HELEN *gathers her things to leave. Feels a small spasm of back pain.*

ZACH You've never got time! Whenever I try and talk to you, you're always doing something else!

HELEN Yes, cooking, cleaning, washing your clothes! Trying to scrape together enough money so I can send you off to university.

ZACH Well, don't bother! I'm going to uni in Singapore, and dad's paying for it.

HELEN Ha!

ZACH What do you mean, 'ha'? He promised!

HELEN Like he promised to take you over for Christmas? Well, fine, go off running to him then, see what happens.

ZACH At least he believes in me. You're such a fucking bitch, you know that?

Without thinking, HELEN *turns and slaps* ZACH *in the face. She instantly regrets it. She's close to tears.*

HELEN I'm sorry. Listen, I've got to go and . . .

His face stinging, ZACH *turns and storms upstairs.*

HELEN Zach!

HELEN *knows she has to leave. She exits and closes the door.*

INT. HALL. NIGHT.

Later that night.

The doorbell sounds. ZACH *answers and finds* BOB *standing there. He holds a bunch of flowers and large, heavy holdall.*

ZACH She's not here.

ZACH *walks away to the kitchen.* BOB *lets himself in and closes the door.*

INT. KITCHEN. NIGHT.

BOB *follows* ZACH *into the kitchen.* BOB *produces an envelope, leaving his mobile phone on the kitchen island.*

BOB I've got some cash for you! From the GGs, double-G.

ZACH I'm not allowed to take it.

BOB Why not? Have you had another row with your mum?

ZACH *doesn't respond.*

BOB *(cont'd)* Maybe I shouldn't have interfered. Here. Yellow roses, double-L.

BOB *hands the flowers to* ZACH.

ZACH Her favourite. Have you been stalking us?

BOB Do you want to put them in some water?

ZACH *takes the flowers and thrashes them against the counter until they are just petals and empty stems. He hands them back to* BOB *and departs.*

BOB *(cont'd)* OK . . .

INT. ZACH'S ROOM. NIGHT.

ZACH *sits in his room.* BOB *puts down the holdall and pushes it under the bed. A moment of silence.*

BOB Have you learned anything yet about the Doppler Effect, double-P, double-F? It describes the change in frequency of a wave in relation to an observer who is moving relative to the source of that wave . . . For example, why a police siren is higher in pitch when it approaches, double-P, and is lower in pitch when it drives away.

ZACH I've never noticed.

BOB It's like time. It drags when you're young, but when you're older . . . it flies by. And you find yourself thinking about all the things you wished you'd done differently, double-F. What you'd say to yourself, if you could go back forty years, to when you were a boy.

ZACH What are you talking about?

BOB What I'm going to tell you now won't be in any of your textbooks, double-O, because it hasn't been invented yet, but in the future, we will be able to manipulate gravitational waves, as I said – as you said – and harness the power of black holes . . .

ZACH Harness is double-S.

BOB It doesn't matter – listen! What we thought was theoretical can actually be achieved. If you get the physics right. And you did.

ZACH Did what?

BOB *rolls up his sleeve to show a tattoo on the inside of his wrist. Faded with time, but still legible: 'Zach'.* ZACH *is freaked out. He looks at his own matching tattoo.*

BOB '62 isn't when I was born. It's where I came from.

ZACH *stares at* BOB. *He can't believe what he's hearing.*

BOB *(cont'd)* Be kinder to your mother, Zach. You only ever have one; science will never change that. And yours – ours . . . She's not going to be around for much longer.

ZACH What do you mean? What are you talking about?

INT. HALL. NIGHT.

HELEN *lets herself in and makes her way to the kitchen. She seems shell-shocked. She puts down her bag and some leaflets on 'Living with a terminal illness'.*

INT. ZACH'S ROOM. NIGHT.

ZACH *is emotional.*

BOB She's dying, Zach. By the time you go away to Singapore, you've stopped speaking to each other, and then it's too late. And believe me – you'll spend the rest of your life regretting it.

ZACH No . . .

BOB You'll close in on yourself. Your own kids will walk away from you. And you'll understand too late just how much she sacrificed for you. How incredibly brave she was. And that guilt will cripple you for life.

ZACH This is bullshit.

BOB *grabs* ZACH.

BOB You've got to believe me.

INT. KITCHEN. NIGHT.

HELEN *enters the kitchen and sees the flower stalks on the counter, the petals on the floor. She's overcome with emotion.*

Suddenly, a phone buzzes on the counter. It's BOB*'s. She instinctively answers it. It's not a good line, quite a lot of static.*

HELEN Hello?

RUDOLPH *(V.O.)* Zach? Can you hear me? What the fuck do you think you're doing?

HELEN Zach's my son. Sorry, who is this?

RUDOLPH *(V.O.)* Oh, God. Please, Mrs Wilson, try to stay calm. I think your son could be in grave danger.

INT. ZACH'S ROOM. NIGHT.

ZACH *backs away from* BOB.

BOB I just need you to tell her I love her. Very much. It won't save her, but it could save you. Just a random act of kindness.

BOB *removes a gun from his jacket.* ZACH *looks scared.*

BOB *(cont'd)* So you can have my time again.

INT. KITCHEN. NIGHT.

HELEN *is on the phone, straining to understand.*

RUDOLPH *(V.O.)* The man whose phone this is, he's not to be trusted, do you understand?

HELEN You mean Bob?

RUDOLPH *(V.O.)* You mustn't leave your son alone with him.

HELEN But he's . . .

BANG! HELEN *hears a gunshot coming from upstairs.*

HELEN Zach! Zachary!

HELEN *drops the phone and runs up the stairs.* RUDOLPH*'s voice can be heard on the phone, fizzing with static.*

RUDOLPH *(V.O.)* Mrs Wilson, let me speak to him, please!

INT. ZACH'S ROOM. NIGHT.

HELEN *bursts into the room.* BOB*'s body lies on the floor, gun in hand, a spray of blood and brains on the wall.* HELEN *is horrified at the sight.* ZACH *sits on the bed, white with shock.*

HELEN Oh my God!

ZACH I'm sorry.

HELEN What happened? Are you alright, did he hurt you?

HELEN *hurries to* ZACH.

ZACH No, I'm fine. I love you, Mum.

HELEN I love you, Zachary. I love you so much . . .

They embrace.

ZACH It's all going to be alright . . . I promise. It's going to be alright.

We tilt down and see BOB*'s holdall under the bed. A green light pulses within.**

FADE TO BLACK.

INT. KITCHEN FLASH FORWARD (2062). DAY.

*The structure of the room is the same, but the dressing is different. Subtly of the future. Pan along some bereavement cards on the table. 'Sorry for your loss,' 'Thinking of you at this sad time.' Flowers in vases. A framed photo of '*BOB*' with an elderly lady:* OLDER HELEN*. He holds a Nobel Prize medal.*

RUDOLPH *picks up the photo and regards it.*

OLDER ZACH *enters, dressed in a black suit. (This is the same actor that played '*BOB*', only he looks smarter.)*

RUDOLPH Oh, Dr Wilson, your daughter let me in.

OLDER ZACH Call me Zach, please. Everybody does.

RUDOLPH Thank you. It was a lovely service.

OLDER ZACH Yes, I think my mother would have said that it went on a bit too long, but then a lot of people said that about her as well.

RUDOLPH How old was she?

OLDER ZACH Ninety-three.

RUDOLPH A very decent age, even by today's standards.

OLDER ZACH She was a tough old bird. So strange being back in her house without her. Sorry, can I offer you a drink?

RUDOLPH I'll have a coffee, thank you.

OLDER ZACH *prepares the drinks, using an app on his iDevice to activate a coffee machine.*

OLDER ZACH So my daughters were telling me you have a Youku channel?

RUDOLPH Yes.

OLDER ZACH That's very retro.

RUDOLPH I do little science videos, for children. Pretty basic stuff.

OLDER ZACH And you wanted to interview my mother?

RUDOLPH That's right. She was one of the first people to trial your anti-cancer serum back in '29. I wanted to hear in her own words what she could remember.

OLDER ZACH Not much, I would have thought. It was a long time ago.

RUDOLPH Time is relative, so . . .

OLDER ZACH *gives* RUDOLPH *his coffee.*

OLDER ZACH So you're an actual scientist, then? You're not just an actor in a white coat.

RUDOLPH Yes, I do dabble. In fact, this . . .

RUDOLPH *picks up the framed photo from the table.*

RUDOLPH *(cont'd)* This could have been me. A world-famous Nobel prize-winner. But you cheated me out of that, didn't you Zach?

OLDER ZACH*'s face darkens.*

RUDOLPH *(cont'd)* In another time, we were partners, you and I. We developed the Wilson–Brann Wormhole together.

INT. LAB (2042). DAY.

Goggled SCIENTISTS *stand around as* RUDOLPH *and* OLDER ZACH *power up a portal of shimmering light.* OLDER ZACH *throws a live bird into the portal, and it disappears.* RUDOLPH *and* OLDER ZACH *embrace excitedly.*

RUDOLPH *(V.O.)* It was a game-changer. Made us billions.

INT. KITCHEN FLASH FORWARD (2062). DAY.

Back in the kitchen.

RUDOLPH But because in this timeline, you never left to study Physics in Singapore, you never came to Cambridge to research black holes, and so we never met. Instead, you devoted your life to chemistry and oncological research, and I ended up doing Youku videos as 'Dr Brann the Science Man'.

OLDER ZACH I'd like you to leave now, please.

RUDOLPH Then one day, I was clearing out my spam folder . . .

INT. TV STUDIO FLASH FORWARD (2062). DAY.

RUDOLPH *stands on the set of his science show, looking at his phone.*

RUDOLPH *(V.O.)* . . . when I found a video message I'd apparently just emailed to myself.

RUDOLPH *frowns as he opens the video message.*

INT. LAB (2062). DAY.

On the phone, we see a video of a slightly more groomed and successful RUDOLPH *giving a frenzied explanation of what has happened:* ZACH *has betrayed him and sent himself back in time.*

RUDOLPH *(V.O.)* I must have known I didn't have long before that version of my life ceased to exist.

INT. TV STUDIO FLASH FORWARD (2062). DAY.

RUDOLPH *is watching the video of his alternate self.*

RUDOLPH *(V.O.)* That you would forfeit my reality by trying to save your precious mother.

INT. KITCHEN FLASH FORWARD (2062). DAY.

OLDER ZACH *and* RUDOLPH *face each other as before.*

RUDOLPH I always had a feeling I was living the wrong life. The life you stole from me. And now I want it back.

RUDOLPH *pulls a small tube-like device from his pocket, somewhere between a taser and a sonic screwdriver.* OLDER ZACH *looks scared.*

RUDOLPH *(cont'd)* Where is it?

OLDER ZACH What?

RUDOLPH Our time machine. The one you used to visit yourself as a boy.

OLDER ZACH That was just junk, I got rid of it.

RUDOLPH I don't believe you.

OLDER ZACH It's true! Bob was . . . insane.

RUDOLPH No. We're going back, Dr Wilson. Time to reset.

RUDOLPH *approaches* OLDER ZACH, *and he backs away.*

OLDER ZACH Please . . . My mother . . .

RUDOLPH Fuck her. I'm not prepared to be your collateral damage.

RUDOLPH *comes for* OLDER ZACH *with the futuristic weapon, but* OLDER ZACH *attempts to grab it. They struggle, ricocheting round the kitchen.*

RUDOLPH *eventually pushes* OLDER ZACH *on to the table, and the cup of coffee is knocked over and spills.*

INT. KITCHEN. DAY.

HELEN *has just knocked over the cup of coffee.*

HELEN Bloody hell!

HELEN *mops up the spilled liquid.*

INT. ZACH'S ROOM. DAY.

ZACH *sits on the bed, using his laptop, earbuds in. Outside, we see birds flying past his window. Suddenly, a bird flies directly at his window, and there is a loud bang.* ZACH *turns to see what the sound was.*

EXT. HOUSE. DAY.

Outside the house, a small bird lies twitching on the path.

INT. KITCHEN. DAY.

HELEN *mops up the coffee. Suddenly, she feels a spasm of pain in her lower back.*

INT. ZACH'S ROOM. DAY.

ZACH *goes back to his laptop. He has a nagging feeling something is wrong.*

EXT. HOUSE. DAY.

The bird lies still on the path. A small twitch. We stay on it for some time . . .

THE END

Episode 6

WISE OWL

CAST LIST

Ronnie – Reece Shearsmith

Mr Blenkin – Steve Pemberton

Dinah – Georgie Glen

Wilf – Ron Cook

with the voices of

Dylan Hall

Isabelle Lee Pratt

INT. FIELD (ANIMATED). DAY.

We see a public information film from the early 70s, rendered in simple 2D animation.

A small BOY *and* GIRL *are flying a kite in a field.*

BOY It's my sister's birthday today.

GIRL I'm six!

BOY She got a new kite. I promised Mummy I would watch her while we played with it outside.

The BOY *turns to his sister.*

BOY *(cont'd)* It's my turn now.

GIRL No, it's my present and I want to fly it.

The BOY *and* GIRL *tussle over the kite, and she lets go of the string. The kite flies away. The* GIRL *starts to cry.*

BOY Don't cry. I can see it up there – look.

The BOY *points to a large electrical pylon, where the kite has become lodged. They approach the pylon, which has a warning sign next to it.*

GIRL It's very high.

BOY That's alright, I can climb up.

The boy passes the warning sign and is starting to climb when he hears a sound from the nearby tree.

WISE OWL *(O.S.)* Twit-you, twit-you!

The BOY *looks round and sees a big brown owl sitting on the branch of the tree. This is* WISE OWL.

He looks stern, his eyes piercing through the feathers on his face, his claws large and sharp.

GIRL Look, it's Wise Owl.

BOY Hello, Wise Owl.

WISE OWL Twit-you! Only a fool would climb up there. Didn't you see the warning sign?

The WISE OWL *flies down from the tree to the warning sign.*

WISE OWL *(cont'd)* Pylons kill. Stay away from them.

BOY I won't touch the wires.

WISE OWL That doesn't matter. The electricity will be conducted through the kite's metal rods.

WISE OWL*'s head spins round.*

GIRL But what about my present?

WISE OWL Let's see if our friend the wind can help.

WISE OWL *blows through his beak, and swirls of wind dislodge the kite, which flutters to the ground. The* BOY *and* GIRL *go to pick it up.*

BOY Thanks, Wise Owl!

GIRL Thanks, Wise Owl!

WISE OWL *(into camera)* Don't be a twit-you. Leave electricity alone.

The legend appears: 'Be a wise owl.' The public information film ends.

INT. SPARE BEDROOM. DAY.

A hand reaches and pulls a plug from a wall socket. We see RONNIE, *a middle-aged man, serious-looking, holding a portable radio. He moves to the window and peeps out through the curtains.*

EXT. STREET. DAY.

We see RONNIE *in the upstairs window, then the curtains twitch closed. The house is old and tired-looking. The front window has a pane crudely boarded up with cardboard where a window has been smashed.*

There is a plaque with an image of an owl and the number 9.

TITLE: *'Wise Owl'.*

INT. BATHROOM. DAY.

An old-fashioned bathroom suite (the house is generally dated in its decor). RONNIE *puts the radio on the side of the bath, puts in the bath plug and turns on the taps.*

INT. STAIRCASE. DAY.

RONNIE *heads down the stairs. He seems quietly determined.*

INT. LIVING ROOM. DAY.

RONNIE *enters the living room and starts to look through drawers and cupboards. The room is full of taxidermied animals: a squirrel, a badger, a crow, a shrew.* RONNIE *finds what he is looking for in one of the old drawers: an extension lead. He takes it back upstairs with him.*

INT. SPARE BEDROOM. DAY.

RONNIE *plugs the extension lead into the wall socket.*

INT. BATHROOM. DAY.

RONNIE *brings the extension lead into the bathroom and plugs the radio into it. He places the radio back on the side of the bath. He turns off the bath taps and stares down at the water as the taps drip into it, seeing his reflection ripple and distort.*

RONNIE *turns on the radio. It hisses and crackles as some classical music blares out. He steps into the bath and sits in the water. He picks up the radio and holds it out in front of him. He takes a couple of deep breaths.*

Suddenly, a voice emerges from the radio speaker.

WISE OWL *(V.O.)* Twit-you, twit-you!

The doorbell sounds downstairs.

RONNIE *hesitates. He switches off the radio and puts it back on the side. The doorbell sounds again.* RONNIE *rises up from the bath.*

EXT. HOUSE. DAY.

A middle-aged man, MR BLENKIN, *stands at the front door, holding a cardboard box.*

RONNIE *can be seen approaching through the frosted glass.*

MR BLENKIN Oh, is that Mr Oliver? Erm, it's Derek Blenkin here, I live on Deerfold. You did my neighbour's bobtail last year. Dr Pepper.

No response, though MR BLENKIN *can see the distorted outline of* RONNIE.

MR BLENKIN *(cont'd)* Sorry, am I at the right house? You do do taxidermy?

INT/EXT. HOUSE/HALL. DAY.

RONNIE *closes his eyes tight. We cut between inside and outside.*

MR BLENKIN Well, what it is – we've just come back from our holidays, and we'd left our cleaner to feed my daughter's pet rabbit, Ferrari. That's the rabbit, not my daughter. Anyway, she wanted to give it a treat, and to cut a long story sideways, she's accidentally fed it a bag of chocolate buttons and now it's dead. Are you there?

RONNIE (V.O.) I'm not meant to talk to strangers.

MR BLENKIN Oh. Well, we've had it in the fridge overnight. My daughter doesn't know yet – she's only five. So I was wondering if you could preserve him for us? Ferrari. She won't know the difference, I'll just tell her it's always tired. My neighbour said you'd do us a good price?

No response from RONNIE.

MR BLENKIN *(cont'd)* I don't need it all dressed up and doing ballet like a Beatrix Potter.

It'll just be in the corner of the hutch, covered in straw. You'll barely see it. It's just we're not ready for the whole death conversation at the moment. We've got all that to come with my mother.

There is a pause. MR BLENKIN *is expectant. The door is yanked open and* RONNIE *snatches the box from* MR BLENKIN.

MR BLENKIN Thank you so much. And, as I say, any discount gratefully received. It needn't even have legs if that's cheaper . . .

RONNIE *slams the door shut again.*

MR BLENKIN OK. Nice to meet you.

He walks away down the path. He seems discomfited.

INT. LIVING ROOM. DAY.

RONNIE *comes in and looks into the box, lifting the lid slightly. Inside is a dead white rabbit. He puts the lid back on and puts the box on the work table.*

Sensing movement behind him, RONNIE *swivels round to look at the rows of stuffed animals. They seem to be staring at him menacingly.*

RONNIE *leaves the room.*

INT. LANDING. DAY.

RONNIE *makes his way up the stairs, back to the bathroom.*

INT. BATHROOM. DAY.

RONNIE *enters the bathroom and is about to unplug the water when he sees, floating in the bathwater, a large brown feather. He stares at it, puzzled. He hears a disconcerting screeching sound coming from next door.*

INT. LANDING. DAY.

RONNIE *comes out on to the landing and walks to a closed bedroom door. He slowly puts his ear to the door. He listens closely. There is a sound like rustling or flapping coming from inside.*

RONNIE *looks frightened.*

EXT. BEACH (ANIMATED). DAY.

We see another public information film. This time, we are on a beach. We see the BOY *and* GIRL *throwing a ball to each other.*

BOY One day on our holidays, the weather was nice so we came to the beach.

GIRL I want to go in the sea!

The MOTHER *comes along and takes the* GIRL*'s hand. The pair walk off to the seashore.*

BOY Mummy took my sister paddling, and I started to make a sandcastle.

We see the BOY *fill a bucket and make a sandcastle.*

BOY *(cont'd)* I was happy playing when a man came to talk to me.

A shadow looms over the BOY*, as we see a pair of adult legs walk up to him and stop. The* BOY *looks up, but the bright sun makes the* STRANGER *just a silhouette against the blue sky.*

BOY *(cont'd)* He said I looked nice and shiny, and did I want to see a starfish? I thought that sounded fun.

The BOY *stands up and the* STRANGER *holds out his hand for the* BOY *to take. The* BOY *is reaching out to hold it when we hear a familiar cry.*

WISE OWL *(O.S.)* Twit-you, twit-you!

We see WISE OWL *flutter down and land on top of the bucket. He is dressed in a stripy bathing suit.*

WISE OWL You don't know who this man is! He may seem friendly, but his intentions might not be.

The STRANGER *suddenly reaches out and grabs the* BOY*'s hand tight. He starts to pull his arm.* WISE OWL *flies off the bucket and pecks the* STRANGER*'s hand, and he lets go. The* STRANGER *runs off. The* BOY *sobs.*

WISE OWL What did your mummy tell you about strangers?

BOY That I shouldn't talk to them?

WISE OWL Exactly. Don't be a twit-you. Always stay safe with your mummy and daddy. Wise Owl knows best!

WISE OWL *flies off. The* BOY *is left alone, crying.*

BOY Mummy! Mummy! MUMMY?!

The animation ends far more bleakly than it should.

INT. KITCHEN. DAY.

RONNIE *takes the large, sharp knives from the wooden block on the side and carefully puts them into a cardboard box. Then he opens the cutlery drawer and takes out all the knives and adds them to the box. He then has a thought, and takes one of the sharp knives back out.* RONNIE *takes the box to the larder and places it inside, out of harm's way.*

RONNIE *is distracted by the hum of the fridge-freezer. He listens carefully as the sound seems to increase. He goes over and unplugs the fridge.*

RONNIE *goes round unplugging everything in the kitchen.*

INT. LIVING ROOM. DAY.

RONNIE *tapes up the sockets in the living room, the stuffed animals looking down on him as he works.*

RONNIE *then stands on a chair and unscrews the bulb from the ceiling pendant light.*

INT. HALL. DAY.

RONNIE *is removing the bulb from the hallway light fitting when the letter box opens and the postman pushes through some letters.* RONNIE *freezes and watches the postman move away.*

He carefully climbs down from the chair and goes to look at the letters. RONNIE *picks up the mail. A couple of bills addressed to Mr W. Oliver, then a brown envelope with a childlike scrawl that reads: 'To Wise Owl'.*

RONNIE *opens a drawer on the console table, and we see a small pile of similar letters addressed to Wise Owl. He adds this one to the pile.*

INT. BATHROOM. NIGHT.

RONNIE *is brushing his teeth at the sink. Behind him, a pink balloon rises past his head.* RONNIE *continues brushing his teeth as he watches it float up.*

BOY *(V.O.)* It's my sister's birthday today.

INT. LIVING ROOM (ANIMATED). DAY.

There is a cake on the table with six candles. A pink balloon is tied to a chair.

The BOY *and the* GIRL *are standing by the table.*

GIRL I'm six!

BOY She got a doll, a tea set and a kite. Now we're waiting for Mummy to get home so we can light the candles on her cake.

GIRL I want to do it now! I know where they keep the matches – look!

The GIRL *takes a large box of matches from the mantelpiece.*

The BOY *takes a match from the box and lights it. He stares at the flame.*

INT. BATHROOM. NIGHT.

RONNIE *looks at himself in the mirror. He pulls back his hair and we see some burn scars.*

INT. LANDING. NIGHT.

RONNIE, *using a small torch to light his way, heads for the stairs. He pauses by the closed door and listens in again. Hearing nothing, he turns the handle and opens the door slightly, but as he does so, he hears loud flapping and screeching noises, and he quickly closes it again.*

INT. LIVING ROOM/DINAH'S HOUSE. NIGHT.

RONNIE *is laying out a sleeping bag on the floor of the living room.*

He comes across a framed photograph on the mantle of a little girl, around five years old. There is another child standing next to the GIRL, *but he has been cropped out.*

RONNIE *regards the photo for a moment, then replaces it on the mantle.*

Suddenly, RONNIE*'s phone starts to ring.* RONNIE *goes to answer it and sees that it is a FaceTime call from 'Mum'. He answers, and we see his mother* DINAH *on the screen.*

RONNIE Hi, Mum.

DINAH Ronnie? Is that you? I can't see you properly.

RONNIE I'm just getting ready for bed.

DINAH It's only quarter past eight! I'm calling you between *Corries.* Are you alright?

RONNIE Yeah.

DINAH I came round earlier today. You weren't in.

RONNIE I've been busy. Got to stuff a Ferrari.

DINAH A what?

RONNIE It's someone's pet.

DINAH Oh.

RONNIE *is silent.*

DINAH *(cont'd)* We had a cat, do you remember? When you and Joanne were little. Mimsy. We got rid of it in the end. It made you wheeze. And it had this way of looking at you all superior, like you were just muck on its shoe.

RONNIE Cats don't wear shoes.

DINAH Well, you know what I mean. Anyway, I'm just checking that you're still coming on Monday?

RONNIE *doesn't respond.*

DINAH *(cont'd)* You haven't been in over three years. You know what Dr Dinetto said.

RONNIE He doesn't know me. He doesn't know anything. I can look after myself.

Silence.

DINAH I know you can. I'd just like you to be there, that's all. For me. Puss in Boots! He wore shoes, so . . .

RONNIE Will Dad be there?

DINAH I'm not sure. I've asked him, but he might not show up, you know what he's like. I don't suppose you've heard from him?

RONNIE *shakes his head.*

DINAH *(cont'd)* We all deal with things in our own way, don't we? Now, promise me you'll come.

RONNIE OK.

DINAH And you won't . . . do anything silly before then?

RONNIE *shakes his head.*

DINAH *(cont'd)* Promise?

RONNIE I promise.

DINAH Alright then. I'll call you tomorrow, sweetheart.

RONNIE Bye.

DINAH I love—

RONNIE *ends the call.*

INT. HOSPITAL (ANIMATED). NIGHT.

The BOY *sits on a hospital bed. His hand and head are bandaged. He is tearful. He can hear a* DOCTOR *by the bed.*

DOCTOR *(O.S.)* I'm sorry, Mrs Oliver, we did all we could.

MOTHER *(O.S., crying)* It was her birthday! Why did you do it Ronnie, why? You knew it was wrong!

WISE OWL *flies in and sits next to the* BOY *on the bed, looking at him accusingly.*

WISE OWL You mustn't say anything.

INT. LIVING ROOM. NIGHT.

RONNIE *lies asleep in his sleeping bag on the floor.*

After a few moments, we hear a scuttling sound coming from the other side of the room. RONNIE *wakes and looks around. He turns on his torch and looks at some of the taxidermy animals, the beam giving them a strange sense of movement. Satisfied there is nothing there, he settles back down again.*

Suddenly, he hears the door creak open. RONNIE *opens his eyes again and sits up.*

He stares in terror at the door as a figure slowly peeps round. It has an oversized owl head that resembles WISE OWL.

RONNIE What do you want?

WISE OWL *steps slowly forward, the large owl's head on a naked man's body.*

WISE OWL Wise Owl knows best.

WISE OWL*'s head starts to turn slowly through 360 degrees. As the head turns to face* RONNIE *again, it screeches . . .*

RONNIE *wakes up. He breathes heavily, looking round the room. He is alone.*

INT. LIVING ROOM. DAY.

It is early morning. Light streams through the curtains. RONNIE *suddenly wakes. He is sweaty, uncomfortable.*

RONNIE *can hear flies buzzing. He gets up to see three or four big bluebottles buzzing around the box on the table that contains the dead rabbit. He gets up and shoos the flies away, peeping inside the box.*

INT. ROOM (ANIMATED). DAY.

The GIRL *is petting a cat on the table.*

BOY *(O.S.)* This is my sister's cat, Mimsy. One day, he got poorly and died.

The cat meows, spins on to its back and dies with its paws in the air. The GIRL *cries. The* BOY *appears.*

BOY *(cont'd)* I told her not to worry, and that he was in cat heaven now.

GIRL I don't want him to go. I wish we could keep him forever.

BOY But that's impossible.

WISE OWL *(O.S.)* Twit-you, twit-you!

We see that WISE OWL *is on the mantlepiece in the room.*

BOY and GIRL *(simultaneously)* Wise Owl!

BOY *(cont'd)* What are you doing here?

WISE OWL Have you children never heard of taxidermy?

GIRL Taxi-what?

WISE OWL Dermy. It's a way of keeping your favourite pets around forever. Let me show you. You will need . . .

We see the items appear on the table next to the dead cat.

WISE OWL *(cont'd, O.S.)* A scalpel, some galvanised wire, a scraper, and tanning chemicals. Always read the label.

The BOY *starts to cut open the dead cat.*

WISE OWL *(cont'd, O.S.)* First, you need to peel the skin off. Make incisions around the legs and tummy, then pull the animal's pelt slowly from its carcass.

We see this animated.

WISE OWL *(cont'd, O.S.)* Then you remove the eyes with the scalpel. I can do this for you.

WISE OWL *pecks the cat's eyes from its head.*

WISE OWL *(cont'd, O.S.)* You can dispose of the body in an incinerator.

The GIRL *throws the cat's pink body into the fire.*

WISE OWL *(cont'd, O.S.)* Next, use the chemicals to tan the skin for twenty-four hours. This is a good time to play a game or have a sandwich.

The BOY *and* GIRL *sit at the table, eating sandwiches among the detritus. The* GIRL *pulls an eye on a stalk from her sandwich.*

GIRL Ew!

They giggle.

WISE OWL Next, make a body shape from foam, using wire to keep it in place. Then pull the tanned hide back on to the model.

BOY Like putting a sausage into its skin.

WISE OWL Exactly! Select glass eyes to match your pet's, and gently force them into the sockets. Scrunch and pull it into position, and use a needle and thread to stitch everything back together. And hey presto! Easy when you know how.

After this procedure, the stuffed cat looks almost like it did before. The GIRL *cuddles it.*

GIRL Thanks, Wise Owl!

BOY He's as good as new!

INT. LIVING ROOM. DAY.

RONNIE *stands at the table, surrounded by the detritus of taxidermy. He looks down at his creation, frowning slightly.*

We see the stuffed rabbit Ferrari on the table. It is an abomination: too-big glass eyes popping from its head, teeth bared in a rictus grin, misshapen body on too-stiff legs, and badly sewn visible seams.

RONNIE *picks up the rabbit and tries to bend down the ears. It still looks odd and frightening.*

The doorbell sounds, and RONNIE *goes to answer it.*

INT/EXT. HOUSE . DAY.

RONNIE *opens the door to find* MR BLENKIN *standing there.*

MR BLENKIN Yeah, we've had a change of heart, and I'd like to get Ferrari back, please. Just as he was. You've not touched him, have you?

RONNIE Erm . . .

RONNIE *looks back over his shoulder towards the living room.*

MR BLENKIN Is the real Mr Oliver in?

RONNIE *doesn't respond.*

MR BLENKIN *(cont'd)* I was chatting with my neighbour, and she said he's a gentleman in his seventies. So that's not you, is it?

RONNIE *shakes his head slightly.*

MR BLENKIN *(cont'd)* So who are you, then? Eh? What are you doing here?

RONNIE *looks down at the broken glass by the boarded-up window.*

MR BLENKIN *(cont'd)* You'd better not have done anything to him.

RONNIE Who?

MR BLENKIN Ferrari! Can I have him back now, please, or am I going to have to call the police?

RONNIE *goes back to the dining room.*

INT. LIVING ROOM. DAY.

RONNIE *puts the stuffed rabbit into its box and takes it back out.*

INT/EXT. HOUSE. DAY.

RONNIE *hands the box back to* MR BLENKIN.

RONNIE Here.

MR BLENKIN Thank you!

MR BLENKIN *looks inside the box and is horrified.*

MR BLENKIN *(cont'd)* Oh dear God! What the hell do you call that?

RONNIE *closes the door.*

MR BLENKIN *(cont'd, O.S.)* This is disgusting! What am I going to tell my daughter now, eh? She'll have bloody nightmares if she sees this! Franken-rabbit. You want reporting. You're sick!

RONNIE *covers his ears so he can't hear* MR BLENKIN *shouting. Eventually,* MR BLENKIN *goes away.*

INT. KITCHEN. DAY.

RONNIE *stands at the stove. He holds a large box of matches. He stands for some time, before sliding open the box and removing a match.*

RONNIE *steels himself, then strikes the match against the side of the box.*

He turns on the gas and lights the gas ring. A whoosh of flame.

EXT. HOUSE (ANIMATED). NIGHT.

The house is ablaze. Black smoke pours from the window. We hear screaming from within.

WISE OWL *flies out of the window and lands in a tree, watching the blaze as the fire engine approaches.*

We move close in on WISE OWL*'s eyes as he watches the house burn.*

INT. KITCHEN. DAY.

RONNIE *shakes the match so the flame extinguishes, just as it was about to burn his fingers. Then he carries it over to the sink and runs the spent match under the tap.*

RONNIE *watches the pan on the gas ring. The water starts to boil, and* RONNIE *drops a boil-in-the-bag fish into the pan. He carefully pushes the pan handle to the side so it isn't sticking out.*

EXT. GRAVEYARD (ANIMATED). DAY.

The BOY *stands at the front of an open grave flanked by his parents (we don't see their heads). He looks at the small coffin as it is lowered into the ground.*

A tear falls from the BOY*'s eye.* DAD *puts his hand on* RONNIE*'s shoulder. He speaks with* WISE OWL*'s voice.*

DAD *(as* WISE OWL*)* It should have been you, Ronnie.

EXT/INT. HALL. NIGHT.

Night has fallen and the house is quiet. A figure appears at the front door and lets himself in with a key. We see the man enter, in a brown coat with swept-back grey hair. This is WILF.

He goes to turn on the light, but it doesn't work. He sees the open drawer. WILF *takes the torch from the table.*

INT. LIVING ROOM. NIGHT.

WILF *tries the dining room light, but this doesn't work either. He scans the room, and spots the sleeping bag on the floor.*

WILF Hello? Is someone there?

INT. STAIRS. NIGHT.

WILF *heads up the stairs with the torch.*

WILF I've no money, you know!

WILF *gets to the top of the stairs.*

INT. BATHROOM. NIGHT.

WILF *enters the bathroom.* RONNIE *crouches on the side of the bath, like a large bird.* WILF *is taken aback. He squints as his eyes adjust.*

WILF Ronnie?

RONNIE Hello, Dad.

INT. LIVING ROOM. NIGHT.

WILF *pours two shots of whisky and hands one to* RONNIE.

WILF Here. You gave me quite a shock. You'll have to give me the money for that window, you know. Cheers!

RONNIE You shouldn't drink so much.

WILF It's only a nip. I've just come back from Pickering. They had a seventies weekend at the Toy Museum, a few of the old buggers like me wheeled out. Ray Brooks. Nigel from *Pipkins*. One of the

Bungles – not the scary one. We had a laugh. I don't suppose you've followed my career over the last twenty-odd years? Did they have a telly in . . . where you were, or were you not allowed?

RONNIE *won't meet* WILF*'s eye.*

WILF *(cont'd)* I didn't do much after *Wise Owl* finished. Couple of theatre tours, nice two-hander with Jeff Holland. Everything was a bit tainted after . . . well, you know.

RONNIE *looks down.* WILF *takes out a bundle of autograph cards from his jacket. They show a younger* WILF *with* WISE OWL *on his shoulder, with the caption: 'Wilfred Oliver is . . . Wise Owl!'*

WILF *(cont'd)* They were thinking of bringing him back three or four years ago. Computer animation – it would have been crap. I said to my agent I'd be happy to do it, then he said they'd asked Stephen Fry! I said, 'Yeah 'cos he needs the work, doesn't he? Throw him a bone.' Anyway, it all fizzled out. So I do this now . . .

WILF *approaches the stuffed animals on the shelf.*

WILF *(cont'd)* You'd be surprised how many people want to preserve something of the past. Keep a memory alive, a freeze-frame of a happy moment.

The biggest thing I've done is a goat. Spent nearly a month on that. A little old lady brought him in; she called him Pan. Probably a witch. Funnily enough, I've never done an owl. I don't think I'd want to. So, are you going to tell me what you're doing here? Did your mum put you up to it?

RONNIE You know what Monday is, don't you?

WILF Monday . . .

WILF *thinks. Remembers.*

WILF *(cont'd)* Oh. That.

RONNIE She would have been fifty.

WILF Really? Time flies.

RONNIE Did you get my letters?

WILF Yes, I had a few. I couldn't read half of them – your handwriting's shocking. I still get quite a bit of fan mail. People asking Wise Owl's advice on this and that.

Daft, really.

RONNIE Did you never want to come and see me?

WILF Your mother said not to. Said it'd only make it worse. It's all water under the bridge now, anyway. Come here . . .

WILF *goes towards* RONNIE, *but he flinches and screws his eyes shut.*

WILF *(cont'd)* You mustn't feel guilty, you know, Ronnie. It was just an accident. I don't blame you if that's what you're worried about.

Big close-up on RONNIE.

RONNIE It was my sister's birthday.

GIRL *(V.O.)* I'm six!

INT. LIVING ROOM (ANIMATED). NIGHT.

When RONNIE *opens his eyes, we are still in the living room, but everything is animated – apart from* RONNIE, *who remains real among the 2D setting.* RONNIE *is holding an animated pink cake, which he places on the table.*

RONNIE She got a doll, a tea set and a kite. Now we're waiting for Mummy to get home so we can light the candles on her cake.

GIRL I want to do it now! I know where they keep the matches – look!

The GIRL *picks up a large box of matches from the mantlepiece.*

RONNIE You shouldn't play with matches, Joanne. Isn't that right, Wise Owl?

RONNIE *turns to* WISE OWL, *who is perched on the armchair in the corner. He is half-asleep. He clutches a bottle of whisky, just as* WILF *did.*

RONNIE *(cont'd)* Wise Owl?

WISE OWL What?

RONNIE Joanne wants to light her candles, but I told her it's dangerous.

WISE OWL Twit-you. What does it say on the box? Can't you read?

RONNIE *reads from the box.*

RONNIE 'Safety matches'.

WISE OWL Exactly. They're safe. If she wants to light her candles, let her light them. It's her birthday.

GIRL Thanks, Wise Owl!

The GIRL *goes to light a match, but* RONNIE *stops her.*

RONNIE Are you sure we shouldn't wait for Mummy?

WISE OWL 'Are you sure we shouldn't wait for Mummy?' Why do you have to ask permission for everything? Grow some balls, Ronnie, for fuck's sake!

The GIRL *laughs. She tugs on* RONNIE*'s jumper.*

GIRL He said *balls*!

RONNIE But . . .

WISE OWL Wise Owl's always right, remember? Now come on, let's leave Joanne to make her wish. You're coming upstairs with me.

RONNIE *looks scared.* WISE OWL *flies to the door.*

RONNIE I'd rather stay here.

WISE OWL Wise Owl knows best.

RONNIE *heads for the door.*

INT. STAIRWAY. NIGHT (AND DAY FOR JOANNE).

RONNIE *follows* WILF *up the stairs. He looks back into the living room through the open door and sees a little girl,* JOANNE, *(the girl from the photograph) striking a match and lighting the candles on her cake.* JOANNE *smiles at* RONNIE *through the open door.*

INT. LANDING. NIGHT.

WILF *gets to the top of the stairs.* RONNIE *is behind him.*

WILF Now what?

We see that RONNIE *is holding a large, sharp knife. He gestures to the bedroom.*

RONNIE In there.

WILF *opens the bedroom door and enters.* RONNIE *braces himself and follows.*

INT. MAIN BEDROOM. NIGHT.

RONNIE *gestures to the bed.*

RONNIE Sit down.

WILF Ronnie . . .

RONNIE Sit. Down.

WILF *sits on the bed.*

RONNIE *(cont'd)* Why did you let me take the blame?

WILF Oh, let's not dredge up the past . . .

RONNIE You said you were on your way home from the pub when you saw the house on fire. Said you climbed in through a window and rescued me. You were the hero. But that's not true, is it? You were in here. With me.

WILF I think you're remembering it wrong, son.

RONNIE I don't think so.

WILF I had a career to protect! I was the voice of the public information films. And my daughter gets burned alive in a fire. Not very 'on brand', is it? What was I supposed to do?

RONNIE I trusted you. I always did everything Wise Owl said. Everything . . .

WILF That was just a game, Ronnie. It wasn't doing any harm; you enjoyed it. I loved you, and Joanne. Now, come on. Come and join me. Don't be a twit-you! Give your old man a hug.

RONNIE *falters. He slowly approaches the bed. Then he raises the knife and plunges it down three times.*

We reveal that he has stabbed it into the pillow next to WILF, *who cowers on the bed.*

WILF Don't hurt me, please. Do you want to be put back in that place? Stop this now and I won't say anything.

RONNIE No. But I will.

RONNIE *throws the pillow at* WILF, *feathers escaping from the holes and floating in the air.*

RONNIE *turns and exits.*

INT. LIVING ROOM. NIGHT.

RONNIE *hurries into the living room and starts to pack his sleeping bag into his rucksack.*

WILF *(O.S.)* Ronnie!

WILF *enters. Some feathers are stuck to his face and coat.*

WILF Ronnie, what did you mean? Where are you going?

RONNIE To see Mum. I'm going to tell her.

WILF Tell her what, exactly?

RONNIE *looks at* WILF *intently.*

RONNIE Everything.

WILF No, no, stop the night here. Let's just talk some more . . .

RONNIE *continues to pack.*

WILF *(cont'd)* You can't go. Ronnie! You mustn't say anything. Wise Owl won't let you.

RONNIE *hesitates.*

WILF *(cont'd)* And we must always do what Wise Owl says, mustn't we?

RONNIE Not any more.

RONNIE *picks up his rucksack and brushes past* WILF.

EXT. HOUSE (ANIMATED). NIGHT.

An animated version of the house. The BOY *exits and walks away.* WISE OWL *flies from the door and hovers in front of the house, tweeting desperately.*

WISE OWL Twit-you! Twit-you! Twit-you!

The BOY *carries on walking. As he strides away, his gait becomes longer and he grows before our eyes into a man, not dissimilar to* RONNIE. *He stops and turns.*

RONNIE *(V.O.)* Get stuffed.

He walks away, leaving WISE OWL *flapping.*

THE END

SERIES
8

Foreword

— This is my father Stephen, and he likes cricket.

Catherine Oakwood, '3 By 3'

Series 8 was commissioned alongside Series 9 - taking us all the way to the magic number and releasing us from having to do any more. We felt that poetically it would be a graceful end to stop at nine series and be in control of our fate, rather than limp on until we were mercifully cancelled. We wanted to be in charge of our demise. Like Dignitas.

But before the final series we had this one - and needed more than ever to make bold choices that would still surprise and delight our audience, well schooled by now in the tricks we tended to play.

We had an idea for a second Christmas Special, so as with Series 3 in 2016, we would film the first episode and have it ready for a festive viewing separate from the body of the rest of the series.

'The Bones of St Nicholas' was our own homage to M. R. James, and a proper 'Ghost Story for Christmas'. We wanted to enjoy the tradition and literally have the characters tell each other ghost stories throughout the episode. After discovering the unusual practice of 'champing' (camping in a church), we found we had the perfect Christmas Eve setting. The notion that a series of apparitions are later revealed to be portents or premonitions of a future event was a twist we had wanted to pull for a long time - and this story allowed us to deploy it with gusto.

'Mother's Ruin' stemmed from wanting to explore the world of gangsters and was violent and graphic in a way that we had never really done before. Getting to the point where a foot is going to be cut off with a chainsaw, we assumed that we wouldn't actually go through with it, but writing it we suddenly thought, 'What if we do?' - and, in a gleeful moment of Grand Guignol, we decided to show the whole thing. The heightened gothic tale of necromancy and black magic ritual seemed to allow us to push the boat out with the excess gore.

In 'Paraskevidekatriaphobia' we constructed a story that centres around trying to maintain control of a situation and, despite best efforts, everything that could go wrong would go wrong. It was a funny conceit that we used to tell the story of a man terrified of Friday the 13th, and it was fun to explore every possible omen of bad luck and use it as the comedic engine driving an ever-escalating farce.

We had toyed with the idea of speed dating before and felt that there was something in exploring the slightly absurd situation of being presented with, and trying to make a connection to, a succession of potential partners. Adding into the mix the threat of a 'killer on the loose' gave the proceedings some lurking peril in the background, but really 'Love is a Stranger' was essentially a series of talking heads – the twist being secondary to the journey of our lonely (and troubled) central character.

The next episode came from our ever-growing desire to totally fool the audience. We knew that one way to truly surprise people would be to construct the circumstances of them believing they were not even watching *Inside No. 9* any more – thereby removing the suspicion from our storytelling altogether. We also thought a 'shiny floor show' (as they call them) would be *so* different to anything we'd ever presented before, so we hit upon a game show. The challenge became: could we write a story that was still possible to sense unfolding *within* an episode of an apparently ordinary quiz show? Throw in a little telekinesis and cast improvisation, and '3 By 3' was born. The fun really started when we decided to also publicise the lie that Series 8 would contain 'Hold on Tight': a fictitious episode set on a number 9 bus!

Series 8 concluded with 'The Last Weekend', which was a true horror show of an episode and another one of our stories that was built from taking the unfolding scenes as 'chapters': in this case, the five stages of grief. Initially you are drawn into a sympathetic, heartfelt love story (one of our 'sad ones'), as a couple deals with terminal illness and saying goodbye. In reality we are watching the end of a long and protracted revenge plot that has taken years to execute, in a reveal that, even by our standards, was truly horrible!

Episode 1

THE BONES OF ST NICHOLAS

CAST LIST

JASPER – Steve Pemberton

DICK – Simon Callow

POSY – Shobna Gulati

PIERCE – Reece Shearsmith

EXT. CHURCHYARD. NIGHT

*A large old church in a remote location. Sinister choral music. A few flakes of snow whipped up by the wind. Flickering candlelight can be seen inside. A man in an overcoat and hat carrying an overnight bag (*JASPER*) steps in and looks up at the church.*

INT. CHURCH. NIGHT.

The front door opens and JASPER *enters.*

The church is large and furnished sparsely but festively. In one corner stands a tall Christmas tree with twinkling lights. There is a small table and a couple of camping chairs, books and a small electric heater near the altar.

JASPER *removes his hat and gazes around the building in awe. He walks up the nave, looking at the stained-glass windows.*

JASPER *passes by the wooden pews, where he finds that one of them has been made into a makeshift bed, with sheets, pillow and duvet. We settle on the small brass number on the end of the pew: 9.*

TITLE: *'The Bones of St Nicholas'.*

INT. CHURCH. NIGHT.

JASPER *puts down his bag on the bed. He spies a stone sarcophagus on one side of the church and goes over to inspect it. He lays his hand on it, fingering a carved but illegible inscription.*

The sound of wind, like a door being opened. Something catches his eye on the other side of the nave, near the Christmas tree. A curtained alcove; the curtain billows slightly. Is there someone watching from behind?

JASPER *slowly moves towards the alcove, but before he can get there, he is interrupted by the arrival of* DICK*, an older man in an anorak.*

DICK Excuse me, I was just draining a kidney. You're Mr Parkway, I take it?

They shake hands, JASPER *somewhat reluctantly.*

JASPER Dr Parkway, yes. You must be Mr Wilson?

DICK Oh, call me Dick, everyone does. So, have you ever been champing before?

JASPER Sorry?

DICK Champing – camping in a church, that's what we call it. Though it does have unfortunate connotations of someone eating with their mouth full . . .

JASPER No I haven't, actually. My wife booked this as a Christmas present, but sadly she–

DICK As I'm sure you're aware, it costs a pretty penny to preserve these old buildings, and 'champing' is our biggest money-spinner. So we let in any creed, faith or culture, as long as they pay the overnight fees. Speaking of which, did you . . . ?

JASPER Oh yes. I only have a card, I'm afraid.

DICK No worries, I've got my swiper.

DICK *pulls out a card-reader from his pocket and inserts* JASPER*'s card before moving off around the church.*

DICK *(cont'd)* Now, I've made your bed up here, as you can see. Some churches put a full-sized Queen Anne in the middle of the transept, but I personally don't think it's in keeping. I said to Canon Berryman, 'We're not an Airbnb'. He said, 'No Dick, we're a *Prayer C of E*!'. Eighty-five and sharp as a blade. Many's the time I've seen him do a Wordle in two.

JASPER *smiles thinly; he's getting a little impatient.*

DICK *(cont'd)* I've created a little lounge area for you, and there's some literature about the history of the place. For example, did you know that in the fifteenth century . . .

JASPER Hmm, can I ask, do you spend the night here also, or will you eventually leave?

DICK Oh yes, I'll be out of your hair soon, don't worry. If you'd care to insert your digits . . .

DICK *hands the card-reader to* JASPER, *and he enters his PIN.*

DICK *(cont'd)* I have to say, we've never taken a booking on Christmas Eve before! Your wife will be joining you later, will she?

JASPER No, she . . . she passed away in the autumn.

DICK I am so sorry. So sorry – I've just charged you a two-person rate. Shall I void it and start again?

JASPER No! No, please don't. I just want to spend a peaceful night here . . . alone with my thoughts and memories.

DICK Oh, I'm sure you won't be alone.

JASPER *looks around the church, checking the curtained alcove – but all is still.*

DICK *(cont'd)* Well, Merry Christmas, Dr Parkway. And God bless us, every one.

DICK *departs.*

INT. CHURCH. NIGHT.

JASPER *carefully opens his holdall and gets out an old book, pulling out papers from within and opening up copies of ancient documents. We see an image of the stone sarcophagus, as well as a floorplan of the church, and a pair of transparencies containing odd markings.*

JASPER *looks up. He peers slowly around the church, his eyes struggling to penetrate the gloomy corners. He scans round to the far end of the church, where a dark* FIGURE *in a red cloak seems to be spying on him behind the Christmas tree.* JASPER *stares, trying to make out the creepy sight.*

JASPER Hello?

The FIGURE *seems to move behind the tree.* JASPER *walks towards the tree to get a better look. The* FIGURE *cannot be seen, but suddenly a bauble falls from a branch and rolls forward.*

JASPER *picks up the bauble (we see a lit candle behind him on a stand). The bauble features the smiling face of Santa Claus.*

JASPER *approaches the tree, and sees there is nobody behind it. He hangs the bauble up again.*

A movement catches his eye, and JASPER *turns to see the candle has just been extinguished and smokes, as if something or someone has just passed by it.*

JASPER Mr Wilson, is that you?

JASPER *approaches the smoking candle. He looks around, but again there is no sign of anyone.*

Suddenly, JASPER *can hear voices. He sinks into the shadows beside the vestry. Behind him is an open door with stone steps leading upward to the bell tower.*

POSY *(O.S.)* Oh my God, it's freezing. I told you it would be.

PIERCE *(O.S.)* It's a bloody church, what did you expect?

The church doors open, and POSY *and* PIERCE *enter: a couple in matching cagoules. They have rucksacks and look more like they are actually going camping.* JASPER *watches from the darkness.*

POSY What did I expect? On Christmas Eve night? Oh, I don't know, a Holiday Inn.

PIERCE Eh, I've told you, don't blame me.

POSY A Radisson, maybe.

PIERCE Blame global warming. Anyway, I asked the old bloke to try and get us some booze. Champers for the champers! That should cheer you up a bit.

PIERCE *kneels in a pew and puts his hands together.*

PIERCE *(cont'd)* Our Lager, which art in barrels, hallowed be thy ale. Thy kegdom come, I will be drunk, at home, as in the tavern. Give us this day our foamy head, and forgive us our spillages, as we forgive those that spill against us. For thine is the beer, the bitter and the lager, forever and ever! Barmen!

POSY You're not funny, you know.

PIERCE 'Course I am. Now come on, do you want to see my little white balls . . . ?

PIERCE *pulls out a sprig of mistletoe and approaches* POSY . JASPER *steps out from the shadows.*

POSY Oh my lord!

JASPER Not quite. He arrives in the morning.

PIERCE You nearly give us a heart attack! Are you the vicar?

JASPER No, no, I'm Dr Parkway. Jasper. And I'm afraid I have exclusive use of this church until 10 a.m. tomorrow.

POSY Use?

JASPER I should explain: my mother passed away this year. She's buried in the graveyard. I simply wanted to spend the night here in quiet contemplation.

PIERCE Oh, well we just booked it on the website this morning. That Dick, the man called Dick, he said he hadn't seen the email. I'm Pierce, and this is my wife Posy.

POSY Like the flowers.

PIERCE Yeah, because when her mam got pregnant with her, the first thing she said was, 'Thanks a bunch.'

POSY Ignore him, he's pathetic. I'm sorry, about your mother. We were supposed to be going to Lapland yesterday, only they rang up and said there wasn't any snow.

JASPER How unfortunate.

PIERCE Yeah. They said we could still go, and they'd put us in a shed instead of an igloo, but we thought, what's the point?

JASPER Well, I hate to disappoint you, but as you can see, there is only one bed set out . . .

PIERCE Don't worry, we've come prepared, sleeping bags at the ready. Who wants a brew?

POSY *and* **PIERCE** *start to unpack.* **JASPER** *looks pained.*

INT. CHURCH. NIGHT.

JASPER *sits on his pew, reading quietly.* **POSY** *is unpacking her rucksack.* **PIERCE** *approaches with some biscuits on a gold plate.*

PIERCE These biscuits are nice, Po. Do you want one?

POSY I don't think they're for us, Pierce. They're like church wafers.

PIERCE You what?

JASPER It's the Eucharist. The body of Christ.

PIERCE Oh shit.

PIERCE *looks up to the Heavens.*

PIERCE *(cont'd)* Sorry! They taste like rich teas, anyway. The most boring of all biscuits. Apart from them Nices – which, ironically enough, are horrible.

POSY I'll go and see if there's anything else. They must have a kitchen somewhere.

PIERCE Yeah. Especially with all these lady vicars now.

POSY Idiot.

POSY *takes the plate and heads off.* **PIERCE** *approaches* **JASPER** *and looks at his books.*

PIERCE So are you a religious man then, Jaz?

JASPER Not particularly, no. It's the building itself I'm most interested in.

PIERCE So you're a history doctor, then? Like Indiana Jones, *Da Vinci Code* stuff?

JASPER You could say that. Though I'm more of an academian than an action-man.

PIERCE Right. 'Doctor, Doctor, I've got a chip up my nose, a carrot in my left ear and a sausage in my right ear. What's the matter with me?' Doctor says, 'You're not eating properly.'

JASPER *goes back to his book without laughing.*

PIERCE *(cont'd)* Tough crowd.

A scream from POSY.

POSY Arghhh! Oh my good godfathers . . .

POSY *is in front of the curtained alcove.*

Standing there is a full-sized model of St Nicholas, complete with a rather tattered red hooded robe and mitre, and a scary bearded face with piercing eyes. He holds a wooden staff, and would not be out of place in the Chamber of Horrors.

PIERCE Who is it?

POSY I dunno. I just pulled back the curtain and he was there. I thought it was Paul Hollywood.

PIERCE You wouldn't want him reaching out and giving you a handshake, would you?

JASPER *joins them.*

JASPER It's St Nicholas. The original Santa Claus.

POSY You mean the Coca-Cola one?

JASPER A little before that, I believe. Patron saint and protector of children, dating back to around 300 AD, possibly even earlier.

PIERCE What's his origin story?

POSY It's not *X-Men*, Pierce!

JASPER Actually, St Nick was an 'Avenger' in his own way. Three small boys were said to be lost one night, after straying too far from their homes while playing in the woods. As it got dark, they came across an old building belonging to a butcher. He offered them food and shelter for the night, and they eagerly accepted his invitation.

However, once inside, the butcher set upon the three boys, slitting their throats one by one.

POSY Bloody hell!

JASPER He then cut up the children's bodies and laid the pieces in a salting tub, preserving their flesh to sell as ham to the nearby villagers.

JASPER *crosses to a stained-glass display showing St Nicholas in his red robes. Three children are at his feet.*

JASPER *(cont'd)* Seven years had passed when Nicholas, Bishop of Myra, was riding in the area and stopped at the house. He demanded the butcher open up his barrels of salt. When he saw the contents, Nicholas performed a miracle, restoring the three boys to life and sending them home to their astonished parents.

POSY Lucky for them.

JASPER The myth also explains why we now have pickles and gherkins as Christmas tree decorations.

PIERCE We've got one of them! A big green one. Posy calls it the Grinch's co–

POSY Pierce!

JASPER It's an unusual derivation; the pickling or preserving of the children's bodies in salt or vinegar.

PIERCE Mmm. *(To* POSY*)* Did you bring any crisps?

POSY *and* PIERCE *wander off.* JASPER *stares at the imposing figure of St Nicholas, who seems to stare back at him disapprovingly.*

JASPER *is unnerved. He pulls the curtain back across.*

INT. CHURCH. NIGHT.

JASPER *is beside the sarcophagus. He is taping some paper over the odd markings and taking a rubbing of them.*

POSY *is wandering the aisle with two Christmas stockings, singing to herself. She's not entirely sure of the words, much to* JASPER*'s annoyance.*

POSY O, little town of Bethlehem / How still we see thee thy / Among the hills and daffodils / Da da da da da by . . .

JASPER Would you be quiet, please?

POSY Sorry?

JASPER Would you please stop singing? I'm trying to work.

POSY Of course, yeah. I'm just getting in the mood. I'm wondering where to hang my stockings . . .

JASPER *(to himself)* How about round your neck?

POSY Pardon?

JASPER Anywhere around the nave.

POSY Have you not got one? I think I've got a spare in here somewhere . . .

POSY *looks through her rucksack and pulls out a pair of thick black tights.* JASPER *goes over to his bag to retrieve a pen.*

POSY *(cont'd)* They're a bit laddered around the gusset, but you could pop a tangerine in.

JASPER That's very kind.

POSY I'll just hang them on the end of your bed for you.

POSY *heads off down the aisle.* JASPER *hears something. A creak.*

He turns to see the door leading to the bell tower is closing slightly. A shadow may be visible in the door's crack. JASPER *heads towards it. He pulls open the door . . . but there's nobody there.*

INT. CHURCH, BELL TOWER. NIGHT

JASPER *looks up into the dark staircase. He can hear a distant guttural, moaning sound coming from above. He slowly climbs the stairs of the tower. The sound is intermittent, but seems to get louder.* JASPER *opens the door to the bell enclosure. Suddenly, the sound stops.*

JASPER Is somebody there?

JASPER *looks around the dark tower. He finds a single black shoe on the floor, but then throws it back down again. He climbs the ladder to the level above.*

There is a narrow plank against the wall, and a lantern hanging from a hook. JASPER *carefully steps across the beams and removes the lantern, lighting it with his Zippo lighter. He steps along the plank towards the wall.*

JASPER *holds up the lantern and sees a series of old bricks with unusual carved symbols. He inches along the creaking plank, but stops when he hears a noise: a scraping sound, like something being dragged over stone. Once, twice, three times. Then silence.*

JASPER *looks round, scared.*

JASPER *(cont'd)* Hello?

Suddenly, DICK *appears below carrying a bottle.*

DICK Only me! Just wondered if you wanted to join us for a little tot of Bristol Cream?

EXT. CHURCHYARD. NIGHT.

We see the church, its bell tower looming against the night sky.

INT. CHURCH. NIGHT.

DICK *is pouring four small glasses of sherry.* DICK, POSY *and* PIERCE *sit around in the lounge area.*

DICK Christmas Eve. The most magical of night of the year.

DICK *hands sherries to* POSY *and* PIERCE .

JASPER *kneels at the sarcophagus, tracing the rubbing he took on to a transparency film with a Sharpie.*

PIERCE I used to love it when I was a kid.

POSY You still are a bloody kid!

DICK Do you have any children?

POSY *and* PIERCE *share a brief look.*

POSY No. No, we don't.

PIERCE We still believe in Santa, though, don't we?

DICK This church has a unique link to St Nicholas, actually - hence the display. Would you like to hear it? It does involve . . . a ghost.

PIERCE Now you're talking. *(To* JASPER*)* Come on doc, pull up a pew.

JASPER I'd rather not, if it's all the same to you.

PIERCE Oh, come on! A ghost story for Christmas!? It's perfect.

JASPER I don't believe in ghosts, and I've no interest in made-up narratives about them.

DICK I can assure you, doctor, that the events I'm about to recount are not made up. I know that. For certain.

DICK *proffers a glass of sherry to* JASPER.

DICK *(cont'd)* Well?

JASPER *looks at his tracing: an unreadable series of straight and curved lines.*

JASPER Seems like I don't have much choice, do I?

JASPER *joins the group.* DICK *sits on a chair in front of them. He clutches his sherry, and his face glows red in the light of the electric heater.*

DICK The body of St Nicholas, as with all the great saints, was harvested for reliquaries and devotionals.

PIERCE Sorry, you've lost me already.

JASPER Relics are the bones or body parts of venerated individuals. Often stolen from tombs and sold all around the world. They used to be a big business.

DICK They still are. What would you say if I told you the jawbone of St Nicholas is hidden in this very building?

POSY Is it?

DICK I can tell you it has yet to be found, but I do believe it resides here somewhere.

JASPER Why do you believe that?

DICK Because of what I saw with my own eyes five years ago, on Christmas Eve night.

POSY Here we go. Hold my hand, Pierce.

DICK I'd locked up for the evening. I'd extinguished the last of the candles, so I was leaving with just the light from my phone screen to see me out.

PIERCE *clicks his fingers.*

PIERCE Why didn't you turn your torch on?

DICK I didn't know it had one.

PIERCE *clicks his fingers again.*

PIERCE Carry on.

DICK I was at the double doors over there when I heard a noise by the Christmas tree.

JASPER *listens a bit more intently. He glances back at the tree.*

DICK *(cont'd)* It sounded like a deep sigh, or perhaps someone yawning, and then a noise on the marble. Like a dragging, shuffling sound. I genuinely thought, if I'm not careful, someone was going to be locked up for the night and they might freeze to death.

POSY We had that at the school where I clean. A homeless man was living in the gym equipment cupboard. Sleeping in the vaulting box. The deputy head bought him a Boneless Banquet from KFC, and Sally Army came for him.

PIERCE Have you finished?

POSY Sorry.

DICK I walked over to the tree, and that's when I saw him. Peeping out from behind the branches. A figure in a dark red cloak, his head bowed. I stood perfectly still. I didn't want him to see me. It felt like if he saw me, that would be the worst thing in the world. Then my phone started beeping. I always set an alarm for when I'm meant to be out of the building, otherwise I'd never leave. I could tell the shape had heard it. Its head slowly lifted. But I wasn't expecting what I saw. It was so . . . sad.

An old man, with kind eyes, but such pain in them. And below this tender, imploring face, there was no bottom jaw. Just a black, lolling tongue, dangling down into the space below.

It moaned and clacked, and started to come towards me. And that's when I ran. I ran and ran, and didn't stop until I got home and locked the door behind me. The next day when I came back, there were footprints, filthy black footprints, all around the church. So that's why I think the jawbone is here somewhere. He was looking for it.

And this night, the Eve of Christmas, is when his presence is strongest. I believe his restless spirit roams this site, longing to be whole again and finally be at peace.

A beat, and then the cheery alarm on DICK*'s phone starts to go off, making everyone jump.*

DICK *(cont'd)* Right, I'll be off then.

PIERCE *and* POSY *laugh after their jump scare.* JASPER *seems pensive.*

PIERCE That was brilliant. I bet that shit you up, didn't it, doc?! Now do you believe in ghosts?

JASPER Of course not. We are pattern-finding creatures, and we rationalise what we don't understand with ridiculous stories. Now, if you don't mind, I'd like to spend the rest of the evening in my own company.

JASPER *goes back to his pew. The others share a look.*

INT. CHURCH. NIGHT.

It is late. The lights in the church are extinguished, save for a few candles, and moonlight shines through the stained-glass windows.

PIERCE *stirs and looks at his digital clock: 2.43 a.m. He sees that* POSY *is not in her sleeping bag; she's sitting in one of the pews. He gets up and approaches her, passing* JASPER*, who is fast asleep on his pew.*

PIERCE You alright, Po?

POSY Yeah.

PIERCE You thinking about Paisley?

POSY *nods.*

POSY I lit a candle for her.

PIERCE Eighteen years next Christmas. I'll book Lapland again.

POSY That'd be nice.

They hold hands.

POSY *(cont'd)* I didn't like Dick's story. Do you believe him?

PIERCE 'Course not. It's his party piece, he'll have one for every season. Giant rabbit at Easter, witch at Halloween.

POSY What's summer?

PIERCE Er, beach ghost. Just some bloke with trunks on, wandering about with a bright red face. Why, did he spook you?

POSY A little bit. It's just . . .

PIERCE What?

POSY That night . . . when I was pregnant and I had the accident. Something happened that I never told you.

PIERCE You saw a ghost?

POSY Not really. I was just mopping the floor in reception when I saw my mother walk past. I thought 'What's she doing here?' I waved, but she didn't say anything. Just stared at me. Then suddenly she put her hand up on the glass and started to cry, mascara running down her face in black lines. Then she turned and went off again. I went to look for her, but there was no one there.

PIERCE That's weird.

POSY Anyway, as I was walking home, I tried phoning her. And it was as I was dialling that the motorbike came off the road and . . . you know the rest.

PIERCE Bloody hell.

POSY A few days later, when I was in the hospital, she came to see me, my mother, do you remember? And she told me the night of the accident, she'd had this awful feeling that something bad was going to happen to me. I didn't tell her what I'd seen, but as she was leaving, she turned and put her hand up on the glass and started to cry, mascara running down her face in black lines.

PIERCE Oh my God.

POSY It wasn't a ghost. It was a warning.

PIERCE Why didn't you tell me?

POSY Because you'd think I was touched. And nothing was going to bring Paisley back. But all this talk of spirits, it just got to me.

They sit in silence for a moment. Suddenly, they hear the sound of a phone ringing from a distant room.

POSY What's that?

PIERCE I'm not sure. Could be one of these new-fangled machines that let you talk to each other through the air.

PIERCE *gets up and heads off towards the vestry.*

POSY What are you doing? Pierce!

POSY *waits for a moment, then follows him.*

INT. CHURCH, VESTRY. NIGHT

PIERCE *and* **POSY** *slowly push open the vestry door.*

The vestry is sparsely furnished, more of a storeroom. The phone is ringing on the desk. They look at each other fearfully.

POSY Don't answer it.

PIERCE *picks up the phone.*

PIERCE Hello?

He listens for a moment.

PIERCE *(to* POSY*)* It's for you.

PIERCE *hands her the phone.*

POSY Yes . . . ?

PIERCE Booooo!

POSY *jumps out of her skin.* PIERCE *laughs.*

POSY You bloody idiot, what are you playing at? Who was it?

PIERCE No one. They hung up; must have been a wrong number. Come on, it's freezing in here.

INT. CHURCH. NIGHT.

POSY *and* PIERCE *come back through into the church.*

PIERCE Hey, we forgot to check our stockings. See if Santa's been yet.

As they walk down the aisle, we are aware of a large, red-robed figure standing in the pulpit. As they stop at the stockings, the ghostly figure slowly makes its way towards them.

POSY What did you put on your list?

PIERCE Socks and undies, obviously.

POSY Yeah, obviously.

PIERCE Hankies with a 'P' on, which'll never come out of the packet.

POSY *smiles.*

PIERCE *(cont'd)* Selection box. They're not as big as they used to be.

POSY Alright, Peter Kay!

PIERCE It's true! What about you?

POSY Oh, bath salts. Chocolates full of some disgusting liqueur, and a shit scented candle.

PIERCE Shit-scented? How do they do that?

POSY Do you really want to know . . . ?

They laugh. A choking sound leads PIERCE *and* POSY *to turn.*

Standing in the aisle, cowled from head to foot in tatty red robes, is the ghastly spectre of St Nicholas!

PIERCE Oh, bloody hell!

St Nicholas advances, groaning and gurgling from under his dark red cowl, no face visible within the hood. PIERCE *and* POSY *scream and run from the church.*

St Nicholas watches them go. When he is satisfied they are not coming back, he lowers his hood to reveal a face wearing thick black tights. The figure tears them open and pulls them down to reveal . . . it is JASPER.

JASPER Finally. I thought they'd never fucking leave.

He checks his watch, then carries his bag over to the stone sarcophagus.

JASPER *then takes two transparencies from his bag which have a series of lines and arcs. When he lays them over the tracing he took earlier and holds them to the light, we can see the markings line up to read 'NICOLA'.*

There is also a shape next to the name, which, with the lines from all three rubbings, makes up a strange symbol. The same one JASPER *saw up in the bell tower.*

JASPER Ho, ho . . .

JASPER *looks towards the church tower door.*

JASPER *(cont'd)* . . . ho.

JASPER *heads for the door, but before he can get very far, he hears* DICK *approaching from the kitchen.*

DICK *(O.S.)* Dr Parkway!

JASPER Shit!

JASPER *panics. He darts behind the nearby curtained alcove, just as* DICK *enters the church.*

DICK Dr Parkway, are you there?

DICK *heads down the nave to check on* JASPER*'s pew.*

JASPER *spies on him through the curtain.* DICK *tries looking under the pew.*

DICK *(cont'd)* I've just had a call from Pierce.

JASPER *sneaks out of the alcove and darts behind the Christmas tree.*

DICK *(cont'd)* He said he saw something rather disturbing . . . Dr Parkway?

JASPER *moves further behind the Christmas tree. He brushes the tree and knocks off one of the baubles, which rolls forward.*

JASPER *looks concerned: has he given himself away?*

DICK *heads slowly forward.* JASPER *pulls out his phone and dials a number. The vestry phone starts to ring, as before.*

DICK *heads towards the vestry.* JASPER *watches him go.*

Once DICK *is out of sight,* JASPER *rushes out from behind the tree, passing a candle and accidentally extinguishing it.*

INT. VESTRY. NIGHT.

DICK *goes to pick up the phone. Behind him we see the red-robed figure of* JASPER *dart down the corridor towards the tower steps.*

INT. BELL TOWER. NIGHT.

JASPER *enters the tower and slowly pulls the door to behind him. He then heads up the steps.*

INT. VESTRY. NIGHT.

DICK *answers the ringing phone.*

DICK Hello?

He frowns and hangs up.

INT. BELL TOWER. NIGHT.

JASPER *opens the trapdoor leading to the bell enclosure. He climbs up on to the plank, looking over at the symbols carved into the bricks. He fixes in on the one from the rubbing downstairs.*

INT. CHURCH. NIGHT.

DICK *emerges from the vestry and is looking around the church with his torch.*

DICK I'm ever so sorry if I frightened you, doctor! What I said earlier, it was only a story.

INT. BELL TOWER. NIGHT.

JASPER *is hacking away at a loose brick with a penknife. He works his fingers round the edge and slowly starts to ease it free.*

INT. CHURCH. NIGHT.

DICK *approaches the door to the bell tower. He opens it and peers inside.*

DICK There is no ghost here, I can assure you!

INT. BELL TOWER. NIGHT.

JASPER *removes the brick and is astonished to find a mouldy bundle in the hollow that is revealed. He carefully pulls it out and holds it. He inches back along the plank.*

DICK *(O.S.)* Like you said, ghosts aren't real!

DICK*'s words echo up the tower.* JASPER *remembers a moment from earlier . . .*

POSY *(O.S.)* It wasn't a ghost. It was a warning.

Suddenly, the plank gives way and JASPER *falls. The tights around his neck catch on the hook.*

JASPER *is now hanging, the tights choking him as he desperately grabs at his throat. He drops the package he was holding. His eyes bulge and his face turns red. He is spluttering, a low guttural sound.*

JASPER *hangs, his life slowly ebbing away. Recent memories fill his head . . .*

INT. CHURCH. NIGHT. (FLASHBACK)

JASPER *sees the alcove curtain billowing.*

INT. CHURCH. NIGHT. (FLASHBACK)

JASPER *spies on* DICK *through the curtain.*

INT. CHURCH. NIGHT. (FLASHBACK)

JASPER *scans round to the far end of the church, where a dark* FIGURE *in a red cloak seems to be spying on him behind the Christmas tree.*

JASPER Hello?

INT. CHURCH. NIGHT (FLASHBACK)

JASPER *hides behind the tree. He brushes the tree and knocks off one of the baubles.*

INT. CHURCH. NIGHT. (FLASHBACK)

A bauble falls from a branch and rolls forward. JASPER *picks up the bauble, which features the smiling face of Santa Claus.*

INT. BELL TOWER. NIGHT.

JASPER *is hanging, gasping for breath.*

INT. CHURCH. NIGHT. (FLASHBACKS)

JASPER *runs towards the door, blowing out one of the candles as he passes.*

JASPER *sees one of the candles by the Christmas tree has just been extinguished and smokes.*

JASPER *reaches the door and heads inside, gently and quietly pulling the door to behind him.*

JASPER *turns to see the door leading to the tower is closing slightly.*

INT. BELL TOWER. NIGHT.

JASPER *realises too late that he has foreseen his own death, his feet scraping helplessly on the wall.*

INT. CHURCH. NIGHT. (FLASHBACK)

JASPER *looks up into the dark staircase. He can hear a distant guttural, moaning sound coming from above.*

JASPER Is somebody there?

JASPER *hears a scraping sound, like something being dragged over stone. Once, twice, three times. Then silence.*

INT. BELL TOWER. NIGHT.

JASPER*'s feet scraping the wall: once, twice, three times. Then silence. He is dead.*

DICK *appears through the trapdoor and is shocked to see the dead body of* JASPER *hanging from the hook.*

DICK Oh no. Oh no. Oh no . . .

A single black shoe falls from JASPER*'s foot. It lands near the bundle that* JASPER *dropped.*

Curious, DICK *picks it up and starts to open it. He looks at the contents, but we don't see what's inside.*

DICK *(cont'd)* Well, I never. Merry Christmas.

Music: 'Ding Dong Merrily on High'.

THE END

Episode 2

MOTHER'S RUIN

CAST LIST

EDWARD – Reece Shearsmith

HARRY – Steve Pemberton

FRANCES – Anita Dobson

REGGIE – Phil Daniels

with the voice of

Maggie Service

EXT. BUNGALOW. NIGHT.

We see the exterior of a bungalow bathed in moonlight. A figure is prowling round the property. A torch briefly illuminates a number 9 hanging by the door.

TITLE: *'Mother's Ruin'.*

INT. BUNGALOW, KITCHEN. NIGHT.

We are inside the kitchen/diner of the dimly lit bungalow. A clock ticks quietly in the still of the night. The light of the torch sweeps across the window, and a shadow appears.

We hear the squeal of wrenching wood as the window is prised open with a crowbar. A serious-looking man, EDWARD, *climbs in through the open window. He carries a rather bulky holdall. He moves his torch around, illuminating the house.*

EDWARD *sees an armchair in the corner of the living room and heads towards it.*

INT. BUNGALOW, LIVING ROOM. NIGHT.

EDWARD *enters and pushes back an item of furniture, then starts to pull up the carpet. As he's doing this, there is a knock at the door.* EDWARD *checks his watch and goes through to answer it.*

INT. BUNGALOW, PORCH/HALLWAY. NIGHT.

EDWARD *unlocks the door from the inside to find* HARRY, *his more emotionally needy brother. They whisper.*

HARRY Hello, Edward.

EDWARD *lets* HARRY *into the bungalow. He carries a big plastic bag in one hand and a large, covered box in the other, holding it from a handle on the top.*

HARRY *(cont'd)* Where shall I put this?

EDWARD Anywhere. Doesn't matter. Stick it down here.

HARRY *carefully puts down the covered box.*

HARRY What did you want it for?

EDWARD It was important to Mum, wasn't it? A lot of value attached to it?

HARRY Yeah. She loved it.

EDWARD More than me and you, probably.

HARRY *goes to hug* EDWARD.

EDWARD What are you doing?

HARRY Giving you a hug. I haven't seen you in ages.

EDWARD *goes back to the living room.*

INT. BUNGALOW, LIVING ROOM. NIGHT.

HARRY *follows* EDWARD *into the living room.* EDWARD *carries on pulling up the carpet.*

HARRY Shall I put a light on?

HARRY *goes to put a light on.* EDWARD *physically stops him.* HARRY *flinches.*

EDWARD Obviously not. People know the new owners are away on holiday. We don't want to attract attention.

HARRY Telling me off already . . .

EDWARD I'm not telling you off.

HARRY . . . attacking me.

EDWARD Calm down, Harry.

EDWARD *rolls the carpet.*

HARRY So, how have you been?

EDWARD I've been busy. Various . . . ventures. Trying my best, you know.

HARRY The bar in Menorca never worked out then?

EDWARD *ignores him.*

HARRY *(cont'd)* 'What about you, Harry?' 'Oh, I've been here, looking after Mum. Then she died and I had to sell her house, don't know if you know that?'

EDWARD *tries to stay patient.*

EDWARD Look, I'm sorry you had to deal with everything, OK? But me and Mum didn't get on.

HARRY *looks around the room.*

HARRY I hate how everyone ends up in bungalows . . . why is that?

EDWARD It's just easier, isn't it? No more stairs; they're manageable. Did you find out anything about them?

HARRY Who?

EDWARD The couple who bought the house.

HARRY No. It all just went through the agent. I'm surprised they haven't decorated. They've been in a year.

EDWARD It's not been a year. Not quite.

HARRY It's weird. They wanted it all just as it was, furniture included . . . Did they even change the locks, I wonder?

EDWARD Don't say that, I just broke in!

HARRY I thought it would feel different, but it's the same. Even the chair in the corner . . .

EDWARD *looks at* HARRY.

HARRY What?

EDWARD You're sure that's where she . . . was?

HARRY Why?

EDWARD Because it really matters, Harry! It really matters *precisely* where she died. Are you sure?

HARRY Yes! I was the one who found her, remember? Me! I was the one looking after her all that time.

EDWARD Alright.

HARRY I was the one bringing her meals and changing her sheets.

EDWARD I know, I know.

HARRY Do you though, Ed? Because it feels like you *don't* know. It feels to me like you've just swooped back in after all this time, trying to fix everything when it's all too late.

EDWARD If it was too late I wouldn't 'kin be here, would I?! We're wasting time.

EDWARD *sets down the holdall and opens it up. He takes out a bottle of red wine, what look like rolled-up cigarettes, matches, a Tupperware box and some chalk.*

HARRY How did you find out about all this? From a book?

EDWARD Yes.

HARRY Did you bring it?

EDWARD This particular book is in the British Library. Behind glass. It's one of the oldest books known to humankind. You have to make an appointment to see it, and you can only touch it with cotton gloves on.

HARRY So that's a no, then. How will you remember what to do?

EDWARD I googled the pages and printed them out.

EDWARD *pulls out a folded set of A4 pages.*

EDWARD *(cont'd)* Did you bring everything I asked?

HARRY Yeah.

HARRY *indicates the plastic bag he has with him.*

EDWARD You go and get ready, then. I'm going to set up.

HARRY *goes off to the bathroom, taking the plastic bag with him.* EDWARD *refers to the printed pages.*

Taking the chalk, EDWARD *draws a large pentagram on the floor. He draws a large circle around the pentagram, but leaves a gap in it. He draws symbols between the spikes of the pentagram, copying from the printout.* EDWARD *then pushes the rocking chair into the centre of the circle.*

HARRY *comes out of the bathroom dressed as a little old lady: pork pie hat, tweed two-piece suit, neckerchief.* EDWARD *smiles.*

EDWARD My God.

HARRY Don't.

EDWARD It's like she's been brought back to us.

HARRY Are you sure this is part of it?

EDWARD I bet you wish now you'd just asked her where all the money was.

HARRY She didn't have any money. She would have told me.

EDWARD Really? Because she was so straight up?

HARRY I told you, she never mentioned her life with Dad, or any of what they got up to.

EDWARD Of course she didn't. They were rotten, Harry. They did some horrible shit and made a lot of enemies. Bad people.

HARRY She was still our mum.

EDWARD Yeah. And by rights, she should have died in prison.

HARRY Well lucky for us she didn't.

EDWARD *opens the Tupperware box and hands it to* HARRY.

EDWARD Scatter the crumbs.

HARRY It's mouldy!

EDWARD Exactly.

EDWARD *reads from one of the pages he's printed as* HARRY *scatters the mouldy black crumbs.*

EDWARD 'For communication with the departed that they may run our requests, these devotions to Azazel, Keeper of the Bones, must be enacted where the dead in life did perish.' Right there.

EDWARD *points at the rocking chair.*

EDWARD *(cont'd)* Let's get on with it. We have to do this in the next hour.

EDWARD *lights the hemlock and mandrake-root roll-ups, and they gently smoke like incense sticks.*

HARRY Why?

EDWARD Why what?

HARRY Why do we have to do it in the next hour?

EDWARD The process has to occur within one year of death, otherwise the necromancer can no longer evoke the chosen person. So, 5 a.m. tomorrow is one year exactly since Mum died, and that's our cut-off point. What's the matter?

HARRY I'm a bit nervous, Ed. A bit trepidatious, if truth be told.

EDWARD Well, have a sit down in the nice chair and I'll get you a drink.

HARRY No – you know what, I don't want to do it.

EDWARD Oh Harry, Harry . . .

HARRY I mean – let's just consider what might happen . . .

EDWARD I already have done. Over and over.

HARRY I know, but . . .

EDWARD We're just going to ask her a quick little question, and we're done.

HARRY What if she's cross with me?

EDWARD What do you mean, 'cross with you'? You're the golden boy, you always were. When did she ever find fault with a single thing you did? Homework, sports day – even making a cup of tea, for God's sake. She'd always let me know I'd slightly let her down. I was the one that was never good enough, Harry. And this was before I abandoned her to have a life of my own.

HARRY You didn't abandon her.

EDWARD I know I didn't. Her words. Not mine. I left knowing, when our stupid, thug arsehole father got himself killed stealing from his own gang, she'd somehow even blame me for that.

HARRY She never blamed you. And she never talked about any other money, Ed! We scraped by on my benefits.

EDWARD She was accessing that money from the day he died. Every month. Did you never see her bank statements, Harry?

HARRY *shakes his head slowly.*

EDWARD *(cont'd)* Because I did. She let us scratch out an existence, but all the while she was sitting on a stolen fortune. And I don't know about you, but I really fucking need that money, Harry.

HARRY What if she won't tell us?

EDWARD She will.

HARRY What if she won't?

EDWARD She has to. She's bound to have to tell us. That's the whole point of necromancy. This isn't like a seance. This is different. We get answers. Alright?

HARRY *tentatively nods.*

EDWARD *(cont'd)* In you go.

HARRY *walks through the gap left in the circle on the floor and sits in the rocking chair in the centre.* EDWARD *completes the rest of the circle with chalk, sealing* HARRY *inside, and sprinkling the rest of the bread.*

EDWARD OK. Now, close your eyes and breathe. Nice and calm.

HARRY *closes his eyes.* EDWARD *gets the bottle of wine and trickles it around the circle.* HARRY *opens his eyes upon hearing the splashing of the wine.*

HARRY That's not good. Red wine on a wood floor. It'll be a deep stain.

EDWARD Harry!

HARRY I think salt gets it out. Or maybe it's rice.

EDWARD Don't worry about it! Concentrate on your breathing.

HARRY *breathes in through his nose and out through his mouth.* EDWARD *gets the pages from the grimoire so he can read out the first part of the ritual. He lights candles as he does so.*

EDWARD 'Oh thou Azazel, Keeper of the Bones, I charge and conjure thee to allow visit to this site as, pure of heart and valiant soul, I undertake these rites as sacred and solemn . . .'

HARRY Baking powder! For the stains. It's baking powder and vinegar. I'll leave them a note. Sorry, carry on.

EDWARD 'Free from fear's grasp, I summon Annie Olivia Blackwood to counsel and abide as Death's Empath questions we are most readily set to pose.' *(To* HARRY*)* Keep your eyes *closed.*

HARRY *looks scared and closes his eyes.* EDWARD *goes to the hall.*

INT. BUNGALOW, HALLWAY. NIGHT.

EDWARD *picks up the covered box that* HARRY *brought. He carries it into the living room.*

INT. BUNGALOW, LIVING ROOM. NIGHT.

EDWARD *sets the item down and removes the cloth. We see for the first time it is in fact a large domed birdcage, and has inside an exotic looking parrot,* MR MACY. *It looks quizzically around the room.*

EDWARD *then removes a package from his holdall. He unwraps it to reveal a small ritualistic knife. He holds the knife horizontally over the cage.*

EDWARD *'Accept this offering as payment in kind. Death for life and back again. With blood, we summon thee. With love, we summon thee . . .'*

EDWARD *opens the parrot's cage and tries to get* MR MACY *out. It squawks loudly. It seems to speak in a cockney accent, to the tune of 'Pieces of Eight'.*

MR MACY What do you want? What do you want?

HARRY *opens his eyes and is alarmed to see* EDWARD *wrestling to get the parrot out of the cage.*

HARRY Edward – stop it! What are you doing?

EDWARD Be quiet, Harry. Sit down and close your eyes.

HARRY You're not killing Mr Macy!

HARRY *gets up.*

EDWARD Stay in the circle!

HARRY Edward, you can't!

EDWARD It has to be something she loved. Come here, Mr Mac . . . Come on . . .

Ouch!

MR MACY *has pecked* EDWARD.

EDWARD *(cont'd)* Right – that's it!

EDWARD *wrestles with the birdcage and eventually manages to get the bird out, but as he is about to kill it,* HARRY *intervenes, fighting with* EDWARD .

HARRY Let him go!

MR MACY *flies up and out of the room, towards the kitchen.*

EDWARD *looks out of the window to see* MR MACY *fly out through the kitchen window into the night, squawking as it goes.*

EDWARD *turns to* HARRY; *he is white with rage. He holds the knife out threateningly.*

EDWARD Sit down, Harry.

HARRY I couldn't let you do it.

EDWARD *smacks* HARRY *hard in the face.* HARRY*'s nose bleeds.*

EDWARD Sit down! It was supposed to be the parrot tonight, but now I'm afraid it has to be you. I need to know where that money is, and you've left me with no option.

HARRY Ed, please . . . I'm your brother.

EDWARD *holds out the knife.*

EDWARD 'Accept this offering as payment in kind. Death for life and back again. With blood, we summon thee. With love, we summon thee . . .'

HARRY Edward!

EDWARD 'With death, we summon thee!'

EDWARD *raises the knife to stab* HARRY *in the chest. Suddenly, the main light is switched on.*

FRANCES *stands in the doorway.*

FRANCES Reggie!

REGGIE *enters.*

REGGIE Yeah?

FRANCES *holds a small suitcase on wheels, and they both wear shorts and summery clothes, and look tanned. A proper Club Med couple.* REGGIE *and* FRANCES *are VERY cockney.*

REGGIE *(cont'd)* What the bloody ding-dong's going on here?

HARRY It's red wine, but it'll come out if you use baking powder . . .

EDWARD Shut up, Harry. *(To* REGGIE *and* FRANCES*)* You two just need to walk away and come back here tomorrow. Like you were supposed to. I don't want any trouble, but you've stumbled upon a family matter that I need to resolve. I haven't got a problem with either of you.

REGGIE *and* FRANCES *look at each other. They nod. Suddenly,* FRANCES *whacks* EDWARD *in the legs with her suitcase. He falls to his knees, dropping the knife.* REGGIE *grabs* EDWARD*'s head and deftly knees him in the face.* EDWARD *collapses with his nose bleeding.*

REGGIE No, but I'm afraid we've got a bit of a fucking problem with you, sunshine.

BLACKOUT.

EXT. BUNGALOW. NIGHT.

MR MACY *sits in the moonlight of a nearby tree, looking back at the bungalow. Light from the open window spills out on to the patch of grass beyond.*

INT. BUNGALOW, LIVING ROOM. NIGHT.

EDWARD *and* HARRY *are tied to chairs, both with bloody noses.*

FRANCES *comes over with a cup of tea for* REGGIE, *who sits opposite the tied-up brothers.*

FRANCES Here you go, love. Keep your fluids up.

REGGIE Cheers, Franny.

FRANCES We had to get an early flight back, 'cos Reggie's been feeling a bit Moby.

Silence.

FRANCES *(cont'd)* Moby Dick – sick.

REGGIE *is looking puzzled at the pages of the grimoire and the matching patterns on the floor.*

REGGIE So you're Harry Blackwood's boys?

HARRY Yes. I'm Harry Junior, and this is Edward.

FRANCES What's that smell? What were you up to in here?

EDWARD Incense.

REGGIE Jesus Christ, I knew it – you dirty bastards. As if it's not bad enough you're fucking each other, one of you has to be dressed like a little old lady as well?

FRANCES Not incest, you silly twat! He's talking about the smell. Incense.

REGGIE Oh, I thought that was just wacky baccy. You want a wheeze on it, Fran?

FRANCES You'll be sick with it, Reg. Leave it.

REGGIE *picks up one of the smoking rolls and sucks on it. He coughs a lot.*

REGGIE Shit that's good.

EDWARD How did you know our father?

REGGIE We were, for a time, members of the same organisation, you might say. We worked together. But your father decided to branch out on his own.

REGGIE *takes another deep drag on the incense for dramatic effect.*

REGGIE *(cont'd)* Do things independent. Not too lemon tart, I'm afraid, as a career move. It didn't end all that well for him.

EDWARD Oh, God. You're Reggie Stone.

REGGIE *smiles.*

REGGIE Fran, go and get us a Xanax from my washbag, will you, love? I think I'm pulling a whitey.

FRANCES You fucking baby. It's not even Harris Tweed you're smoking, it's potpourri!

FRANCES *leaves, shaking her head.* REGGIE *drinks his tea.*

REGGIE She's a good woman, that one. Temper on her mind. You wouldn't want to cross her. Knew your mother well. As did I. We were close.

EDWARD So I've heard.

REGGIE We were *very* close. But unfortunately, when we needed her to talk, we couldn't get a thing out of her. I had to admire her for it in a way. Your father, on the other hand, was a coward. He didn't know anything. I discovered that when I put his foot in a vice and crushed it until it was only about an inch thick. Took some doing, mind; I was sweating. Fran said it looked like spatchcock, which is one of our favourites. See, he didn't want to know where that money was, because he knew he'd squeal. He gave it to your mother, and it was her that stashed it.

EDWARD And when she wouldn't talk, you killed her as well.

HARRY What? No, she died in her sleep.

REGGIE That's right. She died in her sleep.

EDWARD They'll have injected her with something, Harry. All in a day's work for this psychopath.

REGGIE Oh that's pots and kettles, that is. If I'm to think back not fifteen minutes, you were about to stab your own little brother here in the middle of his bleeding heart.

EDWARD How could you kill her, Reggie? You were obviously fucking her for years.

REGGIE *jumps up and smashes his empty tea mug down on one of* EDWARD*'s tied-up hands. The mug shatters, leaving* REGGIE *holding just a piece of handle.* EDWARD *cries in pain. His hand is a mess.*

REGGIE I'm talking, prick. Have some fucking manners, there's a good chap. Now, where was I? Oh yes. May I enquire just what you are doing in my house dressed as Miss fucking Marples?

HARRY *gasps.*

REGGIE What?

HARRY You said Miss *Marples.* Edward hates that. Miss Marples, Cliff Richards, *Trivial Pursuits* . . .

EDWARD Harry, this isn't the time.

REGGIE I don't give a fuck! You want me to spatchcock your foot, junior?

HARRY No, thank you.

REGGIE Keep your fucking north shut, then! Now, come on. Help me out here, gentlemen – as I am, to say the least, a little fucking baffled.

EDWARD *fights the pain of his broken hand.*

EDWARD I don't think you would believe us if we told you.

REGGIE Well you're just going to have to let me be the judge of that now, aren't you? Like the *Mastermind* of old, I've started so I'll finish.

EDWARD I presume you bought this house because my father stole money from you and you hoped my mother had it stashed here somewhere?

FRANCES *comes back in with a pill. She gives it to* REGGIE .

REGGIE We should feel honoured, Franny. Looks like we are in the presence of two giants of the detective genre: Mr Sherlock Holme and Miss Marples, under our very roof.

FRANCES I prefer Father Brown.

REGGIE Father Brown? Father fucking Brown?

FRANCES Don't start, Reg. It's Chesterton's masterpiece. Just because you don't like the actor that plays him.

REGGIE I can only see him as 'Suits you', Franny!

FRANCES I know! That's all you go on about. But I think he's perfect in the role – and I know the books. Do you either of you like thrillers?

HARRY Not really.

FRANCES I like true crime the best. *Women Who Kill.* Have you seen any of them?

HARRY *shakes his head.*

REGGIE I've told you not to watch that programme. It'll give you ideas.

EDWARD Can I ask what time it is, please?

REGGIE It's half four in the morning, Sherlock, and I'm tired. I've just got back off holiday and I was looking forward to some soot.

HARRY *looks confused.*

FRANCES Sooty and Sweep – sleep.

REGGIE But now I find myself inconvenienced. I've got to spend the night chopping up you two turds and finding new places in Epping Forest to bury the bits.

FRANCES I'm not coming with you this time, Reg. I've got to get a wash on. I'll do you a fry-up for when you get back, though.

REGGIE Thank you, sweetheart. What a woman. Considerate is her middle name.

HARRY Really? Mine's Paul.

EDWARD Mr Stone, if you want your money, we don't have long left to find it. There's a window of opportunity, but it's closing fast.

REGGIE Are you saying you can locate it for me?

EDWARD Not exactly.

REGGIE Then you and your brother here are rapidly turning into landfill.

REGGIE *stands up.*

FRANCES I'll fetch the bear's paw.

FRANCES *leaves.* REGGIE *heads to the dining room.*

HARRY Bear's paw . . . ? They're not going to scratch us, are they?

EDWARD It's a saw, Harry.

HARRY Oh.

REGGIE *goes to a drawer and opens it to take out a plastic apron and rubber gloves.*

REGGIE First holiday in God knows how long, and I come back and have to deal with all this. Now it feels like I've never been away!

EDWARD I don't know where the money is, but I was going to ask the one person that does.

REGGIE Who?

EDWARD My mother.

FRANCES *re-enters with a small roll of extension lead, wrapped like a hose pipe, and a bright orange electric saw.*

REGGIE I hate to have to break it to you, son, but your mother is no longer with us.

EDWARD I was going to summon her back from the grave using the power of necromancy to ask her where she hid the cash.

REGGIE *and* FRANCES *look at each other. After a beat, they burst out laughing, wiping tears from their eyes.*

REGGIE Plug me up, Franny.

FRANCES *plugs in the extension lead and the saw.* REGGIE *gives it a whirl, and it buzzes loudly.*

HARRY And there I was worrying about the red wine stains.

REGGIE *puts a clear visor on his head; it's pointing up at the moment. He squares up to them with the electric saw.*

REGGIE Ah, don't worry about that. We've cleaned up worse over the years. Once had two big St Bernards to get rid of – don't ask me why. Picking bits of fur out my teeth for weeks.

HARRY Did you eat them?

REGGIE *just looks at him. He smiles.*

REGGIE Which one of you silly sods wants to go first?

HARRY *and* EDWARD *look at each other.* HARRY *looks like he's going to speak, but* EDWARD *jumps in.*

EDWARD Me. Do me first. And afterwards – maybe let Harry go.

REGGIE That won't be possible, I'm afraid. But very noble of you to volunteer. Here we go, then.

REGGIE *fires up the saw.* EDWARD *has to speak up over the saw noise.*

EDWARD I'm sorry, Harry. This is all my fault.

HARRY It's alright, Ed. I don't mind . . . at least we're together.

HARRY *reaches with his fingers and manages to brush* EDWARD*'s hand.* REGGIE *approaches with the saw blade and flips the visor down over his face.*

REGGIE Try and keep still; it'll be quicker. I'm going to start by taking your head off.

EDWARD *closes his eyes. The blade approaches, but just as it gets to* EDWARD*'s neck, the saw cuts out.* REGGIE *looks behind him.* FRANCES *has pulled the plug on the extension lead.*

REGGIE Franny?

FRANCES Oh, my. Reggie you have to see this.

REGGIE What you got?

REGGIE *lifts up his visor.* FRANCES *has been reading the printed pages of the grimoire.*

FRANCES When I had my tarot done on holiday, it said something like this was on the cards. I got reversed Wheel of Fortune and the Ten of Swords.

REGGIE So?

FRANCES It means betrayal. I think we should let them try this, Reg.

REGGIE Don't be stupid. I need them brown-breaded so I can get some proper kip. I'm dead on my feet!

FRANCES That woman on the beach said I was on the cusp of a life-changing event. Said I needed to protect myself.

REGGIE She was just trying to rent you an umbrella.

FRANCES This is our opportunity to turn things around, Reg. This is what she meant.

REGGIE Is it, though? You just take all these predictions and make them fit.

FRANCES No I don't.

REGGIE You do, Franny. Remember that time Romany Sue said you were going to get attacked by a tiger? You said it came true 'cos a box of Frosties fell on your head at the Lidl.

FRANCES It's got to be worth a try. Their old dear was sitting on the best part of a Georgie.

REGGIE What's a Georgie?

FRANCES George Foreman grill, mill.

REGGIE Oh, well I never. Go on then.

FRANCES *grabs the ritual knife and goes over to* HARRY. *She holds it to his throat.*

FRANCES Sorry about this, but it was going to happen anyway.

HARRY *looks frightened and confused.*

HARRY Ed?

FRANCES *reads out the words from the page.*

FRANCES 'With blood, we summon thee. With love, we summon thee. With death, we summon thee!'

HARRY *screws his eyes tight.*

EDWARD Wait!

FRANCES *stops.*

HARRY Oh, for fuck's sake! I can't take any more of this!

EDWARD I don't think Harry has to die for the ritual to work . . .

HARRY Oh, you remember that now, do you!?

EDWARD Necromancy rituals require a 'sacrifice', but that doesn't always refer to killing a person. I think it can be something else. Flesh and blood, but part of us . . . What if . . . What if you cut one of my toes off?

REGGIE You what?

EDWARD It might not work, but it's worth a try. And there'll be a lot less to clean up!

FRANCES Works for me.

FRANCES *goes to turn the power back on.*

REGGIE Let's get this shoe off.

REGGIE *bends to take off* EDWARD*'s shoe.* EDWARD *turns and smiles at* HARRY.

REGGIE *(cont'd)* Right, let the dog see the rabbit.

REGGIE *lifts* EDWARD*'s foot up on to a stool.* FRANCES *brings over a wooden spoon.*

FRANCES Bite down on this.

EDWARD Thanks. Hopefully it won't be too bad.

EDWARD *bites the wooden spoon.* REGGIE *flips his visor down.*

REGGIE You say that. But I think it's probably best if I take off the whole plate.

EDWARD Hmnggh?

EDWARD *looks scared.* REGGIE *starts up the saw and cuts off* EDWARD*'s foot. Blood splashes on his visor.* EDWARD *screams.* HARRY *can't look.* REGGIE *flips up his visor.*

REGGIE That was tough. Now what?

FRANCES Tie it off.

REGGIE *removes his belt and pulls it round* EDWARD*'s shin.*

FRANCES *pulls some flowers out of a vase and shoves* EDWARD*'s stump tightly into the pot, creating a little peg leg.* EDWARD *is weak with pain.*

FRANCES *picks up* EDWARD*'s severed foot and holds it aloft in the centre of the circle. She reads from the grimoire pages.*

FRANCES 'Accept this our blood offering as a libation, and manifest thyself without dread. For Annie Blackwood, we do request counsel with thee.'

They all stare at EDWARD. *He bows his head. Eventually,* HARRY *speaks.*

HARRY Mum? Mum, can you hear me?

EDWARD *speaks in his mother's voice.*

EDWARD Harry? Is that you, son?

HARRY Yeah, it's me, Mum. How you doing?

EDWARD It's dark, Harry. Who is that with you?

HARRY Erm . . .

REGGIE *pipes up.*

REGGIE It's Reggie. Reggie and Franny.

FRANCES Hello again, Annie. Good to speak with you.

EDWARD Ah, Frances. I'm surprised you're still with that pig of an husband. You not left him yet?

FRANCES Ha ha, no we're still together, Franny. Aren't we, Reg?

REGGIE Yeah – she hasn't got rid of me just yet. Ha ha.

HARRY Mum, I'm sorry I wasn't there . . . at the end. Can you forgive me?

EDWARD Don't worry, son. It's done now. I don't blame you for anything.

FRANCES We wanted to ask you something, Annie, if you've got a minute.

EDWARD Oh yeah?

FRANCES Yeah – something I've been wanting to know for ages.

EDWARD Well, I think I know what that is.

FRANCES Yeah. You see, we've all been wondering . . .

EDWARD Was me and Reg having an affair behind your back for twenty years? Well, yes, we was. And as I say, I'm surprised the horrible fucker hasn't come clean by now.

REGGIE *looks shocked.*

REGGIE What you talking about, Annie? That's not a very nice thing to say, now, is it?

EDWARD All them nights he said he was on a job, Fran? He was half a mile away, hammering me.

FRANCES *looks intently at* REGGIE .

REGGIE Annie . . .

FRANCES Betrayal!

REGGIE She's lying.

HARRY Mum . . .

EDWARD For years, I held out for that selfish bastard. And what thanks did I get? He kills me and goes back to his wife.

REGGIE Shut up, Annie! You've said enough!

FRANCES Yeah, I think she probably has.

FRANCES *stabs* REGGIE *in the chest with the ritual knife. He groans and collapses on the floor, clutching to take the knife out. He dies.* FRANCES *is strangely serene.*

FRANCES *(to* HARRY*)* When your brother wakes up, I want you both out of my house. I'll deal with that mess later. I'm going to catch up on *Women Who Kill.*

FRANCES *leaves the room quietly.* HARRY *is gobsmacked.*

HARRY Mum, I've got one more question for you . . .

The clock strikes 5 a.m. EDWARD *opens his eyes and looks around.*

HARRY Edward? Are you alright?

EDWARD I'm cold.

HARRY You're probably in shock.

EDWARD I expect so.

HARRY Mum doesn't blame me, Ed. She said so herself. I spoke to her.

EDWARD No, you didn't.

HARRY But she was talking . . .

EDWARD My words. Not hers. It was me, Harry. The necromancy didn't work, even with my foot off.

HARRY Oh . . .

EDWARD Maybe I wasn't something she loved. I saved us though, didn't I? Did something right for once.

HARRY *can see* EDWARD *is fading fast and tries to get out of his bindings, but he's tied tight.* EDWARD *sees* REGGIE *dead on the floor.*

HARRY At least we had a sacrifice to Mum after all . . .

Suddenly, MR MACY *the parrot flies in through the window and lands on the top of the cage. It looks quizzically at* REGGIE. EDWARD *and* HARRY *look at each other, then back to the parrot.*

MR MACY What do you want?

HARRY Mum? Mum, we have a question for you.

The parrot looks at them.

MR MACY What do you want?

HARRY Where did you hide all the money?

They stare at the parrot. It looks at them intently. They wait.

BLACKOUT.

THE END

Episode 3

PARASKEVIDEKATRIAPHOBIA

CAST LIST

GARETH – Reece Shearsmith

DANA – Amanda Abbington

SUE – Samantha Spiro

JOHNNY – Steve Pemberton

BETHANY – Ayda Kiiza

SHELLEY – Moyo Akandé

DR ROGERS – Leon Herbert

HIMSELF – Dermot O'Leary

INT. BEDROOM. DAY.

GARETH *sits on his bed in a shirt and tie, looking concerned.* DANA *comes in, wearing a coat and carrying a bag. She affects cheeriness.*

DANA I'm off now!

GARETH OK.

DANA Are you going to be alright getting to work?

GARETH Yep. Don't worry.

DANA I'm not worried. Why would I be worried?

GARETH No reason. Go, I'm fine.

DANA OK. See you later, then.

DANA *looks worried.*

We see that GARETH *is staring at the perpetual block calendar on his bedside table, which currently reads 'Thursday 12'.*

GARETH *slowly turns the day to 'Friday' and the date to '13'.*

EXT. HOUSE. DAY.

DANA *leaves the house and walks off down the street. A black cat sits on the wall outside, and we see the house number by the gate: 9.*

TITLE: *'Paraskevidekatriaphobia'.*

INT. HALLWAY. DAY.

GARETH *locks the front door, pulls the bolts to and puts the chain on.*

INT. KITCHEN. DAY.

GARETH *dials a number on his phone. He puts on a hoarse voice.*

GARETH *(croaky)* Hi Peggy, it's Gareth . . . Yeah, I'm not feeling too great to be honest, it just came on overnight . . . Yeah, I think I better had. Will you tell Dean I'm not going to be in today? . . . Aw, thanks Peggy, bye.

GARETH *hangs up. He fills a mug with hot water and crosses to the window, looking out to see a lone magpie in his garden.* GARETH *sighs, then mutters to himself, tapping his forehead in a salute.*

GARETH One, two, three, good morning, Mr Magpie. I'm sorry you're on your own. So now I've used up my sorrow and nothing bad can happen. Understand?

The magpie flies away.

INT. LIVING ROOM. DAY.

GARETH *sits calmly in the living room with his coffee. The radio plays, and we hear the voice of Radio 2 DJ* DERMOT O'LEARY .

DERMOT *(V.O.)* . . . So, 08081 570685 is the number to call for today's very special phone-in. Hope to hear from you this Friday morning. But it's not just any old Friday – it's Friday the 13th, so no doubt you're all taking extra care of yourselves, and you won't end up in A&E having driven into a lamp post! Our fantastic NHS staff are going to be twiddling their thumbs today, aren't they, everyone being so careful!

GARETH *shakes his head, grabs his phone and dials a number.*

DERMOT *(V.O.)* Well, I hope you get to put your feet up and have a well-deserved rest – and here's a song just for you . . .

Suddenly the doorbell rings, and GARETH *quickly fumbles to turn off the radio, then ducks down to the ground. He stays very still. His phone call is answered.*

RECORDED VOICE *(V.O.)* You have reached BBC Radio 2 . . .

GARETH *hangs up. The doorbell rings again.*

GARETH *slowly moves towards the blinds at the window.* SUE, *a cheery northern postal worker, appears at one of the windows just as* GARETH *is about to close the blind.*

SUE Hello? Oh, you're in, that's lucky. I've got a parcel for you.

GARETH Just leave it on the doorstep, thanks.

SUE I can't, you've got to sign for it.

GARETH Could you come back later? My wife will be in.

SUE Not really, I've got a round to do. Besides, the package is for you, I think – Gareth Beckman? If you can't do it now, it'll have to go back to the sorting office. And with it being Friday, it'll be closed all weekend . . .

GARETH Alright, fine.

GARETH *heads for the door.*

INT. HALLWAY. DAY.

GARETH *gets to the door and unlocks it.* SUE *hands him the parcel and a pen to sign the paperwork.* GARETH *tries to sign, but the pen doesn't work.*

GARETH Your pen's not working – have you got another one?

SUE No, sorry love. We usually have them digital ones where you use your finger, but I dropped mine this morning while I was unwrapping a BelVita and it broke. The device, not the BelVita.

GARETH *heaves an exasperated sigh.*

GARETH Wait there. Please don't come in!

INT. LIVING ROOM. DAY.

GARETH *rushes in and opens a drawer. He roots around among the rulers, paperclips and staplers . . .*

GARETH Not a single bloody pen! What do we do with them all?

GARETH *pulls open another drawer, but it's stuck. He tugs harder on it a couple of times, and it eventually flies out, spilling stationery all over the floor.*

GARETH *(cont'd)* Damn it!

SUE *appears in the doorway.*

SUE Sorry, I couldn't quickly use your loo, could I?

GARETH I literally just told you not to come in!

SUE I'm busting! Dr Mekos says I've got to stay hydrated because of my condition, and I can't just nip behind a privet like a man does, can I? My friend Enid got me one of them She-Wees off *Dragon's Den*, you know, where you funnel it, but my aim was off. Ruined a good pair of Uggs, that did.

GARETH I'm sorry, no.

SUE I'm not going for a crafty poo if that's what you think.

GARETH I–

GARETH*'s phone rings. He turns to* SUE .

GARETH Be quick!

SUE Ta!

GARETH *points the way, and* SUE *goes off to the downstairs loo.* GARETH *answers his phone.*

GARETH Hello? . . . Oh, yes. Well, I just wanted to point out to Dermot O'Leary that a study conducted in 1993 by Scanlon, Luben, Scanlon and Singleton concluded that the risk of hospital admission goes up by as much as 52 per cent on

Friday the 13th – so, you know, get your facts right and stop broadcasting such irresponsible crap. You're welcome, goodbye.

He hangs up. He finally finds a pen and signs for the parcel. Suddenly, he hears knocking from inside the downstairs toilet.

He walks over to investigate.

INT. HALLWAY. DAY.

GARETH *arrives at the door of the toilet.*

SUE *(O.S.)* Hello?

GARETH What's wrong?

SUE *(O.S.)* I can't get out!

GARETH What do you mean? Just unlock the door.

SUE *(O.S.)* I can't, the handle's broke!

GARETH *tries the door from the outside.*

GARETH What have you done to it?

SUE *(O.S.)* Nothing, it just came off in my hand! Hurry up, please, I don't like confined spaces!

GARETH I need to get a screwdriver. Wait there.

SUE *(O.S.)* I don't have much choice do I?

GARETH *turns to go and get his tools from a chest of drawers by the stairs.*

GARETH Unbelievable.

Suddenly, a black cat darts in through the open front door and crosses in front of GARETH *and up the stairs. He starts.*

GARETH No! Out! Hey, get out!

SUE *(O.S.)* I can't!

GARETH Not you!

He runs up the stairs to get the cat.

INT. LANDING. DAY.

GARETH *arrives at the top of the stairs. He listens, and hears the cat meowing from one of the bedrooms. He goes in.*

INT. BEDROOM. DAY.

The cat is under the bed. GARETH *gets down on his knees and starts to reach for it.*

GARETH Come on – what are you doing under there? . . . Ow!

We hear the hiss of the cat, and GARETH *pulls his arm out from under the bed sharply. In doing so, he tears the top seam of his shirtsleeve, which now flaps open. He sees the cat has scratched the back of his hand.*

GARETH Shit.

He looks around and a gets a ball of wool and bounces it around, hoping the cat will come out and play with it.

GARETH Come on! Come on!

The cat comes out and attacks the wool. As it is distracted, GARETH *grabs a beanbag and dives towards the cat. He struggles for a moment, before realising that the cat isn't there. He lifts the beanbag, which has now burst, and its tiny polystyrene balls fall everywhere.*

GARETH *hears the cat meowing in the bathroom.*

INT. BATHROOM. DAY.

GARETH *slowly walks into the bathroom, poised like a cowboy. He looks around and sees the cat sitting at one end of the bathtub.* GARETH *steps into the bath and slowly unhooks the hand-held shower head from its clip, talking gently to the cat as he does so.*

GARETH Do you know, a man came up to me the other day and he said, 'Have you seen my cat? He's got black fur, patchy with mange. He's missing his right ear, he's blind in one eye and he only has three legs due to a recent traffic accident.'

GARETH *reaches slowly for the shower valve, pointing the hand-held shower head at the cat.*

GARETH *(cont'd)* I said, 'What's his name?' And the man said, 'Lucky.'

GARETH *turns the valve. Whoosh! The water pours down from the overhead shower, not the hand-held.* GARETH *is drenched.*

The cat hops down off the bath and trots out nonchalantly. GARETH *turns off the water and sighs deeply.*

INT. STAIRWAY. DAY.

GARETH *comes down, towelling his hair, to find a large ladder leaning against the wall at the bottom of the stairs.*

GARETH Oh, for fuck's sake . . .

A man, JOHNNY, *comes from the kitchen. He wears overalls.*

GARETH Who are you?

JOHNNY Barry Styles, locksmith. Apparently, you've trapped a lady in your downstairs toilet?

GARETH I didn't trap her, she went in of her own accord!

JOHNNY I don't need to know the details, I just need to let you know it's an £80 call out fee.

SUE *(O.S.)* Get me out, I can't breathe . . .

GARETH I'm not paying that. I didn't call you.

SUE *(O.S.)* I'll pay it. I'll pay anything, just get me out!

GARETH I was about to get you out, I just need a screwdriver. *(To* JOHNNY*)* Can you move this?

GARETH *points to the ladder.*

JOHNNY Yeah, sorry about that. I have to bring everything in from the van or it all gets nicked. Kids today, I don't know.

JOHNNY*'s phone starts to ring.*

GARETH Well, can you shift it, please? I can't get by!

JOHNNY One sec . . .

JOHNNY *answers his phone.*

JOHNNY Hiya love, did you find it alright? . . . Yes, of course, I'm at number 9 . . .

JOHNNY *wanders out, leaving* GARETH *on the stairs, the ladder leaning against the wall. He tries to tip it across to one side, but it hits the ceiling and won't go.*

SUE *(O.S.)* Hello, what's going on? I'm getting a bit dizzy . . .

GARETH I'm coming, hold on!

GARETH *steels himself and considers passing under the ladder, but he can't do it. Instead, he climbs over the banister and manages to climb down into the hallway using a chest by the stairs.*

GARETH *collapses the ladder, but it catches his tie, and he is now attached to the ladder. He pulls, but the tie won't come free. He reaches through the ladder to open a drawer in the chest, and pulls out a pair of scissors.* GARETH *then snips his tie free of the ladder.*

GARETH *tries to manoeuvre the ladder out of the front door. There is a lucky horseshoe nailed up above the door, and* GARETH *knocks it with the ladder. It swings downward.*

GARETH Oh no . . .

GARETH *leans the ladder against the door and steps up to try to right the horseshoe. Just as he corrects it, the front door opens and* JOHNNY *comes back in, knocking the ladder and* GARETH *to the floor.*

The horseshoe swings, pointing down again.

JOHNNY Oh, dear me, sorry about that. Are you alright?

JOHNNY *helps* GARETH *up and moves the ladder.*

GARETH Yes, I'm fine; I just want both of you to leave as soon as possible. I can't have people in the house today!

A five-year-old, BETHAN*, runs in holding a doll.*

BETHANY Grandad! Grandad!

JOHNNY Hello, cherub!

GARETH Who's this, now?

JOHNNY It's my granddaughter, Bethany. I've just got to look after her for a couple of hours, my daughter-in-law's got band practice.

GARETH What?

SHELLEY *comes in, wearing a garish costume and a big headdress made of peacock feathers.*

SHELLEY Thanks for doing this, Barry, I won't be long. I'll leave her bag down here.

SHELLEY *turns to* GARETH .

SHELLEY Oh, hello. Are you the fella who's locked a woman in his toilet?

SUE *(O.S.)* Yes, he is!

GARETH No I'm not!

SHELLEY Well, Bethany'll be no trouble. It's just we've got a special gig today, and we need to work on 'My Ding-a-Ling'.

GARETH Can you just step outside, please!

SHELLEY One second, I've got to sort her lunchbox . . .

GARETH I can't have *those* in here.

SHELLEY Those what?

GARETH Peacock feathers!

SHELLEY Are you allergic?

GARETH Yes, to the Evil Eye! You're covered in them!

SHELLEY Don't say that, they're lovely! Feel them . . .

SHELLEY *advances on* GARETH *with her head bowed.*

GARETH Get it away from me!

GARETH *backs up the stairs.*

GARETH *(cont'd)* Just get out, get out, GET OUT!

JOHNNY *is shocked at* GARETH*'s outburst.*

JOHNNY Eh, come on, there's no need for that.

SHELLEY It's alright, Barry. *(To* BETHANY*)* Now, you be a good girl for Grandad, and Mummy'll see you later. *(To* GARETH*)* Is there any chance I could just nip to your upstairs loo?

GARETH Definitely not.

SHELLEY Why?

GARETH Because we can't cross on the stairs.

SHELLEY Well, someone obviously got out the wrong side of the bed this morning.

GARETH Don't say that.

SHELLEY I'll have to dust off my She-Wee. *(To* BETHANY*)* See you later, darling.

SHELLEY *kisses* BETHANY *and leaves.*

JOHNNY Come on, let's go and do a nice picture in the kitchen.

GARETH Oh, make yourself at home, why don't you?!

JOHNNY *takes* BETHANY *through to the kitchen.*

SUE *(O.S.)* Have you got that screwdriver yet?

GARETH I'm getting it!

GARETH *goes to fetch the screwdriver from the cupboard.*

SUE *(O.S.)* I don't know if you want to hear this now, but your flush is broken, by the way.

GARETH Of course it is.

SUE *(O.S.)* What with that and the lock . . . they say bad luck comes in threes.

GARETH What's number two?

A pause.

SUE *(O.S.)* Your flush is broken, by the way.

GARETH *shakes his head.* JOHNNY *comes back from the kitchen.*

JOHNNY Ah, thanking you, sir.

He takes the screwdriver from GARETH. JOHNNY *kneels to look at the lock.*

JOHNNY Right, let's establish what we're looking at here . . .

GARETH *notices that* JOHNNY *isn't wearing his shoes.*

GARETH Excuse me, where are your . . . Oh, no!

GARETH *goes to look in the kitchen.*

INT. KITCHEN. DAY.

GARETH *is horrified to see* JOHNNY*'s shoes on the kitchen table.* BETHANY *sits at the table with Pritt Stick and paper.*

GARETH You can't put shoes on a table!

JOHNNY *(O.S.)* It's alright, they're brand new.

GARETH That's even worse!

GARETH *grabs the shoes and puts them on the floor. When he looks back up, he sees that* BETHANY *has a large container of table salt and is tipping it out on to paper to make a picture.*

GARETH Stop!

GARETH *lurches forward to grab some of the salt and flings it over his left shoulder.* BETHANY *stares at him.*

GARETH It wards off evil spirits.

BETHANY *laughs and copies* GARETH, *throwing salt over her own shoulder. It accidentally lands in* GARETH*'s face. He's temporarily blinded and totters back, falling over the mop and bucket.*

INT. HALLWAY. DAY.

JOHNNY *is using the screwdriver to open the door.* GARETH *appears, looking a mess. One of his glasses lenses is cracked.*

JOHNNY You alright sir?

GARETH Just, please, be quick.

SUE *(O.S.)* Yes, hurry up!

SUE *jiggles the door.*

JOHNNY Alright, madam, can you not do that, please? You're jiggling the mechanism and making my life even more difficult. *(To* GARETH*)* May I ask how the lady came to be inside the bathroom, sir?

GARETH She wanted a wee. What else would she be doing in there?

JOHNNY You tell me. I don't want any nasty surprises.

SUE *(O.S.)* Well, there is one . . .

JOHNNY Especially now there's a child on the premises.

GARETH Yes, a child you brought here! I didn't ask for any of this!

JOHNNY Here we go . . .

JOHNNY *stands and opens the door, and* SUE *emerges, hyperventilating.*

SUE Finally! Oh my God, oh my God, thank you!

JOHNNY Deep breaths; you're alright. Now, just for my own peace of mind, you went in there of your own free will, yes? The gentleman didn't force you? Because I do know the words for a citizen's arrest.

GARETH What?

SUE The room's spinning. I think I'm going to be sick.

SUE *runs back into the downstairs toilet and leans over the sink.* JOHNNY *inspects the lock.*

JOHNNY Yeah, I'd say the internal mechanism's buggered. It'll be another £150 to replace the tailpiece - plus labour, of course.

GARETH Of course.

JOHNNY I might have been able to salvage it, but she's been hacking away at it with this screw by the look of things.

JOHNNY *holds up a screw.*

GARETH Where's that come fr– Oh, my God!

GARETH *notices that the mirror on the bathroom wall is swinging precariously by a single screw, the other one having been removed by* SUE.

GARETH Help me, don't let it drop!

GARETH *steps into the downstairs loo to hold the mirror and straighten it on the wall.*

GARETH *(cont'd)* Can you put it back in?

JOHNNY It'll cost you.

GARETH Just do it!

JOHNNY *starts to screw the mirror back on to the wall as* GARETH *holds it.*

GARETH I don't need any more bad luck today.

BANG! The door slams shut behind them.

INT. HALLWAY. DAY.

BETHANY *stands by the handle-less toilet door, laughing. She runs back to the kitchen.*

EXT. HOUSE. DAY.

Establishing shot of the house.

INT. KITCHEN. DAY.

BETHANY *sits in the kitchen, colouring a picture of a school bus.*

INT. DOWNSTAIRS TOILET. DAY.

JOHNNY, GARETH *and* SUE *are squashed into the downstairs toilet.* SUE *has her eyes closed and breathes deeply.*

JOHNNY Now, imagine you're on a beach, and you're looking out at the wide open horizon. You can feel a cool breeze on your face . . .

JOHNNY *motions to* GARETH.

JOHNNY *(cont'd)* Can you feel it?

GARETH *reluctantly blows on to* SUE*'s face.*

SUE Yes . . .

JOHNNY There's not another soul for miles around. The waves lapping, the sun shining . . .

SUE Have I got sunblock on? Because I burn easily.

JOHNNY Yes, you put it on earlier. Factor 20.

SUE Only 20?!

JOHNNY Sorry, 50. I've not got my glasses on. Just think about how calm you are. Not a care in the world.

SUE This breeze smells of coffee. It stinks.

GARETH *stops blowing.*

GARETH Look, this is ridiculous, sorry. There's a toddler out there. God knows what she's getting up to.

JOHNNY My daughter-in-law's on her way over, I told you. Bethany's a good girl; she won't get up to any mischief.

GARETH I never should have answered the door. Today of all days. I knew it, as well. I knew it!

JOHNNY You don't believe all that Friday the 13th stuff, do you?

GARETH Yes, of course I do! Look where I am. Locked in a toilet with you two.

JOHNNY That's nothing to do with the date, it's just circumstance.

GARETH So says Mr Shoes-on-the-table. You're inviting bad luck.

SUE From who, though?

GARETH From the universe! I let you in, and boom! Utter chaos.

JOHNNY That's a very negative attitude, if you don't mind me saying.

GARETH Tell that to Jesus. Crucified on so-called Good Friday. After the Last Supper, when there were thirteen guests.

SUE I didn't know they had Fridays in them days.

GARETH Of course they did! Chaucer says it in the 14th century: 'And on a Friday fell all his mischance.' The Knights Templar were tortured by King Philip IV of France on Friday 13th, 1307. Public hangings happened on Fridays, and there were thirteen steps up to the gallows.

SUE And what about all them kids that were chopped up by a madman at that lake in America? That was . . .

GARETH Friday the 13th.

SUE Yeah. They made a film about it.

JOHNNY There's plenty of good things happen on a Friday too, though. End of the working week, fish and chips . . .

SUE I got my big telly on Black Friday. Mind you, it was half the bloody price a month later. It's swings and roundabouts, isn't it?

GARETH You've pepped up all of a sudden. What happened to your claustrophobia?

SUE Oh, it's being on this lovely beach – makes me feel relaxed. What time is it?

JOHNNY I don't know, my watch has stopped . . .

GARETH Oh no.

JOHNNY Thirteen minutes past.

GARETH Right, that's it . . .

GARETH *starts to kick at the door, and it bursts open. He storms into the living room.*

INT. LIVING ROOM. DAY.

GARETH *enters the room to find his wife* DANA *playing with* BETHANY. *A suited* DR ROGERS *stands in the corner of the room.*

GARETH Dana, what . . .? What are you doing here? Is everything OK?

DANA It's fine, I'm fine.

GARETH Why didn't you let us out? And who's this?

DR ROGERS I'm Dr Marcel Rogers. Your wife asked me to prepare this treatment for you.

GARETH What treatment? What are you talking about?

DANA I didn't know what else to do.

SUE *and* JOHNNY *come through.*

DR ROGERS Allow me to introduce my friends Sue and Johnny Brabbins, from the Little Marlow Amateur Dramatic Society.

JOHNNY *bows and removes his fake moustache. He and* SUE *are now very well spoken.*

JOHNNY At your service.

SUE And don't forget our juve lead, Shelley. Come in, don't be ashamed.

SHELLEY *enters, still in her outfit.*

SHELLEY Such a pleasure working with you. I hope we weren't too annoying!

DR ROGERS They've very kindly taken time out from rehearsing *Half a Sixpence* to be here today.

SUE I do hope we gave you what you wanted?

JOHNNY The reviews are in – and you were excellent, dear, as always.

SUE I never read reviews, darling, you know that.

GARETH Dana, what is all this?

DANA I know it's extreme, but Dr Rogers thought it was the only way.

DR ROGERS Exposure therapy, or 'exposure *in vivo*', as we call it. Putting you, Mr Beckman, into direct contact with your greatest fear. Your wife explained to me that your paraskevidekatriaphobia was becoming unmanageable.

GARETH My what?

DANA Paraskevidekatriaphobia. Fear of Friday the 13th.

JOHNNY Puts me in mind of the Gilbert and Sullivan we did last year: 'I am the very model of a paraskevidekatriaphobiac . . .'

GARETH So you've just been tricking me? To what end? Trying to give me a stroke?

DR ROGERS I appreciate that the experience has been very anxiety-inducing, Mr Beckman, but you needed to stay in the situation long enough for your irrational fears to subside. And for that, we needed to create a fully realised worst-case scenario. Hence the arrival of your unwanted guests.

SUE I loved all the improv stuff we did on the doorstep. I mean, 'BelVita' – where did that come from?!

JOHNNY It was magnificent. So, so funny.

SUE Bless you. But that's the accent, I think. I just read her as northern.

SHELLEY She was exactly the same in last year's Ayckbourn.

SUE Maybe not exactly the same, but thank you, darling. And Johnny here went all method, didn't you? We've had tools out all over the living room . . .

JOHNNY I read a very good article about Cumberbatch in the *Mail* and I thought that was the way to go with 'Barry Styles'. But I shall miss him, that's for sure.

GARETH Sorry – what the fuck are you talking about?

DANA Gareth!

GARETH *points to* BETHANY.

GARETH And who's this, then? Did you get her from Sylvia Young?

DR ROGERS No, but she is on the waiting list. My granddaughter – who did a wonderful job, I thought.

JOHNNY Absolutely, bravo! She'll make a first-class Rosalind when she's older.

GARETH I'm sorry, but this is bullshit! You're all talking as if what I'm saying is irrational, but it isn't, as I just explained in there.

SUE That was a lovely scene, by the way.

GARETH It wasn't a scene, it was real! I was explaining the real-world history of this phenomenon.

DR ROGERS What phenomenon?

GARETH Bad luck!

DANA It's not luck, though, Gareth! You avoid walking under a ladder because something might fall on your head. You don't want shoes on the table because you're going to eat off it. Actors don't like saying *Macbeth* because there are sword fights in it, and people have been genuinely injured!

JOHNNY Oh no, she mentioned the Scottish play!

JOHNNY *and* SUE *turn round on the spot, spit over their left shoulders, then link pinkies.*

JOHNNY and SUE Piss-pots!

GARETH And you think I'm the one who needs to see a fucking therapist.

SUE Well, I think that's our cue for the interval. Shall we?

SHELLEY Come on Bethany, there's some lovely cake for you in the green room.

BETHANY *runs over to* SHELLEY, *and they leave with* SUE *and* JOHNNY .

DR ROGERS Perhaps we ought to address what's really going on here, Gareth.

GARETH What do you mean?

DR ROGERS Your wife tells me there was an inciting incident. Can you tell me about the 13th of October 1978? I believe it was a Friday.

GARETH *looks at* DANA.

GARETH How could you?

DANA I had to, Gareth. It's taking over our lives. Every Friday the 13th, three times a year. You're obsessed.

GARETH I'm not obsessed. And it's not three times a year; it's twice this year, twice next year, and one time the year after that.

DR ROGERS Why don't you tell me what happened?

GARETH *looks down.* DANA *takes up the story for him.*

DANA You were on a school trip to France. Skiing in Le Corbier. But on the Friday, you had a stomach ache and you didn't want to go. You watched as all of your classmates got into the coach and drove away. And that was the last you ever saw of any of them. The coach skidded on black ice and came off the road.

GARETH All of them died.

DR ROGERS Except you. Your survivor's guilt and its association with that date has blighted you ever since. But now it's time to confront your fear and put an end to it.

DR ROGERS *nods to* DANA, *who leaves momentarily.* DR ROGERS *hands* GARETH *a hammer.* DANA *returns with the mirror from the downstairs toilet. She holds it up in front of* GARETH.

DANA We want you to smash this mirror.

GARETH What? No.

GARETH *is terrified.*

DANA Break it.

GARETH I can't.

DR ROGERS Friday the 13th is just another day. A day when something terrible happened in 1978 that wasn't your fault.

GARETH It's seven years' bad luck.

DR ROGERS Break the mirror, Gareth, and set yourself free.

SUE, JOHNNY *and* SHELLEY *have come in and are looking on.* BETHANY *stares too.* GARETH *looks at them. Looks in the mirror. Looks at the hammer. He is in turmoil.*

GARETH I'm sorry . . .

GARETH *closes his eyes and hits the mirror with the hammer. When he opens his eyes, he sees the cracked pieces of mirror still in the frame.*

There are 13 shards. In each one, GARETH *sees a schoolchild from the bus crash, bloodied but staring back at him.*

GARETH *looks away, then back again. The faces of the children are gone. Just his own reflection in kaleidoscope across the broken pieces.*

DR ROGERS Well done.

Ding-dong! Suddenly the doorbell rings.

Everyone turns to the front door. GARETH *looks round, concerned.*

GARETH What now?

DANA I don't know.

DANA *leaves to answer the door. We hear murmured voices.*

DANA *(O.S.)* Oh my God!

DANA *returns, beaming, followed by* DERMOT O'LEARY, *holding a microphone, and a* PRODUCER, *wearing headphones and recording the events on a phone.*

DERMOT Oh, hello, hello! Blimey, I feel like I've crashed a party! Which one's Gareth?

GARETH Er, me . . .

DERMOT Well, tah-dah! Congratulations, Gareth: you were the one millionth person to call into our Radio 2 show earlier this morning, and you have won a whopping great cheque for £130,000!

An ASSISTANT *in a full-size cat costume enters, holding a huge cheque made out to* GARETH *for that amount.*

DERMOT *(cont'd)* I think this must be your lucky day!

The others laugh and cheer. DERMOT *and the* CAT ASSISTANT *hand over the cheque, and the* PRODUCER *films* GARETH *receiving it, looking bewildered.*

GARETH Thank you! I don't . . . is this really happening?

DERMOT It certainly is, my friend!

SUE *(to* DERMOT*)* Can I just say, Dec, if you and Ant would like tickets for *Half a Sixpence*, I'm pretty sure I can get a couple of house seats . . . You'd be most welcome to come and see if we've got the X-Factor!

DERMOT *forces a smile.*

DERMOT Oh, that's . . . unbelievable. I'll check my diary. Now, Gareth, if you don't mind, we wanted to do a quick interview to play out on the show tomorrow morning when we make the big announcement – is that OK?

GARETH *looks around at the celebrations. He finally starts to relax and begins to smile.*

GARETH I'd love to.

INT. BEDROOM. DAY.

GARETH *is asleep in bed. He is smiling. He opens his eyes and sits up sharply.*

GARETH Oh no . . .

He stares at the perpetual block calendar on his bedside table, which reads 'Friday 13'.

GARETH *(cont'd)* No . . .

DANA *comes in wearing a coat and carrying a bag.*

DANA I'm off now! . . . What's wrong?

GARETH I thought I'd fixed everything, but it turns out . . . it was all a dream.

DANA What are you talking about, 'a dream'?

DANA *turns the blocks over to 'Saturday 14'.*

DANA Today is Saturday, you idiot. You just haven't turned it round yet.

GARETH Oh. You mean – Dermot O'Leary, that was real?

DANA Yes! Dermot bloody O'Leary, in our living room! I nearly died of shock. Now come down, your interview is on in a minute.

INT. LIVING ROOM. DAY.

GARETH *is having a coffee at the table, a window into the street behind him. He looks at the huge cheque for £130,000.* DANA *is getting ready to go out.*

DANA I'm meeting Paula for breakfast, so I'll listen to you later. Oh, you should open this.

GARETH What is it?

DANA The package from yesterday. Open it.

GARETH *opens the package. It is an umbrella.*

DANA One last test for you. Just to be sure.

GARETH *looks at her, then presses the button on the umbrella handle. It springs open.*

DANA Well done, darling. I'm so proud of you. See you later.

DANA *kisses him.* GARETH *hands her the brolly.*

DANA Enjoy your interview!

DANA *leaves.* GARETH *puts on his headphones to listen to the radio.*

DERMOT *(V.O.)* Coming up, I chat to our one millionth caller, who yesterday won an incredible £130,000! We'll be hearing from him about what it feels like to be so unbelievably lucky. Speaking of which – here's Kylie!

'I Should Be So Lucky' by Kylie Minogue starts to play. GARETH *smiles and sips his coffee.*

Behind him, we see DANA *come out of the house.*

As GARETH *happily nods his head to the music, we see* DANA *struggle to collapse the umbrella. She absent-mindedly walks into the street, and gets knocked down dead by a car.*

THE END

Episode 4

LOVE IS A STRANGER

CAST LIST

VICKY – Claire Rushbrook

EDGAR – Mathew Horne

NORMAN – Reece Shearsmith

MANNY – Steve Pemberton

POLLY – Menyee Lai

LESLEY – Frances Barber

JAI – Asim Chaudhry

INT. VICKY'S FLAT, BATHROOM. NIGHT 2.

Romantic piano music plays. VICKY *is getting herself ready for a date. She applies a little make-up, and tries putting her hair up, before deciding against it. She squirts perfume in the air and walks through it.*

She looks at herself in the mirror and smiles. We hear a radio news report in the background.

NEWSREADER *(V.O.)* . . . and there were reports that the Chief Whip had quit just hours after the Foreign Secretary resigned . . . There's been another body found on waste ground just outside Kettering. Police are linking the case to the so-called 'Lonely Hearts Killer' . . .

EXT. VICKY'S FLAT. NIGHT 2.

Close on a series of numbered buzzers on a door-entry system. A menacing shadow looms across the metal plate, and a gloved hand pushes buzzer number 9.

INT. VICKY'S FLAT, BATHROOM. NIGHT 2.

VICKY *reacts to the buzzer, then checks herself in the mirror one last time.*

EXT. VICKY'S FLAT. NIGHT 2.

Close on the buzzers. We hear VICKY *through the intercom.*

VICKY *(O.S.)* Hi! Come on up.

The dark figure passes, and we see buzzer number 9.

TITLE: *'Love is a Stranger'.*

CUT TO BLACK.

INT. VICKY'S FLAT. NIGHT 1.

We are watching a series of internet dates on VICKY*'s computer. The site is called Palm Dates. We can see* VICKY*, more dowdily dressed, sitting in her flat and looking at the laptop, but we only ever see her dates via the screen.*

Suddenly, a man appears: EDGAR. *In his 40s, attractive, nice smile.*
A clock at the top of the screen counts down from four minutes.

VICKY Oh, hello!

EDGAR Hi!

VICKY That took me by surprise.

EDGAR I know, yeah. It's weird, isn't it?

VICKY and EDGAR *(simultaneously)* I . . .

VICKY No, go on.

EDGAR I was going to say, I don't know if we're allowed to say our names?

VICKY Oh, I'm not sure. The email said to keep things anonymous, what with everything in the news.

EDGAR Well, statistically, you're more likely to be killed by someone you know rather than a complete stranger, so . . . let's live dangerously. I'm Edgar.

VICKY *seems unsure.*

EDGAR *(cont'd)* You don't have to tell me if you're not comfortable.

VICKY Vicky.

EDGAR Hi, Vicky. Nice to e-meet you.

They mime shaking hands.

VICKY You too. So, have you done one of these before?

EDGAR I've done one in real life where you go along the line . . .

VICKY IRL.

EDGAR Sorry?

VICKY Oh, that's . . . in real life. IRL.

EDGAR Yeah, where you jump along one every five minutes.

VICKY Like musical chairs!

EDGAR Exactly. Though mine was more like 'Pin the Tail on the Donkey'. Sorry. Anyway, nothing came of it, so I thought I'd try this. See who randomly pops up.

VICKY Well, I'm glad you did.

EDGAR So am I.

VICKY So what do you do, Edgar?

EDGAR I'm a landscape gardener. I do designs and planting – basically the kind of thing you see on the *Chelsea Flower Show*.

VICKY I love that! I've never been, I used to love watching it on the TV. I've always enjoyed gardening.

EDGAR Really?

VICKY I've actually written it down as one of my passions.

VICKY *refers to her list.*

EDGAR Well, that's a good start! What else is on that list?

VICKY Ah, that would be telling! Got to keep some feminine mystique.

EDGAR Absolutely right. So, how big is your plot?

VICKY Sorry?

EDGAR Your garden? Do you want me to come round and give you a quote?

VICKY *laughs.*

VICKY Oh, it's only a little patch. Well, it's a window box, but I've got all my herbs and some potted plants for a splash of colour.

EDGAR Sounds great. I love a window box. Peonies can be good; they can grow in a tight space. If you water them regularly . . .

EDGAR*'s trying to flirt, but* VICKY *isn't getting it.*

EDGAR *(cont'd)* So how about you, Vicky, do you work?

VICKY I'm a carer – *was* a carer. And now I do a little bit of volunteering, just in the local charity shop. So that's me!

EDGAR OK!

VICKY *smiles.* EDGAR *smiles too, but not as convincingly. His interest is waning.*

EDGAR And . . . And do you have a family, or . . . ? What's your situation?

VICKY My brother moved to Canada a while ago, and he's got two little girls now. So I'm an auntie!

EDGAR Cool. Whereabouts?

VICKY Winnipeg. I'm going to go over, definitely, when he gets settled.

EDGAR How long has he been there?

VICKY Six years.

There's an awkward pause. EDGAR*'s eyes flick up to the clock.*

VICKY Tell me more about you, anyway! There's me, wittering on.

EDGAR Yeah, like I say, landscape gardener. I golf, occasionally. Music-wise, Dire Straits, Dylan, Simply Red . . .

VICKY I love them. What's your favourite album?

EDGAR Erm . . . *Greatest Hits*, probably. Anyway, Vicky, it's been lovely to meet you . . .

VICKY Oop, we've still got a minute.

EDGAR Well, fifty-five seconds.

VICKY That's half a lifetime in speed dating! You never know – I might be The One.

EDGAR Of course! Erm . . .

Awkward pause.

VICKY Sorry, I shouldn't . . . I was getting ahead of myself.

EDGAR No, no, it's my fault. But when you go shopping for a new sofa, for example, you don't just buy the first one you see, do you? You have to sit on a few first, get a feel for them. You know – some are saggy, some are sleek and hard.

VICKY And some are fluffy and comfortable, and can last you a lifetime.

EDGAR True. Anyway, good luck. Hope you get to Canada someday.

VICKY I will. Thanks, Edgar. It's been nice chatting to you.

EDGAR You too, I've really enjoyed it. And it's been good practice for the next one . . .

EDGAR*'s image disappears.* VICKY *is left a little deflated.*

INT. VICKY'S FLAT. NIGHT 2.

BUZZZZ! The intercom buzzer sounds. VICKY *hurries in and picks up the intercom phone.*

VICKY Hi, come on up.

VICKY *presses the entry button and looks round. The table is set for dinner for two. She lights the candles.*

There is a knock on the door. VICKY *checks her reflection in the hallway mirror, goes to the door and opens it. The dark shadow of a figure at the door.*

VICKY I'm really glad you came.

INT. VICKY'S FLAT. NIGHT 1.

VICKY *is still deflated. After a couple of beats,* NORMAN *appears on the screen in front of her. Quite stiff and military.*

NORMAN Right, victim number two! Good evening.

VICKY Hello there! This is weird, isn't–

NORMAN Could you sit up for me, please.

VICKY Sorry?

NORMAN Sit up a little, would you? The lighting is very poor your end. Is that deliberate?

VICKY No, but maybe if I tilt the screen back . . .

VICKY *tilts the screen back a little.*

VICKY *(cont'd)* Is that better?

NORMAN Marginally. Now, I have a brief checklist, if you don't mind my going first? Always best to have a plan, I find. So, you are . . . ?

VICKY I thought it was supposed to be anony–*(relenting)* Vicky.

NORMAN *(writing this down)* Victoria. Age?

VICKY Well, is that . . . ?

NORMAN Ballpark figure will do. I know you fillies like to shave half a decade off if you can.

VICKY I'd rather not say, to be honest. I'm as old as my gums and a little bit older than my teeth!

NORMAN Hmm, I'll put fifty-eight. And location?

VICKY I'm not comfortable telling you that at the moment.

NORMAN For goodness' sakes, do I look like an axe murderer? I just need to know if you have direct transport links to Kettering.

VICKY Erm, yes.

NORMAN That's fine, then. Now these you can answer in any order you like, but I'd like to know the following: occupation and salary, pastimes and interests, family and domestic expectations.

VICKY Oh, right. You're very prepared, aren't you? Ha ha. I just . . . Anyway, I'm a carer - was a carer - and now I work in a charity shop locally.

NORMAN Is that a salaried position?

VICKY No. I get first dibs, though, every time a new bag comes in! Sorry, what was your name?

NORMAN Norman Jenkins. Pastimes?

VICKY I like to garden . . . erm, walks, cooking.

NORMAN Hmm, standard stuff.

VICKY Family-wise, I've got a brother in Canada, but other than that I'm footloose and fancy-free. So . . .

NORMAN *spends a little time writing this down.*

NORMAN Hang on! 'Loose . . . and free.'

VICKY Sorry, Norman, what did you mean by 'domestic expectations'?

NORMAN I've recently been cut open from here to here.

NORMAN *points to his chest.*

VICKY Sorry to hear that.

NORMAN Don't be sorry, it saved my life. I'm fitted with a pacemaker which regulates my heartbeat to between 60 and 80 bpm. However, my surgeon warned me against energetic activities, including housework and bedroom antics, so my enquiry about 'domestic expectations' has to do with that. Is that clear?

VICKY Oh, right. Well, it's too soon to be thinking about . . .

NORMAN Suffice to say, I'm unable at present to deliver on certain aspects of what you might be looking for.

VICKY That's fine. But thank you for being so honest. I appreciate it. I've had some big life-changing stuff going on myself. It's just nice to talk to someone, isn't it?

NORMAN I'm not lonely, if that's what you mean.

VICKY Good. I'm pleased for you. I am, a bit, but I've been doing these dating apps and whatnot, trying to find the right man. It's just hard, isn't it?

NORMAN Not really. It's a question of preparation.

VICKY *smiles.*

VICKY Can I turn the tables now? Interrogate you?

NORMAN If you wish, yes. Only fair.

VICKY So, Norman, if we were going to go on a date, where would you take me?

NORMAN Hmm, good question. I suppose, off the top of my head, it would have to be Kensington Palace Gardens. Peter Pan statue. Mother used to take me there when I was a boy. Every Sunday, once a month. Before I was returned to boarding school. She'd buy me an ice cream with strawberry sauce – monkey blood, we used to call it – and then drop me off at the station. And I'd sob my little heart out all the way back to Surrey.

VICKY That's so sad. Is your mother still with us?

NORMAN No. She died in 2014.

VICKY I'm sorry. I lost my mother last year. It untethers you, doesn't it? You lose your bearings. Do you think you'd like to maybe meet up for a coffee some time to talk about it?

NORMAN Certainly not. You look nothing like her.

NORMAN*'s half of the screen cuts out.*

VICKY *is left feeling bemused, a little shocked. She makes a note in her notebook. Another man pops up on screen: a jolly-looking* MANNY.

MANNY Ooop, hello, I'm Manny.

VICKY Erm, Vicky.

MANNY You look like you've lost a shilling and found a penny. Am I that ugly?

VICKY No, no, not at all, sorry. I just had the rudest man.

MANNY Oh, there's some nutters on here, aren't there? Well, you've only got to read the paper! My last one didn't go to plan either.

VICKY Really?

MANNY Yeah, screen comes up and there's nobody there. I just hear this voice: 'Sorry, I'm having a wee!' I said, 'It's alright, love – when you've got to go, you've got to go!' Then she comes out of the toilet and starts unloading the dishwasher.

VICKY No!

MANNY I swear down! I said, 'Are you not going to have a quick look, just in case you've got Cary Grant sitting here.' So she comes over, puts her glasses on and says, 'Cary Grant? More like Russell Grant!' Then she frigs off again.

VICKY Aw. I like a cuddly man.

MANNY Well, I go up and down, but it's hard, isn't it?

VICKY Hmm. I think my previous date was after a mother rather than a partner. You don't know who you're going to get, do you?

MANNY True. You've got lovely eyes.

VICKY Thank you.

MANNY So, do you work, Vicky?

VICKY Yes, I'm a landscape gardener.

MANNY Really?

VICKY *seems surprised by her own lie, but goes with it.*

VICKY Hmm. I do designs and planting, the kind of thing you see on the *Chelsea Flower Show*.

MANNY Wow. I was going to say something about a neat bush, but I stopped myself. Don't blow it, Manny!

VICKY *laughs and has a sip of her wine.*

VICKY It's nice to laugh. I've not laughed in ages.

MANNY Oh yeah, it's the best medicine. Even if nothing comes of these things romantically, I always try and have a bit of fun – but that's just me. You can't go wrong if you're just straight-up with people, you know what I mean? Be honest, and if they like you, they like you. And if they don't . . . it's four minutes out of your life.

VICKY Yes. You're right . . . I'm not a landscape gardener. I just said it, I don't know why. It's a confidence thing.

MANNY Oh, don't be daft, I'll talk to anyone, me. Well – you're not a traffic warden, are you?

VICKY Ha ha, no. I'm . . . I'm nothing. Forget it. Tell me what you do, anyway?

MANNY I run a premium phone line for people who are stuck on their Rubik's Cube.

VICKY Honestly?

MANNY Yeah, swear down. People ring up, they've got three sides done, they want to know how to progress. Occasionally, I get the speed-cubers phoning in with a DNF . . .

VICKY What's that?

MANNY Did Not Finish. But most of the calls are just taking muggles through to solve-completion using the Fridrich method: you know, starting with your basic white cross, then inserting pairs of corners using OLL. Sorry – orientation of the last layer. I do go a bit geeky when I get on the subject.

VICKY No, it sounds fascinating. So how long are you on for?

MANNY Average call time is seventeen minutes, pound a minute. You do the maths.

VICKY Seventeen pounds.

MANNY Exactly. Then throw in your internationals, your Chineses, your Thais . . . I only need three or four calls a day, and I'm laughing.

VICKY Sounds perfect.

MANNY I wanted to franchise it, take it on *Dragon's Den*. To me, it's the next Trunki or Tangle-Teaser, but I don't think they'd get it. Well, the new lad they've got on, Stephen – he might. You've got to get it on social media.

VICKY You get everything on social media nowadays, can't you?

MANNY Yeah. Including someone to have a bit of fun with.

MANNY *smiles.* **VICKY** *looks down, embarrassed but also slightly coquettish.*

VICKY I wish I had a hobby I could turn into a job.

MANNY Oh, it's the best. But it does make it hard to meet people. So that's why . . .

Behind **MANNY**, *the door opens and a woman,* **POLLY**, *comes in.*

POLLY Manny, have you seen the key to the shed? I want to get the kids' bikes out for the morning.

MANNY Yeah, I'll be down in a bit, love.

POLLY Who's this?

MANNY No one . . . One of my cubers.

POLLY You fucking liar. You're doing it again, aren't you?

MANNY No . . .

POLLY Listen, he's married! You sad cow.

POLLY *holds up her hand and shows her wedding ring.*

VICKY Sorry, I didn't–

POLLY Keep your desperate, clammy hands off! If I catch you sniffing round again, I'll find out where you live and I'll break your ribs, do you hear me? I've done it before.

MANNY She has.

POLLY Piss off and get your own man, bitch!

POLLY *slams the laptop shut.* VICKY *is stunned and shaken.*

INT. VICKY'S FLAT. NIGHT 2.

We are in VICKY*'s date's POV. The door to flat 9 is opened by a smiling* VICKY.

VICKY I'm really glad you came. Come in!

We enter, still with the date's POV as she closes the door. A gloved hand passes a bottle of wine to VICKY.

VICKY *looks at the bottle. It's only three-quarters full.*

VICKY Oh, you opened it already, did you? Bit of Dutch courage, I suppose.

The camera pans around the flat as the date looks around. VICKY *appears and ushers the date towards the sofa.*

VICKY Here, come and sit down, and I'll pour us a glass.

VICKY *moves towards the kitchen. Still in the date's POV, we watch her as she leaves. Then he looks down and starts to remove his gloves . . .*

INT. VICKY'S FLAT. NIGHT 1.

VICKY *pours her wine, then looks to the screen again. Up pops a middle-aged lady,* LESLEY. VICKY *frowns, confused.*

LESLEY Hello! Who've we got here, then?

VICKY Oh, hi, erm . . .

LESLEY No, don't worry, it's been happening all night. I think they've got me on the wrong track because of my name, Lesley. It's one of those bipolar names, isn't it? Although that shouldn't mean anything in this day and age, what with all the mixing of gender fluids.

VICKY I suppose so, yes.

LESLEY Anyway, I'm not a lesbian! I'm not even bi-curious; I couldn't imagine anything worse. What's your name, lovey?

VICKY Vicky.

LESLEY 'Vicky . . .' Aaah! Is that with a 'c- k-i' or a 'k-k-i'?

VICKY No, just 'v-i-c-k-y'.

LESLEY *writes this down.*

LESLEY . . . 'c-k-y' – aaah. And do you go by Vicky or by Victoria?

VICKY Vicky, mainly. Victoria's a bit . . .

LESLEY Old-fashioned. Yes, I agree. Though I have a friend my age called Ivy, and she's got tattoos and a labia ring, so go figure! Now tell me, have you seen any potential Mr Rights out there, or have they all been . . . ?

VICKY Mr Lefts, as my mother used to say.

LESLEY Ha! Mr Lefts, I love it!

LESLEY *writes this down.*

VICKY No, a couple of potentials, maybe, but no one's really jumped out at me.

LESLEY I should hope not! That's the beauty of it being online – safety first. You know they found another body this morning? Ring finger chopped off. Terrible. You could be talking to the 'Lonely Hearts Killer'!

VICKY Oh, don't say that . . .

LESLEY Well, who knows? You can't trust anyone. I tell you what, though, Vick, I've been laughing with some of my other ladies about the descriptions guys use, compared to what they look like. Do you know what I mean?

VICKY Yes. My last one described himself as Cary Grant. I thought, 'More like Russell Grant.'

LESLEY Ha, that's priceless! Mind you, we're just as bad, aren't we? Saying 'bubbly' when you mean 'fat'. Or 'homely' when you mean 'a frump'.

VICKY 'Lives life to the full' – i.e., 'raging alcoholic!'

LESLEY Or my favourite, 'Footloose and fancy-free,' meaning, 'A totally empty existence.'

LESLEY *laughs.* VICKY *forces a laugh and takes a sip of her wine.*

LESLEY So, what's your current status, Vick? Are you divorced, single? Married and looking for a bit of fun on the side?

VICKY No, no, I've not really had the time for a serious relationship.

LESLEY Ah, you're a career woman, like me.

VICKY Not really, I just . . . I always worried that if I found a man, he'd have to share me with Mum.

LESLEY Sounds kinky!

VICKY No, not like that! But up until recently, I've had to put her needs first. Dad walked out when we were little. Then she had boyfriends, but they weren't very nice, so it was down to me. And that was my life.

LESLEY *casually makes notes as* VICKY *talks.*

VICKY *(cont'd)* Through my fingers before I even knew it.

LESLEY So you found solace in food?

VICKY Not really.

LESLEY Aaah, we're so hard on ourselves, aren't we? I mean, how many items of clothing have you got that you can't fit into any more?

VICKY Oh, don't!

LESLEY One to five, five to ten, or eleven and over?

VICKY Erm . . . five to ten, probably, if I . . .

LESLEY *writes this down.*

LESLEY Good. And sometimes, Vick, when I'm stepping into a bath of an evening and I glance in the mirror, I think, 'what three words would I use to describe my body shape?' Do you ever think that, and if so, what would they be?

VICKY What?

LESLEY The three words. Take your time, we've still got a minute left.

VICKY Sorry, what's this about? Why are you writing everything down?

LESLEY Vicky. What if I were to tell you that there's a brand-new miracle product which is just about to launch in the UK. It's a supplement, not a meal replacement, and I'm able to offer you . . .

VICKY So, what, you're just trying to sign me up to some diet plan?

LESLEY Ha ha, no – we don't call it a diet plan, we call it a gateway to a new you. Have you got an email address?

VICKY No! I mean, yes, I have, but I'm not giving it to you.

LESLEY Why not, lovey?

VICKY Because you've tricked me! I bet you deliberately put yourself down as a man, didn't you?

LESLEY Well, it's fish in a barrel, isn't it? Where else am I going to find an endless supply of ladies like you?

VICKY What do you mean, ladies like me?

LESLEY . . . Bubbly! Now, I do need that email address, Vick, if you want to set up the direct deb–

VICKY *(suddenly angry)* Fuck off!

LESLEY*'s screen goes blank.* VICKY *is despondent. Another five seconds pass.*

A man (JAI) *appears, who has an animated filter on his face making him look like a mouse. The eyes and mouth move as he speaks.*

VICKY *looks at him, unimpressed. A long pause.*

JAI Hello.

VICKY Is that supposed to be funny?

JAI No. I'm really sorry. I've been trying to turn it off for the past half an hour. I let my kids use the laptop to watch *Lazy Town* on CBeebies and the next thing . . . At least I'm not a turd! There's one that's a turd. Sorry.

VICKY *doesn't respond.*

JAI *(cont'd)* I can keep on fiddling on my computer and try and fix it, or I can just concentrate on talking to you properly. Or you can switch off now and save yourself four minutes; I wouldn't blame you.

VICKY No, it's fine. I'm not doing anything else.

JAI Can I ask your name?

VICKY I'd rather not say.

JAI OK. Sorry.

VICKY You don't have to keep saying sorry. You sound like me.

JAI What have you got to be sorry about?

VICKY Daring to exist, according to most of the people on here.

JAI It's not easy, is it? Being gazed at and picked over by half a dozen random strangers. I've never done this before, and I don't think I'll bother again.

VICKY Why not?

JAI It's just . . . too painful. It confirms all the worst things I think about myself.

VICKY Come on, don't be like that. There'll be someone out there for you. Are you a man or a mouse?

VICKY *laughs.*

VICKY *(cont'd)* Sorry.

She picks up her wine glass.

VICKY *(cont'd)* Here's to us, anyway!

JAI Cheers.

JAI *raises his glass of beer and goes to drink some. The filter over his face flickers off and on as he drinks.* VICKY *sees that he has a large port-wine birthmark on one side of his face.*

VICKY My name's Vicky, by the way.

JAI Jai.

VICKY How old are your kids, Jai?

JAI Eleven and twelve.

VICKY And they still watch CBeebies?

JAI . . . Yeah.

VICKY What are their names?

JAI Sally and Lindsay.

VICKY Like the actress!

JAI I suppose, yes.

VICKY I used to sit Mum in front of CBeebies. She liked the colours. So I know that *Lazy Town* hasn't been on for nearly ten years. You put that filter on yourself, didn't you?

JAI *nods.*

JAI I don't have kids. Thing is, I've got this . . .

VICKY I know. When you took a drink, I saw. Why don't you turn it off? Then we can talk properly.

JAI *removes the filter.* VICKY *smiles.*

VICKY That's better.

JAI So, tonight's been a bit of a washout?

VICKY Yeah. Up until now, anyway.

JAI I don't get to meet that many women IRL. It's not easy, you know, with the constant stares.

VICKY Tell me about it, I live on the top floor with no lift.

JAI No, I meant . . .

VICKY I know you did; I was making a joke, I'm sorry.

JAI People react in different ways. I'm either the Invisible Man or the Elephant Man. They either don't see me or they can't stop looking.

VICKY It must be hard. I get overlooked as well. No man, no job. Unless you count being a carer, which most people don't. So this is me, finally coming out to the world. Like a flower starting to bloom. Except no one wants to smell me.

JAI I do! Sorry, that sounds a bit . . .

VICKY Quick, twenty seconds left. What can you say in twenty seconds?

JAI *presses a couple of buttons and another filter appears on his screen, showing love hearts swirling round his head.*

VICKY *laughs.*

JAI *writes his phone number on a pad and holds it up to the screen.*

JAI I hope you've got a good memory, Vicky.

VICKY *quickly writes down the number before* JAI*'s screen disappears. She closes her laptop, then sits back in her chair and smiles. Finally happy.*

INT. VICKY'S FLAT. NIGHT 2.

VICKY *is in the kitchen, pouring two glasses of wine.*

VICKY I've made a lasagne – hope that's OK. Just with salad and a bit of garlic bread. It's nice to have someone to cook for. Mum only ever wanted tinned stuff. It became quite boring after a while.

VICKY *comes through to the living room and hands the glass of wine to . . .* JAI. *He takes it and smiles.*

VICKY *(cont'd)* Cheers. Nice to see you in the flesh. Here's to no more masks.

JAI No more masks.

They clink glasses and sip wine.

VICKY So, how are Sally and Lindsay?

JAI Oh right, yeah. They're tucked up in bed. Watching *Lazy Town*!

VICKY I'm glad to hear it. Sit down.

They sit.

VICKY So, have you been working today? I never asked you what you do.

JAI I'm in investments. Stock market and stuff. I'm getting some Bitcoins soon, so I've just been running the numbers.

VICKY Ooh, exciting.

JAI It is. That's an interesting dress. You're the third person I've seen wearing it this week.

VICKY Really?

JAI Yeah, must have been in the sales.

VICKY No it's . . . quite old. One of Mum's, I think. What makes you say that?

JAI I got you a present.

JAI *fetches a cheap pendant on a chain from his pocket.*

JAI *(cont'd)* It's a mouse. To remind you of how we first met.

VICKY Oh, that's lovely.

JAI Can I put it on you?

VICKY Er, yes, thank you.

JAI *stands and goes behind* VICKY. *She's feeling a little tense as he moves her hair aside to place the small mouse pendant round her neck.*

JAI I can smell you now. There you go. Looks nice.

VICKY *smiles and fingers the pendant.*

VICKY I'll get some crisps.

VICKY *goes to the kitchen to dish up some crisps, and* JAI *follows.*

JAI You seem nervous. Hope it's not because of me.

VICKY No! No, it's . . . As I said, I've not been on many dates, what with Mother and her condition. You can't be going out for a romantic meal for two at Zizzi when your mum's bag needs emptying every four hours.

JAI Sounds draining.

VICKY It was. Literally. But she passed, and now I'm free to start a new chapter, so . . . every cloud. Do you still have your mother?

JAI How do you mean?

VICKY Is she still alive?

JAI Yes. I think so.

VICKY *is disconcerted.*

VICKY I don't think we ever really get over–

JAI *lunges in and tries to kiss* VICKY. *She pushes him away.*

VICKY What are you doing? Stop!

JAI Shit, sorry.

VICKY We haven't even had any food.

JAI I know, I messed up. I thought I could miss out a few steps and it would still be alright. Can we start again?

VICKY What do you mean 'steps'?

JAI I dunno, I just . . . OK, Vicky, I'm going to level with you. I didn't know how to get to the next level with women – you know, bedroom-wise. So I did a pick-up course.

VICKY A course?

JAI Yeah, it gives you a structure, sort of like a script. You know, how to demonstrate higher value, like with the Bitcoin stuff. Then remembering to throw in the odd neg . . .

VICKY What's a 'neg'?

JAI Saying your dress is shit is meant to make you like me more, or something. I don't know why, I had to go the toilet in that bit.

VICKY*'s expression darkens.*

VICKY Oh. Well, that's very disappointing. You've let yourself down, Jai.

JAI Great. So I wasted my money on these now, have I?

JAI *takes a packet of condoms from his pocket.*

JAI *(cont'd)* And the wine. Fuck's sake.

JAI *throws the condoms down.*

The oven alarm goes off.

VICKY I'll just . . . go and set the table.

VICKY *turns off the oven and leaves the kitchen.* JAI, *frustrated, looks around.*

JAI I'm not being funny, but I don't even want the lasagne. That's not what I came here for, you know what I mean?

VICKY *is opening the sideboard.*

VICKY I'm surprised anyone's thinking about dating at the moment, with all this stuff on the news. We're either very brave or very stupid.

JAI *is looking at the glass jars on the kitchen shelf.*

JAI Are you negging me now?

VICKY *(O.S.)* Not really. Just an observation.

JAI *sees a jar of pasta, a jar of lentils . . . The next jar has something fleshy inside. He opens it and empties the contents out on to the side – and is horrified to find four severed ring fingers. Belonging to men. He backs away from them in fear.*

VICKY *(O.S.)* Lonely Hearts Killer. I hate that name.

JAI *spins round to see* VICKY *approaching slowly, smiling, eyes slightly glazed. She carries a large lump hammer.*

VICKY *(cont'd)* Makes me sound like a victim. And that's not me. I refuse to end up like my mother.

JAI Oh, God . . .

VICKY There's so many nasty men out there. But one good thing I've found about these dating sites. If a person's not good enough for you . . .

VICKY *suddenly swings the hammer across* JAI*'s head, and he falls to the ground.*

VICKY *(cont'd)* . . . just 'swipe left'.

She looks down at JAI*'s dead body as the blood pools around his head.* VICKY *smiles.*

THE END

Episode 5

3 BY 3

CAST LIST

HIMSELF – Lee Mack

MAISIE – Tiajna Amayo

GAVIN – James Bailey

SHINDU – Kiran L. Dadlani

ENID – Mary Keegan

MARGARET – Gemma Page

BELLA – Ronay Poole

NIALL – James Rastall

STEPHEN – James Tucker

CATHERINE – Saskia Wakefield

INT. TV STUDIO. DAY.

A studio set for 3 By 3, *a TV quiz show.*

Three podiums, each for a team of three players, are in the centre of the set, with a host's podium to one side. Each team's podium has a scoreboard showing how much money they have won. A large screen behind the host bears the logo of the show, '3 By 3'.

A studio audience can be heard, with laughter and applause.

Punchy music and graphics introduce the show, and the host, LEE MACK, *addresses the TV audience.*

LEE *(reading autocue)* Hello, I'm Lee Mack, and welcome to *3 By 3*, the brand-new quiz show that gives three teams of three people three chances to win a big money prize. Well, I say 'big money' – this *is* the BBC. In fact, if the set doesn't fall over, we'll be happy! Anyway, let's crack on and meet tonight's teams. Threesome one, will you introduce each other, please?

We cut to Team One, ENID, NIALL *and* SHINDU, *who introduce each other along the row.*

ENID This is Niall. He lives in Knutsford, and he works in financial services.

NIALL This is Shindu. She's a software consultant, and she's from Chester.

SHINDU And this is Enid, who lives in Huntington. She's a retired teacher.

LEE So, Niall, it's not often you hear this phrase on BBC quiz shows, but what makes you a threesome?

NIALL We are members of Sing-Along-a-Chester, which is a come-and-sing choir formed in lockdown, and we just carried it on.

LEE It's a what choir?

NIALL Come-and-sing choir.

LEE Oh, a come-and-sing choir. I genuinely thought that was a Welsh word I'd never heard of. A come-and-sing choir. OK, great. And . . . Enid. Retired teacher.

ENID Yes.

LEE What did you teach?

ENID Oh, well, I taught in a junior school, so I taught everything, really.

LEE You're supposed to say 'kids', because it always gets a laugh.

ENID *(laughing)* Oh, right.

LEE Yeah. So, what do you teach?

ENID Kids.

LEE That was my joke. Shindu, you're a software consultant?

SHINDU Yes, I'm currently working for an engineering technology company, looking after the company system to make sure we are delivering things correctly.

LEE Great stuff – and so, do you have a team name?

NIALL Yes. We'd like to be known as The Three Tenors.

Their team name, 'Tenors', appears on their podium.

LEE Well let's hope you manage to win more than that tonight. The Three Tenors!

Applause.

LEE Threesome number two, will you introduce each other, please?

Team Two, STEPHEN, MARGARET *and* CATHERINE, *introduce each other.*

STEPHEN This is my wife, Margaret. She's an clinical trial manager, and she makes the best fruit scones in Letchworth.

MARGARET This is my daughter Catherine, and she's about to start an online master's degree in applied neuroscience.

CATHERINE This is my father Stephen, and he likes cricket.

LEE Alright, so a family team. OK, Stephen, the cricket fan. Who do you follow?

STEPHEN I quite like Nottingham.

LEE OK. You obviously sound like a devoted fan . . . Is it just the three of you at home?

STEPHEN No, Catherine's great-grandmother will be at home watching this.

LEE Ah! And what's her name?

STEPHEN Rosemary.

LEE Rosemary. *(To camera)* Hello Rosemary, how are you? I've always got *thyme* for you. *(To* STEPHEN*)* It's a herb gag.

He turns to MARGARET.

LEE And Margaret – clinical trials manager. I feel clever just saying it.

MARGARET It's basically research and development of new medical protocols, controlled experiments – but we like to have fun as well, doing quizzes and board games and things like that.

LEE Always a bit of a worry when you find out scientists are at work playing Buckaroo. And Catherine, an online degree? That must be tricky. I know students find it hard to get out of bed at the best of times!

CATHERINE Yes, but I get a lot of help from Dad and Mum.

LEE Sounds like my parents when I was a kid. Apart from the online bit. And the degree bit. And the help bit. Actually, sounds nothing like my parents. Margaret, what's your team name?

MARGARET We'd like to be known as The Oakwoods.

The team name 'Oakwoods' appears on their podium.

LEE The Oakwoods, let's hear it for them!

Applause.

LEE *(cont'd)* And our final threesome of the evening – blimey, sounds like a very busy swingers' party. Will you introduce each other, please.

Team Three introduce each other: BELLA, GAVIN *and* MAISIE.

BELLA This is Gavin, and he works for a recruitment company in Farnham.

GAVIN This is Maisie, and she works for a recruitment company in Farnham.

MAISIE And this is Bella, and she works for a recruitment company in Farnham.

LEE Right, I see. And how do you all know each other? . . . I'm actually going to guess that you're flatmates. I don't know why. You all look about the same age.

GAVIN No – well, we have been. So, Bella and I used to be together – we used to be in a relationship. But we are no longer–

LEE I genuinely asked you for light entertainment reasons. Now I feel like I've opened a huge can of worms. I'm so sorry.

They all laugh.

GAVIN Now, to add awkwardness to this, Maisie and I are now together. But we're all–

LEE Oh, you're now with Maisie?

GAVIN Yes, we live together now.

LEE Bella, if you could at some point go out with Maisie, that would wrap everything up perfectly.

BELLA *laughs.*

LEE Well, that's nicely awkward on national television.

Laughter.

LEE Bella, what do you like doing in your spare time?

BELLA Um, Gavin enjoys this as well, actually. We go LARPing.

LEE LARPing?

BELLA Live action role-playing.

LEE The *Dungeons and Dragons*-type thing?

BELLA You can do *Dungeons and Dragons.* We–

LEE I can't, I'm afraid.

BELLA You could.

LEE No, because I'm happily married.

Laughter.

LEE Gavin, what does your character do? What's his personality?

GAVIN He's a knight, so he's very chivalrous. And I've got a big, long sword that–

LEE You don't have to tell Bella or Maisie that!

Laughter.

LEE *(cont'd)* Maisie, could you suggest a character for me?

MAISIE You could be, like, an elf or something.

LEE How dare you! Is an elf a real thing in your world?

MAISIE Yeah, in certain worlds. Yeah, you can be an elf.

LEE Do you speak English?

MAISIE Elven . . . is it?

BELLA Elvish.

LEE Elvish! *(Does an impression of Elvis's voice)* I'm a big fan of his early work. *(To* GAVIN*)* Gavin, have you got a team name for us, please? In English!

GAVIN We'd like to be known as Quiztopher Bigwins.

Their team name 'Bigwins' appears on the podium.

LEE Best of luck to you, Quiztopher Bigwins!

Applause. LEE *addresses the TV audience.*

LEE So, those are our gleesome threesomes. Let's see how they get on with round one: '3's a Crowd'!

Music sting and graphic wipe for the round '3's a Crowd'.

LEE Now, because I'm in a generous mood, I'm going to start off by giving each team £300 . . .

We see each team has £300 on their podium.

LEE *(cont'd)* In the first part of this round, they'll each be playing as individuals. Get a question right, and we'll add another a hundred to their kitty; however, get it wrong, and they'll lose a hundred and be frozen out of the game. Their teammates will then have to choose whether to buy them back using their hard-won cash, or send them home with their tail between their legs. So, let's play *3 By 3*!

Music and lighting change as the round begins.

QUESTION CARDS: LEE *asks each contestant a question, reading from question cards. The dialogue below is the template, but will vary from take to take depending on how* LEE *leads the chat.*

LEE Starting with The Three Tenors. Enid, the good news is, it's a music question for you: who was the first act to win the Eurovision Song Contest for the UK? Any ideas?

ENID Yes, it's either Cliff Richards or Sandie Shaw. I'm going to say Sandie Shaw.

LEE Is the right answer – that's £100!

The Tenors' podium shows £400.

LEE *(cont'd)* 'Puppet on a String' in 1967. Niall, a question for you on Greek mythology – do you know much about that?

NIALL No!

LEE Me neither; it's my Achilles elbow. Who was the ancient Greek god of the sea?

NIALL Ah, we have a fish and chip shop near me called this. It's Poseidon.

LEE Correct! Thank God you didn't say Harry Ramsden! That's another £100.

The Tenors' podium shows £500.

LEE *(cont'd)* And last but not least, for a full house, Shindu: on what continent would you find the world's largest desert?

SHINDU *thinks.*

LEE *(cont'd)* On what continent would you find the world's largest desert? OK, I need an answer, Shindu . . .

SHINDU Africa?

LEE No, the answer is Antarctica! So you lose a hundred pounds, and you are frozen out of the game . . .

SHINDU*'s light goes out, and the team's prize pot goes down to £400.*

LEE Hold tight for now, Shindu, and we'll see if your teammates want to buy you back.

LEE *turns to the OAKWOODS.*

LEE The Oakwood family! Who came up with that imaginative team name?

MARGARET No, it wasn't.

LEE It was you, was it Margaret?

MARGARET No, we wracked our brains, but we just couldn't think of anything else.

LEE Well, don't worry; my parents had nine months, and all they could come up with was Lee. Think you can improve on the Tenors' score, Stephen?

STEPHEN I hope so, yes.

LEE Let's see how you get on. Question for you on geography. What is the smallest US state by area? . . . Margaret knows it, look. Do you know, Catherine?

CATHERINE *nods.*

LEE *(cont'd)* Stephen, your wife and daughter know, but do you? Smallest state in the US.

STEPHEN *shakes his head.*

STEPHEN No . . . Hawaii?

LEE I'm sorry, it's Rhode Island. You lose a hundred, and you're frozen.

The Oakwoods' kitty goes down to £200, and STEPHEN*'s light goes out.*

LEE Is that what you thought, Margaret?

MARGARET Yes.

LEE Unlucky. Let's see how you get on with your question on football. Ooh, she doesn't like that. Who was captain of the England team who lifted the Jules Rimet trophy in 1966?

MARGARET Bobby Charlton. Moore! Bobby Moore!

LEE It *is* Bobby Moore, but I'm afraid I have to take your first answer. Sorry, Margaret – you lose a hundred from your kitty and you're also frozen.

The kitty goes down to £100, and MARGARET*'s light goes out.*

LEE Catherine! It's all down to you to you keep your family in the game: the mighty Oakwoods. Are you ready?

CATHERINE Yes.

LEE What is the only Shakespeare play with an animal in the title? Fan of Shakespeare?

CATHERINE Not really.

LEE I don't suppose he comes up much in a science degree, does he? Apart from 'Much Ado About Photosynthesis.'

CATHERINE *is thinking, and doesn't laugh.*

LEE *(cont'd)* Nothing from Catherine on that one. What is the only Shakespeare play with an animal in the title?

CATHERINE *The Taming of the Shrew.*

LEE Is the right answer!

The Oakwoods kitty changes to £200.

LEE *(cont'd)* Phew. Well done, Catherine, you've kept yourselves in the game – just. But you have two players frozen and only £200 in your kitty.

He turns to the final team.

LEE Quiztopher Bigwins, your turn. Starting with Bella, question on movies: who directed the Oscar-winning film *Slumdog Millionaire*?

BELLA Oh, yes . . . Danny Boyle.

LEE Straight in there, and there's an extra £100 in your kitty!

Their kitty shows £400.

LEE Gavin let's see if you can match that: which London Underground line is represented by the colour green on the tube map?

GAVIN We used to live in London for a while, so I think that's the District line.

LEE That it is, well done . . .

They now have a kitty of £500.

LEE *(cont'd)* You're on £500 now, and no freezes – Biggins would be very proud. Let's all take a moment to imagine Biggins standing proud. Finally, Maisie: a history question for you. Who was the first monarch to live in Buckingham Palace?

MAISIE *frowns.*

LEE *(cont'd)* The first monarch to live in Buckingham Palace? I need an answer.

MAISIE I'm going to have a guess . . . Queen Victoria?

LEE Is the right answer, for another £100.

Their kitty goes up to £600. GAVIN *congratulates* MAISIE.

LEE *(cont'd)* What a good guess. So, at the midway point of round one, we have The Three Tenors on £400, The Oakwoods on £200, and the current leaders Quiztopher Bigwins on a maximum £600.

Studio applause. LEE *addresses the audience.*

LEE So, now the Tenors and Oakwoods have a decision to make. In the quick-fire round, they can win a hundred for each correct answer, so more players could mean more pounds. However, if they want to buy a player back, it will cost them and we will take 'a ton' from their kitty. *(To* ENID*)* That's £100, Enid. I'm down with all the street slang, me. So Tenors, what do you want to do? Is Shindu worth a ton? Look at that face – she's got to be, hasn't she?

NIALL We all agreed before the game if we were one person down, we'd definitely buy them back – so yes please.

LEE That's what we like to hear. All singing from the same hymn sheet. So Shindu, you are back in the game.

The Tenors' kitty screen goes down to £300. SHINDU*'s light comes back on.*

LEE Now, Oakwoods. The burden is on you, Catherine. You can bring back Mum or Dad – or both, if you wish, but that would wipe out your kitty. Sounds like something my vet said, but that's a sadder story. What's it to be?

CATHERINE Um, I'd like to unfreeze . . . Mum.

The Oakwoods' kitty goes down to £100. MARGARET*'s light comes back on.*

LEE Well done, Margaret, you're all thawed out and back in the game. Does that feel good?

MARGARET It does.

LEE So, what do we do about Stephen?

CATHERINE *looks to her mum.*

CATHERINE What do you think?

MARGARET Well, you know what I think.

LEE *raises his eyebrows. The audience laugh.*

LEE Say what you mean, Margaret!

MARGARET It puts us a long way behind. Do you think we could do it between us?

LEE Just to remind you, if Stephen isn't bought back, that is him out of the game for good.

CATHERINE *looks to her dad. He smiles.*

STEPHEN It's alright, Cathy. I don't mind.

LEE Are we saying goodbye to Dad, Catherine?

CATHERINE Yes.

LEE Aw, so sorry about that, Stephen! You've been bowled a googly and sent back to the pavilion, I'm afraid! Have you enjoyed it?

STEPHEN I've loved it, yes.

LEE Well, hopefully your sacrifice will mean your family can carry on and get through to the next round. Let's hear it for Stephen, everyone!

The audience clap. LEE *addresses the audience.*

LEE Quiztopher Bigwins still have a full house, so they're looking strong as we begin the quick-fire questions. Our teams have 60 seconds: they'll win £100 for a correct answer, but they lose £100 if they're wrong. The team with the least amount of money at the end of this round will be going home. Fingers on buzzers, here we go. Your time starts: now.

The lights change for dramatic effect. Tenors £300, Oakwoods £100, Bigwins £600.

LEE What is the name of the snowman voiced by Josh Gad in the animated film *Frozen*?

The Oakwoods buzz.

LEE Oakwoods?

CATHERINE Olaf.

LEE Correct.

The Tenors are on £300, Oakwoods £200, Bigwins £600.

LEE A pink ball is worth how many points in snooker?

The Tenors buzz.

LEE Tenors?

NIALL Six.

LEE Correct.

The Tenors are on £400, Oakwoods £200, Bigwins £600.

LEE Who was the longest-serving 20th-century prime minister?

The Oakwoods buzz.

LEE Oakwoods?

MARGARET Winston Churchill.

LEE Incorrect.

The Tenors are on £400, Oakwoods £100, Bigwins £600. SHINDU *buzzes in.*

LEE Tenors?

SHINDU Margaret Thatcher.

LEE Correct.

The Tenors are on £500, Oakwoods £100, Bigwins £600.

LEE In which year did George Orwell write *1984*?

Bigwins buzz.

LEE Bigwins?

GAVIN 1948.

LEE Correct.

The Tenors are on £500, Oakwoods £100, Bigwins £700.

LEE Which element in the periodic table has the abbreviation 'Fe'?

The Oakwoods buzz.

LEE Oakwoods?

CATHERINE Iron.

LEE Correct.

The Tenors are on £500, Oakwoods £200, Bigwins £700.

LEE In *The Teletubbies*, what colour is Dipsy?

Bigwins buzz.

LEE Bigwins?

GAVIN Green.

LEE Correct.

The Tenors are on £500, Oakwoods £200, Bigwins £800.

LEE In the *Harry Potter* books, how many players make up a Quidditch team?

Bigwins buzz.

LEE Bigwins?

GAVIN and MAISIE *(simultaneously)* Seven.

LEE Correct.

The Tenors are on £500, Oakwoods £200, Bigwins £900.

LEE Which planet has moons called Io and Europa?

Bigwins buzz.

LEE Bigwins?

GAVIN Saturn.

LEE Incorrect.

The Oakwoods buzz.

LEE Oakwoods?

CATHERINE Jupiter.

LEE Correct.

The Tenors are on £500, Oakwoods £300, Bigwins £800.

LEE Which Roald Dahl heroine has the surname Wormwood?

We see the Bigwins team trying to buzz, but frustrated that their buzzers seem to not be working fast enough. The Oakwoods buzz.

LEE Oakwoods?

CATHERINE Matilda.

LEE Correct.

The Tenors are on £500, Oakwoods £400, Bigwins £800.

LEE Who was the self-appointed–

The Oakwoods buzz.

LEE Oakwoods?

CATHERINE Matthew Hopkins.

LEE Witchfinder General, correct.

The Tenors are on £500, Oakwoods £500, Bigwins £800.

LEE Which TV family lives at 742 Evergreen Terrace in–

The Oakwoods buzz.

LEE Oakwoods?

CATHERINE The Simpsons.

LEE Correct!

The Tenors are on £500, Oakwoods £600, Bigwins £800.

The time runs out, and the lights change for the end of the round. Applause.

LEE That's it, your time is up. So looking at the scores at the end of the quick-fire round, we have The Three Tenors on £500, The Oakwoods on £600 and Quiztopher Bigwins on £800! *(To* CATHERINE*)* Catherine, a strong finish for you there. You've finally woken up, have you?

CATHERINE I've been practising.

LEE Practising? How do you practise general knowledge? Have you learned the whole internet?

CATHERINE Pretty much, yes.

LEE Maisie, what do you think - you've got a game on your hands, haven't you?

MAISIE Definitely.

GAVIN I think our buzzer wasn't working.

LEE Give it a try.

GAVIN *buzzes.* LEE *looks wryly on.*

LEE It seems to be working now. Blimey, some poor props man was almost collecting his P45 there!

LEE *turns to The Three Tenors.*

LEE Three Tenors, I'm so sorry, but we have to lose you. Have you enjoyed it, Enid?

ENID Yes, we've had a wonderful time - and best of luck to the other teams.

LEE But you go back to Cheshire with £500. Niall, what are you going to do with the money?

NIALL Well, every now and again, we sing at an old folks' home round the corner from where Enid lives. And we thought that we would like to make them a CD of some of their favourite songs that we sing for them.

LEE Well, that's a lovely thing to do. And you've been great sports. Best of luck with your choir, and thanks for playing *3 By 3*!

Applause.

LEE So now we move to the second round, '3 Point Turn'.

Music and a graphic wipe for '3 Point Turn'. When we return, there are just two podiums, and The Three Tenors have departed.

The large screen shows a three-by-three grid, each square with a question category on it. From top left, the categories are Bat, Donkey, Monkey, Dog, Zebra, Octopus, Eagle, Lion and Snake. LEE *addresses the audience.*

LEE Our remaining teams have a three-by-three grid with a total of nine categories. Get a question right and they turn that square; make a line of three horizontally, vertically or diagonally, and they've won the round, and they're through to the big-money final.

It's basically just noughts and crosses. Someone got paid for coming up with this. In this round, there's £300 for a correct answer, but they lose £100 if they get a question wrong – and the other team gets the chance to steal. Let's play *3 By 3*!

Music and lighting change as the round begins.

LEE Quiztopher Bigwins, you have the biggest kitty, so you get to go first. What's tickling your fancy up there?

BELLA Zebra, please.

LEE OK, your question on zebras for that all-important middle square. Ha! Which member of the Beatles went first across the zebra crossing on the famous *Abbey Road* album cover?

The team start to think.

MAISIE Oh, I know this . . . They're all in a line . . .

LEE That's a good start. You've got a choice of four. I'll give you a clue: it wasn't H from Steps. Oakwoods, get ready to steal if they get it wrong.

CATHERINE *is thinking.* MARGARET *looks composed.*

BELLA I don't think Paul was at the front, I think he was in the middle . . .

GAVIN Wasn't one of them barefoot?

LEE Hang on, what's that got to do with anything?

GAVIN Process of elimination.

BELLA What are we going to say? I think it's either George or John . . . Erm, maybe George?

MAISIE I think it's John.

LEE I need an answer.

GAVIN OK, I'll go with Maisie and say John.

LEE Let's see, is it right or wrong? Give us the three-point turn . . .

The middle square turns three times, ending with a picture of Christopher Biggins' face and a 'correct' ping sound.

The Oakwoods are £600, Bigwins £1,100.

LEE Correct! And there's the lovely Biggins. The last time I saw him, he was eating a kangaroo's testicle. It wasn't in the jungle – he's just a very odd man. *(To the Oakwoods)* Oakwoods, you've lost control of the centre. Which category would you like?

MARGARET What do you think?

CATHERINE I can't tell.

MARGARET We'll take Bat.

'Bat' is the top left square.

LEE Bat. Oh, you're not going to like this. Question about cricket.

MARGARET *smiles and shakes her head.* LEE *shouts into the wings.*

LEE Stephen, are you still there? Come back, we need you. *(To* CATHERINE*)* You know much about cricket, Catherine?

CATHERINE Not really.

LEE Well let's hear the question – you never know. Who was the first player to score 10,000 runs in Test cricket. The first player to score 10,000 runs in Test cricket. What are you thinking?

CATHERINE That I wish I'd picked Dad. I don't know any cricket players.

MARGARET We just need to put our minds together. All I know is Tiger Woods.

MARGARET *looks to* CATHERINE.

LEE I need to hurry you.

MARGARET Catherine?

CATHERINE Sunil Gavaskar.

LEE Sunil Gavaskar. Let's see if you're right – give us the three-point turn.

The square turns to reveal an oak tree. The Oakwoods have £900, Bigwins £1,100.

LEE Correct! Sunil Gavaskar of India! Fantastic. Bet you're glad you didn't go for Tiger Woods! He's a *golfer*, Margaret. So, Quiztopher Bigwins, where do you want to go next?

GAVIN Erm . . . I think we'll go with Donkey, because I have a feeling I know what the question will be.

'Donkey' is the top middle square.

LEE 'Donkey' to block the Oakwoods and give yourselves the chance to form a line down the middle. So, here's the question: who provided the voice for the character of Donkey in the 2001 film *Shrek*? Is that what you thought it would be, Gavin?

GAVIN Yes, and I knew it – but it's just gone out of my head now.

LEE Well that's unfortunate, isn't it?! Bella, Maisie, any idea?

MAISIE I was only born in 2001, so . . .

LEE What?! You were born in 2001? My toothbrush is older than that.

BELLA I think it's the same guy that did *The Nutty Professor* or something like that.

GAVIN I keep seeing an image of David Jason, so there must be a connection there . . .

BELLA No, I think . . . I think it was an American.

LEE I've got to hurry you . . .

GAVIN I can't get David Jason out of my head.

MAISIE Well, if that's your instinct, then go for that – because you thought you knew it.

GAVIN Yes . . . OK, we'll say David Jason.

LEE David Jason. Was David Jason the voice of Donkey in *Shrek*? Give us the three-point turn.

The square turns three times and turns red with an 'incorrect' sound. The Oakwoods have £900, Bigwins £1,000.

LEE No, he wasn't! You lose £100, and the Oakwoods have a chance to steal.

MARGARET Catherine knows it.

CATHERINE Eddie Murphy.

LEE Eddie Murphy. Let's see if you're right – give us the three-point turn.

The square turns three times, and shows a picture of an oak tree with a 'correct' sound. The Oakwoods have £1,200, Bigwins £1,000.

LEE It is Eddie Murphy, you steal the square. You were right, Bella,

Eddie Murphy was in *The Nutty Professor* also; your teammates should have listened to you.

MAISIE *and* GAVIN *share a look.*

LEE So now, Oakwoods, Margaret and Catherine, where do you want to go next? I think I know the answer already . . .

MARGARET We'll go for Monkey please.

'Monkey' is top right.

LEE Monkey, to win the round and go through to the big-money final. Good luck to you. A question on music. The Arctic Monkeys had a number-one hit with their first-ever single – what was it called?

MARGARET *frowns. The Quiztopher Bigwins team whisper to each other:* MAISIE *knows it.*

MARGARET This is more your cup of tea, Catherine.

LEE You don't like the Arctic Monkeys, Margaret?

MARGARET No. Sounds like a research project I was once involved in. Erm . . . What do you think, darling?

CATHERINE I'm not sure.

LEE You a music fan?

CATHERINE We're not really allowed to have music at home.

MARGARET We're more of a Radio 4 house.

LEE Quiztopher Bigwins is chomping at the bit for this one – get ready to steal . . .

MARGARET Just say what comes into your head.

CATHERINE I don't actually know it.

MARGARET *just stares at* CATHERINE *for a long time.*

LEE I need an answer.

CATHERINE 'I Bet You Look Good on the Dancefloor.'

LEE Thank you very much. Oh, that's your answer, is it? Let's see if you're right – give us the three-point turn . . .

The square turns three times, but doesn't stop. It turns three more times. Laughter.

LEE Oop, what's going on here, then? This is a nine-point turn. Don't worry, they'll cut this out in the edit.

More laughter.

LEE Oh, it got a laugh – keep it in. And *that* got a laugh – keep that in as well.

Finally, the square lights up with an oak tree and flashes for a three in a row.

Applause.

The Oakwoods have £1,500, Bigwins £1,000.

LEE It's the right answer! Catherine, you've done it again! Oakwoods, you are through to the final round, congratulations!

MARGARET *nods at* CATHERINE *and half-hugs her.*

LEE Quiztopher Bigwins, you've been great contestants. It was so close on that final round, wasn't it?

BELLA Yes, but the best team won in the end.

LEE Gavin, I bet you're kicking yourself about David Jason, aren't you?

GAVIN Yep, I honestly don't know where that came from. I knew it was Eddie Murphy, but . . .

LEE Well, it's hard with the cameras and the studio lights. But look, you've managed to build up quite a nice kitty, you've got an amazing £1,000. Maisie, what are you going to spend it on?

MAISIE Well, Gavin and I fancied going to the Isle of Wight Festival next year, so this'll hopefully pay for that.

LEE I'm sure it will – and I'm sure there'll be enough left over for a new jerkin for you, Bella. Thanks for playing, and give my best to Farnham, won't you? Quiztopher Bigwins, everyone!

The team depart to applause.

LEE So! Catherine and Margaret, mother and daughter from Letchworth, currently have a very healthy-looking kitty of £1,500. But we want to give you more than that. Is there a particular amount you'd love to go home with today?

MARGARET No, I don't think so, is there? It's just been the experience, really.

LEE Fantastic stuff. Well let's see what happens in the final round: '3 Blind Twice'.

Graphic of the final round, '3 Blind Twice'. When we come back, there has been a small scene change, and there is now a soundproof booth onstage and one podium. LEE *addresses the audience.*

LEE So, here's how it works. The Oakwoods have the choice to play three final questions, where a correct answer will treble their kitty, but a wrong answer will see it drop back down to £1,500. For this round, there's no conferring, and I'll be putting one of them into the soundproof booth. To win the cash, they both need to give me matching correct answers. *(To the contestants)* So, who wants to be locked up? Catherine?

CATHERINE *shakes her head.*

MARGARET I will.

LEE Very good. Let's pop you inside, then.

MARGARET *sits inside the booth and then* LEE *closes the door.*

LEE Right, hopefully you can hear me now, can you?

MARGARET Yes, I can hear you.

LEE And when we switch the sound off . . .

A lighting change inside the booth.

LEE *(cont'd)* Margaret, do you want a double gin and tonic?

No response.

LEE She definitely can't hear anything. So, Catherine, anything you want to get off your chest while Mum can't hear?

CATHERINE *looks unsure.*

CATHERINE Erm . . .

LEE Oooh, she's thinking about it, look! Brilliant. Right, let's bring the sound back up, and I'll explain the rules of '3 Blind Twice'. I'll ask a question, then I'll come to you first, Catherine, then to you, Margaret, and both of you must be correct in order to progress. So, here we go with question one – good luck. Let's play *3 By 3.*

Heartbeat/tension music begins. We occasionally use split-screen here to see both CATHERINE *and* MARGARET.

LEE For £4,500 . . . What is the longest river in Europe? The longest river in Europe. Turn Margaret's booth off, please.

The booth turns to silent mode.

LEE *(cont'd)* So, Catherine. Geography question – how is that for you? Have you seen much of Europe?

CATHERINE No. I haven't really been anywhere.

LEE So, longest river – tricky one, that. Do you have an answer for me?

CATHERINE Yes.

LEE What is it?

CATHERINE The Volga.

LEE The Volga. Let's see if Mum agrees, and if it's right.

The light on the booth comes up.

LEE Margaret, you still with us?

MARGARET Yes.

LEE Mother and daughter, so you're obviously very close, but are you on the same wavelength?

MARGARET I knew this one, anyway. It's the Volga.

LEE OK. So for £4,500, they both think the Volga River is the longest in Europe – is that correct?

The lozenge caption below their names shows two green ticks under each name. Applause.

The Oakwoods have £4,500.

LEE It is! Congratulations, you were both right, so now you have a choice.

You can leave with your £4,500, or you can get your second question and treble your money again, to £13,500.

MARGARET I think we'll play on.

LEE Catherine, Mum seems pretty definite – are you happy with that decision?

CATHERINE I just have to go with what she says, really.

LEE Ooh dear, is everything alright at home? You don't need me to call Esther Rantzen or anything?

MARGARET *smiles thinly.*

CATHERINE We'll play on.

LEE They're playing on, very brave.

Applause.

LEE For £13,500. Which influencer was the first person to reach 100 million followers on social media app TikTok? I'll give you a clue: it's not H from Steps. Turn Margaret's booth off, please.

The booth light changes to silent mode. Tension music plays.

LEE Catherine. I don't even know what an influencer is, do you?

CATHERINE Charli D'Amelio.

LEE OK, no messing about, you're giving me the answer Charli D'Amelio. Do you follow her on TikTok?

CATHERINE No. I thought it was a boy.

LEE Now, do you think this is something your mum will know?

CATHERINE I doubt it.

LEE Let's switch her back on and see, shall we? . . . Margaret, can you hear me?

MARGARET Yes, I can.

LEE Are you ready?

MARGARET As I'll ever be.

LEE What's your answer?

MARGARET Well, I know TikTok is a thing, because I've heard the girls in my lab talking about it.

LEE What are you thinking?

We see MARGARET *thinking intensely and* CATHERINE *staring at her.*

MARGARET All I'm seeing is an image of David Jason . . .

LEE Oh, not him again!

MARGARET I know that's not right. Don't know why I should be thinking of him.

MARGARET *thinks hard.* CATHERINE *seems to be straining too. There's an intensity between them.*

MARGARET I'm just getting a mental block for some reason . . .

CATHERINE*'s nose starts to bleed slightly, and she wipes it away.* CATHERINE *seems to relinquish her thoughts.*

MARGARET Ah, yes, it's come to me. I think it's Charli D'Amelio.

LEE Charli D'Amelio – that's what Catherine said. We have two matching answers, but are they right answers?

The lozenge caption shows green ticks under each name. The kitty is now £13,500.

LEE They are! What a result! Mother and daughter both coming up with the goods for a whopping £13,500!

Applause.

LEE *(cont'd)* I need a lie down after that. Now, the final question is worth an incredible £40,500. What would you do with that, Catherine? That's a hell of a lot, isn't it?

CATHERINE I'd like to go travelling, see the world. New Zealand, maybe. I'd like to do the Hobbit tour.

LEE New Zealand, sounds brilliant! Margaret, what about you?

MARGARET Well, we had talked about digging out our basement at home. Catherine's going to need a place to practise and pursue her studies, so that would be a nice gift to be able to give her.

CATHERINE *doesn't look too happy about this.*

LEE Well, who knows? Maybe you could do both. As you've reached the final question, if only one of you is right, you'll still win your original kitty of £1,500, but if both of you are wrong, you go away with nothing. I hardly dare even ask you: do you want to take home your kitty now, or do you want to gamble?

CATHERINE OK, let's gamble.

MARGARET *smiles and nods.*

MARGARET Yes.

LEE They're going to gamble!

The audience applaud.

LEE Right, the very best of luck to both of you. Deep breaths. For £40,500. Tracy Lauren Marrow is better known as which US rapper? I'll give you that again: Tracy Lauren Marrow is better known as which US rapper? Turn the booth off, please.

The booth is turned to silent mode.

LEE Now, personally, I wouldn't have a clue. You said earlier you're not a big musical house. Is that ringing any bells for you?

CATHERINE Well, I'm thinking of the name Tracy, which could be male or female . . . But Tracy starts with a T, so I'm going to say Ice-T.

LEE Ice-T. Let's see if Margaret agrees.

The booth is turned back on.

LEE Margaret, can you hear me?

MARGARET I can.

LEE Tracy Lauren Marrow is better known as which US rapper?

Heartbeat music. MARGARET *is thinking and* CATHERINE *is staring. A tense moment.*

MARGARET Fur Q.

LEE I'm sorry?

MARGARET I think the answer is Fur Q, F-U-R-Q. Final answer.

LEE Fur Q. Well, I have to tell you now that Catherine gave me a different answer, so I'm afraid you won't be taking home the jackpot tonight.

The audience groan. The kitty shows £1,500.

LEE *(cont'd)* But for £1,500, did either of them get it right?

The lozenge caption shows a green tick on CATHERINE*'s side and a red cross on* MARGARET*'s side.*

LEE There we go, the answer is Ice-T, Margaret!

MARGARET *(to* CATHERINE*)* And you knew that, did you?

CATHERINE *nods.*

LEE But all's not lost; you're still going away with a fantastic £1,500. That could get you to New Zealand, couldn't it, Catherine?

CATHERINE One way, maybe.

MARGARET *(to herself)* Over my dead body.

LEE *moves to his spot at the front of the set.*

LEE Come and join me ladies . . .

Applause. MARGARET *starts to open the door to the booth. Suddenly, the handle flies out of* MARGARET*'s hand, and the door slams closed.*

MARGARET Catherine, open this door.

CATHERINE *stands her ground, concentrating hard.*

MARGARET *(cont'd)* Open it!

LEE Well, that's all we've got time for this week on *3 By 3*. Thanks to all our fantastic threesomes. Catherine, come and join me . . .

CATHERINE *is still concentrating hard.* MARGARET *gives up trying to open the door and turns to face* CATHERINE *from the booth.*

The scoreboard and virtual background start to glitch. The three-by-three grid briefly flickers on, with images of Christopher Biggins, the oak tree and, in one square, the image of a bronze hare.

LEE Erm, sadly the Oakwood family didn't manage to win the jackpot tonight . . .

MARGARET The doctors were right; I should have destroyed you when you were bor–

BANG! MARGARET*'s head explodes in the booth. Red viscera and brains coat the Perspex.* LEE *looks utterly astonished and afraid.*
The smallest hint of a smile from CATHERINE.

THE END

Episode 6

THE LAST WEEKEND

CAST LIST

CHAS – Reece Shearsmith

JOE – Steve Pemberton

MOLLIE – Sheila Reid

with the voice of

Maggie Service

EXT. LAKESIDE. DAY.

*A car drives towards an isolated holiday home beside a lake. Lovely views, lots of nature. Two men (*JOE *and* CHAS*) get out of the car with shopping bags and a suitcase. Painted on to a rock by the driveway is the house number: 9.*

TITLE: *'The Last Weekend'.*

INT. LAKESIDE HOLIDAY HOME. DAY.

CHAS *enters and carries bags filled with food through the living room.* JOE *brings in the suitcase.*

CHAS It's back again, that musty smell. Can you not smell it?

JOE Not really.

CHAS It's because she doesn't ventilate it when we're not here.

JOE Honestly, I can't smell anything.

CHAS There's something wrong with you, then. It's like a brie farted.

CHAS *heads into the kitchen.*

CHAS *(cont'd)* And she's left the fridge closed. Frigging hell!

CHAS *puts down the shopping bags, and on one of them we now see the word 'Denial'. We hold for a moment.*

CHAS *starts loading food into the fridge.*

CHAS *(cont'd)* I said, 'Unplug the fridge and leave the door open, please.' I'm going to send her one of my snotty emails.

JOE Don't do that, you'll hurt her feelings.

CHAS I don't care, she's absolutely useless.

JOE She's eighty-two!

CHAS So? It annoys me. It's the absolute bare minimum, because she knows we're in the middle of nowhere and we don't have a choice. Oh my God, and there's ants all over the surfaces. I'm going to have to get the Dustbuster out. I can't bear it.

JOE Chas, please, we've had a long drive . . .

CHAS It's fine – you unpack, I'll clean. What's the problem?

INT. BEDROOM. DAY.

JOE *takes the case into the bedroom, plops it on to the double bed and starts to unpack clothes and toiletries.*

We can hear the sound of the Dustbuster from the kitchen.

CHAS *(O.S.)* And I told her to plant some lavender round the back to keep the mozzies away; I bet she's not done that, either.

JOE *goes to the window and looks out at the view. He seems lost in thought.*

CHAS *comes in holding a small plastic item from a board game.*

CHAS Do you know what this is from? It was behind the fridge.

JOE Dunno. Just put it in with Mouse Trap.

CHAS You want to put everything in with Mouse Trap!

JOE No I don't.

CHAS You do! It's like a whole compendium in there now. I don't know how you're meant to catch the poor thing with a bathtub, two Rummikubs and Captain Peacock.

JOE It's *Mrs* Peacock. Captain Peacock's *Are You Being Served.*

CHAS Alright, Nelly, you know what I mean.

CHAS *heads back into the living room.*

INT. LIVING ROOM. DAY.

CHAS *heads for the window blinds, and* JOE *follows.*

CHAS And I bet she hasn't dusted those blinds.

JOE Chas . . .

CHAS You've got to lower them and get the cloth between each slat . . .

JOE It's fine. Come here.

CHAS *embraces* JOE *and looks out at the view.*

JOE And *breathe.*

CHAS I love you, Joe Madison. Right, I'd better get peeling those spuds. I was going to do the moussaka tonight.

JOE Hang on, before you go. I got you something.

CHAS What? How come?

JOE I know we don't really do anniversaries, but it's been nine years.

CHAS No! That's not now, is it?

JOE Well, depends when you take it from. First date, first kiss. First . . . coupling.

CHAS *Coupling*? What are we, fucking Jane Austen characters?

JOE But I'm taking it from when I first approached you in that awful bar . . .

CHAS Awful bar, what was it called? The Pink Sock?

JOE The Purple Sock.

CHAS Purple Sock, Jesus.

JOE Anyway, I told you then we'd end up together for at least nine years and, in spite of a few . . . bumps and lumps, we made it. So here.

JOE *gives* **CHAS** *a box containing a copper bracelet.*

CHAS Aw! Isn't this what they give to old biddies with arthritis?

JOE Don't be mean. Copper's the traditional gift; I googled it.

JOE *puts the bracelet on* **CHAS***'s wrist.*

JOE *(cont'd)* Apparently, its beauty and malleability–

CHAS What-e-ability?

JOE Malleability. Symbolises the way a couple can bend to accommodate each other after nine years together.

CHAS That sounds absolutely filthy. I love it, thank you.

CHAS *kisses* **JOE**.

JOE *gathers together the toiletries and takes them to the bathroom.*

INT. BATHROOM. DAY.

JOE *puts the toiletries away.* **CHAS** *stands in the doorway, watching him.*

CHAS You know, if you stopped working, we could have more than just weekends together. I'm only thinking of you.

JOE I like working. It keeps me busy, takes my mind off things.

CHAS But don't you want to . . . make the most of every day?

JOE I love our life the way it is; I love coming home and catching up on all our news. Please don't make me change.

CHAS As if I could. I just wish we could have done more . . . Now, I do need to get going with that moussaka.

CHAS *turns to head for the kitchen.*

CHAS *(cont'd)* Hey. Here's to the next nine years.

JOE . . . Yeah.

CHAS *leaves.*

JOE *looks at the bottles of pills he's just loaded on to the shelf, including strong painkillers.*

He goes to the toilet and starts to pee.

INT. KITCHEN. DAY.

CHAS *starts to peel the potatoes. A love song plays on the radio, and* CHAS *seems sad.*

JOE*'s phone starts to ring from inside his coat pocket.*

CHAS Joe! Phone!

CHAS *goes to take* JOE*'s phone from his coat. The screen shows 'Mick', with a tongue emoji.* CHAS *thinks about answering it, but decides to replace the phone and go back to his cooking*

INT. BATHROOM. DAY.

JOE *looks down to see that there is blood in the toilet bowl. He lowers the lid.*

EXT. LAKESIDE HOLIDAY HOME. NIGHT.

Establishing shot of the holiday home at night. We can see lights on in the windows.

INT. LIVING ROOM. NIGHT.

JOE *and* CHAS *are eating their dinner.* JOE *pours some wine.*

JOE What did Mollie say?

CHAS About what?

JOE About the ants.

CHAS *(putting on a Scottish accent)* 'Och, I'm awful sorry, Mr Gregory, I do hope it hasnae spoiled your weekend.'

JOE *smiles and puts down the bottle. Close on the wine label, which reads 'Anger'.*

CHAS *(cont'd, still putting on the accent)* 'I just love cheese. I like to sprinkle a wee bit of cheese out the back to keep the ants at bay.'

JOE She actually did that once.

CHAS I know she did! No wonder it stinks. I wouldn't mind, but a big fucking family of rats came out to eat it!

JOE *smiles.*

JOE I like her. At least she makes us laugh.

CHAS Hmm, nothing's that funny. Next year I'm going to get some sturdy Polish lady in. They're half the price and twice as thorough.

JOE What about Mollie?

CHAS She'll be dead by then, surely.

JOE *looks down at his food.*

CHAS Sorry.

JOE It's fine.

CHAS I didn't think.

JOE You're allowed to say it.

JOE *puts his knife and fork on his plate.*

CHAS You've not eaten much.

JOE I'm not that hungry.

CHAS *gets up to clear the plates.*

CHAS Well, you'll be having it for lunch tomorrow, and every day after that until it's all gone. Got room for some pud?

JOE What is it?

CHAS 'Milk, milk, lemonade, round the corner chocolate's made.'

JOE Sounds delicious.

CHAS Made by my own fair hand.

CHAS *starts to wash up.* JOE *sips his wine. He seems niggled.*

JOE It's 'chocolate cake', anyway.

CHAS What is?

JOE 'Milk, milk, lemonade, round the corner, chocolate cake.'

CHAS What are you going on about?

JOE Nothing. You always say it wrong, that's all.

CHAS What do you mean, wrong? It's: 'Milk, milk, lemonade, round the corner, chocolate's made.'

JOE No. 'Milk, milk, lemonade, round the corner chocolate *cake*.'

CHAS Oh my God, he's trying to gaslight me!

CHAS *fills the kettle.* JOE *moves to the sofa.*

CHAS Do you want a herbal tea?

JOE Sure.

CHAS I think I only brought chamomile.

JOE That's fine.

JOE *is brooding. Can't let it go.*

CHAS Oh, that water pump's leaking again; you can see it's all stained down the back. We'll have to dig out that card from the guy we used last time.

JOE Hmm. You see, in my version, they're all different foodstuffs.

CHAS What are?

JOE *(pointing)* The milk comes from there, the lemonade from there and the chocolate cake from there. There's a logic to it, like you're creating a banquet with your body.

CHAS Oh, Joe, leave it, for fuck's sakes!

JOE Excuse me, you're the one who's learned the wrong rhyme.

CHAS Yeah, well your version doesn't rhyme! You can't rhyme lemonade and chocolate cake.

JOE It's called a slant rhyme; the vowel sounds match up but the consonants are different.

CHAS Alright Professor Plum, let's see. Alexa!

JOE Chas, don't do that. You know it annoys me.

CHAS Alexa, is it, 'Milk, milk, lemonade, round the corner chocolate's made' . . .

JOE It doesn't matter.

CHAS . . . or 'Milk, milk, lemonade, round the corner, chocolate cake'?

JOE *(shouting)* Alright, I said it doesn't fucking matter!

ALEXA I'm having trouble understanding you.

CHAS You're not the only one! *(To* JOE*)* Why are you picking a fight with me?

JOE I'm not; I'm just pointing out that sometimes it is possible that you are wrong.

CHAS There is no wrong! I say 'chocolate's made' and you say 'chocolate cake.' So what? An American girl at the gym says, 'Push a button, fudge is made.' They're just different versions.

JOE Alright, if you're so desperate to win every little argument, then I concede.

CHAS I'm not desperate to win, I'm just pissed off that you're having a go at me when I've done nothing wrong.

JOE I'm going to bed.

CHAS What's got into you?

JOE *(putting on a whiny voice)* 'Alexa, is it, "Milk, milk, lemonade, round the corner, chocolate's made"?'

CHAS I don't talk like that.

JOE *(still in the whiny voice)* 'Alexa, Mollie didn't close the fridge door properly.'*(in his own voice)* Well, boo fucking hoo. Is that the extent of the things you have to worry about?

CHAS I have a right to be angry, Joe.

JOE What, and I don't? You don't know what anger is, true fucking anger that drives you absolutely insane. You have no idea!

CHAS Of course I do, you stupid fucking idiot. Do you not think I'm angry at the life I've missed out on the past nine years? The work I could have done, the holidays I could have been on, the men I could have shagged! I've dropped everything, ground my whole life into this tiny space so I can look after you and be there for you. So don't tell me I don't have a right to be pissed off, because I do!

JOE I didn't ask you to, did I? I didn't ask you to throw your whole life away looking after me. You wanted to!

CHAS And I still want to! And if you think I'm going to walk away and leave you now because you're picking a fight with me, then you're wrong, Joe. I'm here till the bitter end, sorry.

JOE *hangs his head.* CHAS *embraces him.*

CHAS *(cont'd)* Anyway, I'm not pissed off at you, I'm pissed at that . . . *thing* inside you. The bloody . . . chocolate cake.

JOE *laughs.*

JOE I've never heard it called that before.

CHAS Why don't you go to bed, let me clean up.

JOE OK.

CHAS I love you.

JOE *leaves.* CHAS *goes to get the plate from the table, and spots* JOE*'s phone. He looks round to check he's not being watched, then picks up the phone and sees it has a pattern lock.*

He tries drawing a letter 'C' to open the phone, but it doesn't work.

CHAS It's not 'C' for Chas, then.

He then tries a letter 'M', and the phone opens.

Scared of what he might find, he puts the phone down and takes the plate to the sink.

EXT. LAKESIDE. DAY.

Establishing shot of the house and the lake. Clouds of midges hover. We can hear laughter and voices from inside.

CHAS *(O.S.)* Don't give in to him, Mollie! Don't!

INT. LIVING ROOM. DAY.

CHAS *and* JOE *are playing Monopoly with their elderly housekeeper* MOLLIE.

MOLLIE Hold your wheesht, man! So, I will take Piccadilly and Marylebone Station . . .

CHAS He's just going to put hotels on; look how much cash he's got!

JOE Let her speak!

MOLLIE And on top of that, I want £500.

JOE Deal.

They shake hands and exchange the cards.

We see other boxes of games on the sideboard, one of which is titled Bargaining.

CHAS Oh that's it, then – game over!

JOE What are you moaning about? You've still got your greens.

CHAS The greens are shit, no one ever lands on the greens.

MOLLIE Well, I did two turns ago, but you never noticed.

CHAS Oh my God, Mollie Grayson! What a cheat!

MOLLIE It's not cheating if you don't see it.

CHAS The silent assassin.

JOE Right, so I'm going to put two houses on all my reds, which is £900 . . .

CHAS I told you! I'm going to be better off in jail.

JOE *(to* CHAS*)* And remember you still owe me four pounds from when you landed on Vine Street.

CHAS Yes, alright, Nelly. Wait till I've got some change.

MOLLIE Why do you call him Nelly?

CHAS 'Cos he's like an elephant; he never forgets. At least I won second prize in a beauty contest – don't forget!

JOE Who came first, Shane MacGowan?

CHAS Cheeky bastard.

JOE *gets up slowly. He winces.*

CHAS You OK?

JOE Yep. Can I get you any more cheese, Mollie?

MOLLIE Oh, no thank you, I've had quite enough. I do love my cheese, though!

JOE *and* CHAS *exchange a smile.*

JOE We know you do. Right, I just need to go to the little boys' room. I may be some time.

CHAS Are you sure you're alright?

JOE Yes, you carry on. Keep an eye on that bank, Mollie, he's a cheating little so-and-so.

MOLLIE Oh, I will.

JOE *goes to the bathroom.* CHAS *shakes the die and moves.*

MOLLIE He seems in good spirits.

CHAS Yeah. We love coming here. You can leave all your troubles behind. Well, most of them.

MOLLIE *pats* CHAS*'s hand comfortingly.*

MOLLIE If you ever need to talk.

CHAS Thanks.

CHAS *picks up a Community Chest card.*

CHAS 'Doctor's fee, pay £50.' Fucking brilliant.

CHAS *pays the money.*

MOLLIE I hope you don't mind me saying, but I did hear raised voices while I was out with the doggies yesterday.

CHAS Yes, I'm sorry about that.

MOLLIE Oh, don't be sorry, dear. Anger is one of the five stages.

CHAS I think it's the one I'm stuck on. Like a really hard level on *Candy Crush*. I can't get past it.

MOLLIE I'll just nod and pretend I know what you're talking about.

CHAS I thought there were seven stages, anyway? Dopey, Grumpy, Bashful . . .

MOLLIE *chuckles.*

MOLLIE I went through it all when I lost Frazer. Someone bought me the book, *On Death and Dying* by Elisabeth Kübler-Ross.

CHAS I bet that cheered you up.

MOLLIE She actually wrote it for people who were facing up to their own end of life, but it also applies to those who are left behind. It's the same whether you're mourning the end of a relationship or the death of a pet. Not everyone feels the same things in the same order, but you can take comfort from the fact that you're not the only one to have been through it.

MOLLIE *throws the die and moves.*

CHAS Did I ever tell you that was very nearly a pop star?

MOLLIE Goodness me, no!

CHAS Yeah. It was in the late nineties; I'd been slogging away in the clubs with a boy band, Atlantic 5. We got to number 112 in the charts with 'Blue Jeans Baby'. I'm surprised you don't remember.

MOLLIE Och, if it's after Johnny Mathis, I wouldn't know it.

CHAS Anyway, we were dropped by our record label, so it all came to nothing . . . Tried to launch a solo career – classic denial. I started going online to other people's Myspace pages, where they'd posted their own music, and leaving abusive messages. 'Don't call us, we'll call you' – that type of thing. All because I was so angry at what I'd lost and what they stood to gain.

JOE *is listening in the hallway.*

CHAS *(cont'd)* I certainly felt depression – and then, after I met Joe, acceptance. But the bargaining bit . . . I never really understood it. Why I'm so crap at *Monopoly*, I suppose.

MOLLIE From what I remember, it's just a big game of 'What if?'. Either to make yourself feel better or to torture yourself.

CHAS Why torture yourself when you can pay good money to have it done to you?

MOLLIE Maybe coming here is the bargain: 'We're on holiday; we can eat and walk and play games, and death doesn't exist. Joe's cancer doesn't exist'.

CHAS So it's a bit like saying, 'I'll swap my Water Works for your Park Lane and Mayfair'?

MOLLIE You never know, miracles can happen.

JOE *appears.*

JOE I'd swap your Water Works for my water works any day.

CHAS You were listening?

JOE Alexa, please play 'Blue Jeans Baby' by Atlantic 5.

A pop song starts to play. JOE *dances to the intro.*

CHAS Oh don't, Joe, it's embarrassing.

JOE What?

CHAS Stop it!

JOE There's a whole video, Mollie, it's hilarious.

CHAS If you're going to do it, do it properly.

CHAS *gets up and does his boy band dance with* JOE. *They sing along to the track.*

CHAS and JOE *(singing)* She's my blue jeans baby / Driving me crazy / Just one step closer / My heart's a roller coaster! Blue jeans baby / Ripped-knee lady / And when she passed by, I popped my fly!

As CHAS *and* JOE *dance and sing,* MOLLIE *watches them and laughs. She surreptitiously steals £500 from the bank.*

INT. KITCHEN. DUSK.

JOE *is in the kitchen preparing food.*

JOE Do you want it serving hot or cold?

CHAS *(O.S.)* What is it?

JOE Quiche.

CHAS *(O.S.)* Hot, please. As long as the pastry doesn't go all soggy.

We see a pot of honey on the side. Its label reads 'Depression'.

JOE How's it going?

CHAS *(O.S.)* I look like I've got leprosy!

JOE Let's have a look!

CHAS *emerges from the bedroom. He wears a silk dressing gown and has a home-made face mask on. He's carrying a glass of champagne and is a bit tipsy.*

CHAS What's in it?

JOE Oatmeal, honey, baking soda and buttermilk.

CHAS Tasty. Will someone be getting their oats tonight?

JOE Maybe. Depends how hungry I am.

CHAS You know what I'd love now? A massage.

JOE Seriously?

CHAS Yes! You said it was my pamper night!

JOE Yes, I did, didn't I? Come on then, let's get you between my legs.

JOE *sits on the sofa and* CHAS *sits on the floor in front of him.* JOE *massages* CHAS*'s shoulders.*

CHAS Did Mollie get back alright?

JOE Yeah, she had to go and feed the dogs.

CHAS Do you think she ever spreads a bit of Primula on her noo-noo and lets the doggies lick it off?

JOE *slaps* CHAS*'s shoulder.*

JOE Chas! That's disgusting!

CHAS I know. I've had too much to drink.

JOE *massages.* JOE*'s phone pings with a message alert, but he ignores it.* CHAS*'s face darkens.*

CHAS Aren't you going to get that?

JOE No, it'll only be work.

CHAS *sips his drink, looks sad.*

CHAS Why are you being so nice to me?

JOE We don't know what the future holds, do we? This could be our last weekend here.

CHAS That's depressing.

JOE I don't want to be a Debbie Downer, but it's true. I just want you to know that, however hard it's been . . . I've never stopped thinking about you.

CHAS I know.

JOE Right, wait there and don't come in. I've got a surprise for you in the bathroom.

JOE *heads to the bathroom.*

CHAS Wow, you're really spoiling me! You must have a guilty conscience.

Sounds of running water from the bathroom. CHAS *sips champagne. He fondles his copper bracelet.*

CHAS Joe?

JOE *(O.S.)* Yeah?

CHAS Who's Mick? He tried calling you earlier. And yesterday. He sends you messages with kisses and aubergine emojis. I don't mind – it's just we usually tell each other when we're flirting with someone, and we laugh about it. But this Mick . . . you've never mentioned him before. Should I be worried?

JOE *comes back in, wiping his hands on a towel.*

JOE What are you saying? I couldn't hear you.

CHAS OK I'm a bit pissed, but cards on the table. I kissed a man while you were away at one of your treatment centres. He asked me to go to his place and I was tempted, really tempted, because we hadn't . . . coupled for such a long time. Years, in fact. But I stopped myself because . . . I'd made a commitment to you. And I've never wavered from that, however hard it's been. Plus, he smoked liquorice roll-ups, and that repulsed me a little bit.

JOE What are you talking about?

CHAS I'm talking about Mick.

JOE Mick? Mick's great, you'd love her.

CHAS Her?

JOE Yeah, Michaela. She's one of my Macmillan nurses, but she gave me her own number because we hit it off. Why do you ask?

CHAS *laughs.*

CHAS No reason. No reason at all. Oh my God, I've never been so happy. I couldn't bear it if . . .

JOE What?

CHAS *goes to kiss* JOE, *but he dodges away.*

JOE Get off! Now, close your eyes.

CHAS *closes his eyes, and* JOE *leads him to the bathroom.*

INT. BATHROOM. DUSK.

JOE *leads* CHAS *into the room.*

JOE Remember when you'd booked us that hot-spring spa in Iceland, and we couldn't go because I was ill? And you said you'd always dreamed of lying in hot mud with a face mask and a glass of champagne? Ta-dah!

CHAS *opens his eyes. There are lots of candles around the bathtub. The bath is filled with a dark brown mud, and rose petals are scattered on top.*

CHAS Oh my God! Joe!

JOE Go on, get in quick. It won't stay warm for long. I'll get your glass.

CHAS *smiles as he removes his dressing gown.* JOE *heads back to the living room.*

INT. LIVING ROOM. DUSK.

JOE *refills* CHAS*'s champagne glass.*

CHAS *(O.S.)* This is amazing! What's it all in aid of?

JOE I just wanted to pay you back, that's all. Happy anniversary!

JOE *removes a paper sachet from his pocket and tips it into the champagne. He stirs it with a straw, then carries the glass to the bathroom.*

INT. BATHROOM. DUSK.

CHAS *is now lying in the mud-bath.*

JOE How is it?

CHAS It's a bit claggy. But lovely. Thank you.

JOE Here.

JOE *hands* CHAS *the champagne.*

CHAS I should be doing this for you.

JOE No. You deserve it.

JOE *leaves, closing the door behind him.*

JOE *(cont'd)* You really deserve it.

INT. HALLWAY/UTILITY ROOM. DUSK.

As JOE *closes the bathroom door, we pull back and find a sack of quick-drying cement in the cupboard.*

EXT. LAKESIDE HOLIDAY HOME. NIGHT.

It's quiet and pitch-black outside. We see insects dance around the outside light.

INT. BATHROOM. NIGHT.

Close-up of on one of the pill bottles on the shelf. The label reads 'Acceptance'.

We pull back to see CHAS *lying in the bath, groggy from the drugged champagne. The cement has hardened around him, just his head sticking out of one end. He comes to, to find* JOE *sitting on the toilet watching him. The candles are burned low.*

CHAS Joe . . . ? Fuck . . . I must have passed out.

JOE Xanax. Those meds came in handy eventually.

CHAS I can't . . . move . . .

JOE I know you can't.

JOE *knocks the concrete with his fist.*

CHAS What's happening?

JOE So, you were asking me about Michaela?

CHAS No, that was just a misunderstanding. I didn't know she was a nurse.

JOE She's not a nurse; she's a finance manager. I am fucking her, though. We're engaged to be married next year. Shame you can't sing at the wedding. *(He sings)* 'Blue Jeans Baby, driving me crazy . . .'

CHAS What? No, you're winding me up . . .

JOE It's true, I assure you. I live with Mick in London through the week, then I tell her I've got to visit my elderly father at the weekends when I come and see you. It's not been easy, but it's been a couple of years now, and she's not aware you even exist.

CHAS Why?

JOE Why what?

CHAS Why didn't you just split up with me?

JOE Because I wanted to be able to look you in the eye and tell you that you have completely wasted the past nine years of your life. All the sacrifices you made, they were pointless.

CHAS I love you.

JOE I know you do, you kept telling me. But I never responded in kind, did you notice? I did a lot of things I wasn't proud of, but I wouldn't do that.

CHAS Joe . . . what . . . ?

CHAS *starts to cry.*

JOE Hey, don't do that. You'll wash all your lovely face pack off.

JOE *crosses to the bath and reapplies some of the oatmeal and honey concoction.*

CHAS You're just confused, your medication . . .

JOE I'm not dying, by the way. Just a splash of Vimto in the toilet pan every now and again. A few mocked-up emails. You never really wanted to engage with my little tumour, did you? It repulsed you, just as you repulsed me. But I accepted that was the price I had to pay. Just as you have to accept your punishment.

JOE *gets up and produces a framed photo of a schoolgirl.*

CHAS Joe, what the fuck is this? Let me out . . .

JOE This is my daughter, Olivia. She was thirteen, and a big fan of Atlantic 5. One of the few people to buy 'Blue Jeans Baby'. She worshipped you, and you inspired her to start writing songs of her own. Until you found her on Myspace and started to take the piss. But it was worse than that, wasn't it? It wasn't, 'Don't call us, we'll call you.'

CHAS Joe, please . . .

JOE It was: 'You're so shit, why don't you go away and kill yourself?' So she did. Or tried to, at least. My wife found her in the bath with an empty bottle of bleach. Assisted coma for – guess how long? Nine years. Nine years, before my ex-wife and I – we were separated by this time, we just couldn't make it through – were gently encouraged to switch her off. So we did.

CHAS I'm sorry.

JOE We were never sure exactly why she did it, but I did my research. And that's when I sought you out. Chazz with two z's. Approached you in The Purple Sock, where you were doing that tragic PA, and I started my campaign. Nine years of your life wasted, loving someone who hated you. And now you're going to die, but I won't switch you off. That would be too kind.

CHAS You're going to leave me here? On my own?

JOE No. You won't be on your own.

JOE *opens the bathroom window. He extinguishes the candles one by one, apart from one by* CHAS*'s head.*

JOE *(cont'd)* The ancient Persians devised a form of execution called scaphism. The victim would be taken to the edge of a lake, tied between two boats and covered with milk and honey. This soon attracted all manner of insects, who would bite and feed on the body, lay their eggs. Which in turn attracted rats and other vermin. Until you're literally eaten alive.

JOE *squeezes some honey on to the window ledge and bath.*

JOE *(cont'd)* It's said the Persian soldier Mithridates managed to last seventeen days.

CHAS No, no. Joe, please . . . Please don't do this. *(He shouts)* Mollie! Mollie!

JOE Oh, I sacked her, just like you suggested. She's gone away to Glasgow to lick her wounds, so to speak. She won't be back for ages.

CHAS Joe, please listen. I know what I did was wrong, but you can't do this to me, you can't, you can't . . .

JOE Ah, Chas, I've already done it. You're just in denial. Goodnight.

JOE *leaves.* CHAS *is weak, stunned, terrified. He looks at the photo of Olivia, which* JOE *has left on the bath.*

CHAS I'm sorry!

We hear the sound of a mosquito in the room, the horrid whine moving closer and closer. CHAS*'s face turns in horror.*

INT. LIVING ROOM. NIGHT.

JOE *prepares the food.* CHAS *cries out from the bathroom.*

CHAS *(O.S.)* Joe!

JOE I hope you're hungry. You've got to keep your strength up. Do you still want it heated up?

CHAS *(O.S.)* Oh God, no, please . . .

JOE I think I'm going to have mine cold.

CHAS *(O.S.)* Joe!

JOE *sits and eats his quiche as* CHAS *cries out from the bathroom.*

THE END

SERIES
9

Foreword

> — I think it's right for them to end it now, don't you? It has got a bit self-indulgent.
>
> Katherine, 'Plodding On'

How do you give an anthology show a fitting ending? This was the question looming over us as we started to kick around ideas for the ninth and final series. *Inside No. 9* had been so many things throughout its lifetime, from knockabout comedy to psychological thriller, from poignant drama to chilling horror. In the end we set out to make a final series that would live up to any of its predecessors and hoped that we wouldn't end up like Spencer Maguire in 'Simon Says', arguing with fans over the disappointing finale of *The Ninth Circle*.

We both had theatre commitments during the first half of 2023. Reece was playing in Steven Moffat's *The Unfriend* at the Criterion Theatre and as soon as that finished Steve would begin rehearsals for Martin McDonagh's *The Pillowman* at the Duke of York's. We had to fit the writing of Series 9 around these runs, which meant long working days and a disjointed writing schedule. Having trawled through the notebooks for one last time to pick up on all the ideas we'd discussed but never fully written, we began with a title that had been waiting patiently for its time to come: 'The Curse of the Ninth'.

We'd almost written this as part of Series 8 but decided that it had some similarities to 'Paraskevidekatriaphobia', so we held it over to the final series. The 'curse' that a composer would die after writing their ninth symphony really began and ended with Mahler, but it has remained a superstition in the world of classical music to this day. Mahler sought out a session with psychoanalyst Sigmund Freud to discuss this and other issues, and we were very tempted to try to dramatise this meeting as a way of exploring writer's block. After all, we were embarking on our own ninth 'symphony' and feeling the weight of our previous work cramping our creative decisions. In the end we went with a fictional composer and wrote a gothic chiller that would allow us to explore the same themes and to dress up in lovely Edwardian costumes for a rare period piece.

Having seen the proliferation of found-footage true-crime documentaries, we wanted to create a story using a single-shot doorbell camera. The chilling Netflix film *American Murder: The Family Next Door* begins with police body-cam footage, and we discussed how this might be an interesting way into a story, but for the police to be in attendance a crime needed to have been reported already and we wanted a viewpoint that would be more objective. The fixed-point camera perspective of 'Mulberry Close' gave us the ability to create short scenes where the viewer could become detective and try to work out what was going on for themselves. A deceptively simple but very satisfying premise, and one of the funnier episodes in the series.

The third story we wrote was 'CTRL/ALT/ESC'. Two ideas had been floating around for a long time: setting an episode in an escape room and exploring the medical condition of locked-in syndrome. It seems obvious now but the idea of bringing them together was the light-bulb moment that provided us with the story and its 'twist'. Ever since Ian turned out not to be Ian in Series 1's 'Sardines' we'd enjoyed the huge power that a well-seeded surprise ending could deliver to an episode. An anthology of single stories might easily become unmemorable and slight if the denouement doesn't pack a punch. But after eight series our audience was constantly on the lookout for the story we might really be telling within the story we were presenting, and delivering an endless supply of shock endings became a tyranny of its own. So even though we had to make Jason a coma victim instead of a locked-in patient (who wouldn't be in danger of being thought 'brain dead'), and even though it might be possible for the seasoned *Inside No. 9* viewer to work out this wasn't a straightforward, puzzle-solving escape room, we hoped there would be enough in the story to provide human drama and scary thrills to make for a satisfying and emotionally resonant episode.

'Boo to a Goose' was another story that had had a full nine-series gestation. In our initial meeting with BBC Two controller Janice Hadlow, where we'd loosely pitched the idea of an anthology (see the foreword to Series 1's scripts), we'd talked about seeing a couple in identical anoraks eating apples whilst on a tube journey. Okay, it's not *War and Peace*, but our impression of them tickled her and she wanted to know more. So, we'd discussed a scenario where a group of disparate passengers became stranded in a tunnel and fell into a conversation, which would end up resembling a trial by jury. Anyway, we couldn't make it work, and wrote the ensemble comedy of manners 'Sardines' instead. At the start of every series the apple-munchers would be wheeled out for discussion, but no idea stuck. But the image of a second train whizzing past with the same couple sitting there as a pair of eerie doppelgängers was introduced, and eventually 'Boo to a Goose' was born. So never throw away those half-baked ideas or single images - sometimes they are all you need to prompt a creative breakthrough.

The last episode to be written, 'The Trolley Problem', was a true two-hander, the only story that we would fully carry on our own. A psychological cat-and-mouse game, the power balance was constantly changing between the two characters, and it felt like a good summation of everything we'd learned - the drip-feed of information, the use of humour to keep at least a little toe in the world of comedy, and a brutally horrible ending. There are no winners here. You'll see from the script that we took out a big section where Drew is telling his (made-up) backstory, which leads to a comically slowed-by-drugs fight. We had a lot of fun filming this, though partly for reasons of time it had to be cut. But the truth is that it didn't work to shift the tone so much - the gears were crunching and we were happy to make the story work without it.

Another challenge we set ourselves was to create an episode that would have a verbal or a visual reference to all fifty-four preceding stories, and hopefully you'll enjoy reading them in 'Plodding On' even if you couldn't spot them while watching the episode. We pitched to our executive producer Adam Tandy the idea of a wrap party where we would invite back several actors from past series. He half-smiled, half-winced and said we'd have difficulty a) making it work with the budget, and b) making sure it wasn't self-indulgent. He suggested an area away from the party, so we plumped for the toilets. Katherine Parkinson coming in, washing her hands, Tim Key standing patiently in one of the cubicles. Is it indulgent? Hell yeah. But at least we get to demolish our own show as 'half-hour little nothings, every fourth one a dud', before walking out into that room full of talent to enjoy a few clips of our former glories. An unforgettable day's filming and a satisfying way to end the series.

We then decided to create a West End stage show to open early in 2025 at the Wyndham's Theatre, so the door to Number 9 isn't fully closed and bolted just yet. After all, you've got to keep plodding on, haven't you?

Episode 1

BOO TO A GOOSE

CAST LIST

RAYMOND – Mark Bonnar

GERRY – Reece Shearsmith

EDITH – Siobhan Finneran

HAROLD – Matthew Kelly

ELENA – Philippa Dunne

WILMA – Steve Pemberton

CLEO – Susan Wokoma

FINN – Joel Fry

MOSSY – Charlie Cooper

DRIVER – Dan March

STATION ANNOUNCER – Melissa Woodbridge

INT. UNDERGROUND STATION PLATFORM. NIGHT.

A metro carriage approaches the quiet platform.

ANNOUNCEMENT *(V.O.)* For the purposes of safety and security, CCTV is in operation at this station and across all underground lines. Thank you.

RAYMOND, *a serious-looking man carrying a newspaper, steps from a corridor on to the platform. Further down the platform,* GERRY *and* EDITH, *a smartly dressed couple, rise as the train pulls into the station.*

INT. TRAIN. NIGHT.

The train doors open. GERRY *and* EDITH *enter, and walk down the aisle past* ELENA, *a meek-looking NHS worker in her overalls and lanyard, carrying a large raffia bag.*

They approach HAROLD, *an elderly dishevelled man who nods along to music on his headphones. A few plastic bags are strewn around him. He smiles a lot and always appears to slyly know everyone's secrets.*

He smiles up at EDITH. *They decide not to sit near him, and find seats at the far end.*

Ahead of them, we see RAYMOND *boarding and avoiding some departing football lads. He turns down the aisle, avoiding a litter-strewn seat, passing* CLEO, *a grungy-looking young woman with a nose ring sharing a pair of earbuds with her friend* WILMA, *a drag queen.*

CLEO *glances over at* GERRY *and* EDITH *settling into their seats.* GERRY *fetches an apple from his bag and hands it to* EDITH, *then fetches another apple for himself. They eat their apples in silence, reading a theatre programme.*

RAYMOND *finds a seat, and glances over at* FINN, *a shifty-looking young man with a rucksack on his knee. He nervously watches all the other passengers.*

RAYMOND *gets out a pen, puts on his glasses and starts doing a word puzzle. He looks disapprovingly across at* WILMA.

WILMA *flashes a nipple at him, and* CLEO *laughs.* RAYMOND *shakes his head and goes back to his paper.*

The doors close and we see that there is a small 'C9' sticker next to the carriage doors.

TITLE: *'Boo to a Goose'*

The train whizzes off and disappears into the tunnel.

INT. TRAIN. NIGHT.

The train driver's voice comes through the speakers.

DRIVER *(O.S.)* Ladies and gentlemen, I've just been informed the next station is closed. This train will not be stopping at the next station.

FINN Argh! God's sake . . .

FINN *seems annoyed and stands up to check the map, his crotch almost in* RAYMOND*'s face.*

HAROLD *lifts the headphones from his ears. He turns to* ELENA.

HAROLD What was that? I missed it.

ELENA We're not stopping at the next station.

HAROLD Ah. Thank you so much.

ELENA *smiles.* HAROLD *puts his headphones back on.*

FINN *is standing right in front of* RAYMOND *as he surveys the map.* RAYMOND *is irritated.*

RAYMOND Do you mind?

FINN Sorry, I'm trying to read the map! Do you know what the next stop will be?

RAYMOND No.

At the other end of the carriage, GERRY *is perusing the theatre programme over* EDITH*'s shoulder.*

GERRY I thought I recognised her from something.

EDITH Who?

GERRY The lady with the teeth.

EDITH You'll have to narrow it down, Gerry.

GERRY She was the maid or whatever she was.

EDITH What maid? There wasn't a maid. It was set in a shoe factory.

GERRY The boss, then. I can't remember all the details. She was in *Crown Court.*

EDITH That was fifty years ago.

GERRY Not *Crown Court, The Crown.*

EDITH Who was she in that?

GERRY I think she was Princess Margaret.

EDITH Lesley Manville?

GERRY Well, it might have been. People have to work, Edie.

EDITH We haven't just seen Lesley Manville in an amateur production of *Kinky Boots*, Gerry.

The door at one end of the carriage opens and MOSSY *comes in. He is a homeless man. He has a paper cup.*

WILMA *spots him approaching.*

WILMA Frig me, is there a homeless convention in town this week?

CLEO What?

WILMA Up there, you blind bitch. *(To* MOSSY, *while pointing at* HAROLD*)* If you're looking for your dad, he's over here.

CLEO Don't Wilm, he can't help it! I think he's quite cute.

WILMA Fine, go off and shag him then. At least you won't have to pay for his taxi home.

CLEO *hits* WILMA *playfully. Only* ELENA *listens to* MOSSY*'s speech; the others ignore him.*

MOSSY Ladies and gentlemen, very sorry to bother you. I hope you're all having a wonderful evening. But as you can probably tell from my appearance, I'm sleeping on the streets at the moment, so am asking if it would be possible for any of you good people to help me out with a little bit of spare change. I'm so embarrassed to have to ask you like this, but I don't have many options at the moment. I would really appreciate anything you can give to help me out at this difficult time.

MOSSY *starts to make his way down the carriage, pausing in front of people, holding out his cup.* RAYMOND *doesn't acknowledge him.* CLEO *and* WILMA *giggle.*

CLEO Sorry darling, I don't have any change.

MOSSY No one does. I need a card machine.

FINN What! Why would you do that, brother? They can track you if you use cards.

MOSSY Who can?

FINN Them! They're watching us right now.

FINN *surreptitiously looks up at the CCTV camera on the ceiling of the carriage.*

FINN *(cont'd)* No cards, cash only!

MOSSY Do you have any cash?

FINN No.

ELENA Here you go, dear.

ELENA hands MOSSY a two-pound coin from her purse.

MOSSY Thank you.

ELENA Sorry it's not much.

MOSSY That's OK, I appreciate it.

EDITH smiles.

EDITH Every little helps.

MOSSY Yeah.

GERRY Stop it, Edie – he won't know Tesco's.

EDITH I didn't mean Tesco's. I was saying it as a phrase.

GERRY Just don't get involved.

MOSSY waves his cup towards GERRY, who doesn't meet his eye, becoming very interested in his trousers. MOSSY heads back up the carriage.

Suddenly, the train jerks to halt. MOSSY falls to the floor, FINN on to ELENA.

MOSSY Aargh!

RAYMOND What the hell?

EDITH gets up to help MOSSY.

EDITH Are you OK . . .?

GERRY He's fine. Come and sit down.

MOSSY Thank you.

Suddenly all the lights go off, plunging the carriage into darkness.

WILMA Oh, you're kidding me!

DRIVER *(O.S.)* Very sorry for the power outage, ladies and gentlemen. Do please sit tight while we try and get things up and running again. Hopefully won't be long.

Everyone sits quietly for a few moments.

A torch is switched on by HAROLD. He illuminates his own face.

HAROLD I heard some passengers got stuck in a tunnel for two weeks on the Berlin U-Bahn system. Power failed and they were trapped inside.

HAROLD shines the torch around the carriage.

HAROLD *(cont'd)* The authorities couldn't get to them. They sat in the dark, panic slowly setting in. Then they ran out of water . . . they turned on each other in the end. The weakest ones got eaten.

WILMA Jesus, I'd rather eat my own tits than chow down on his gamey old meat. Be like eating a pigeon.

HAROLD Beg your pardon?

WILMA I mean my gag reflex is legendary, but I draw the line at that.

CLEO Stop it!

MOSSY You should have more respect.

WILMA Oh, keep your nose out, Melania Tramp, or I'll put a button in with your change.

MOSSY *approaches* WILMA.

MOSSY What did you call me . . . ?

FINN Stop it. We don't want to attract attention.

MOSSY Think you're funny, do you?

Suddenly, there is a scream from ELENA.

ELENA Argh!

RAYMOND What is it?

ELENA Someone grabbed me!

GERRY Who did?

The lights come back on. ELENA *is on the edge of her seat, looking panicked.* MOSSY *and* RAYMOND *are standing close to her;* FINN, HAROLD, WILMA *and* CLEO *sit near by.* EDITH *and* GERRY *stand by their seats.*

CLEO Are you alright?

ELENA I think so. They pulled at my bag; I dropped it.

RAYMOND Are you hurt?

ELENA No, I don't think so.

GERRY Were they going for the breasts, do you think?

EDITH Gerald!

GERRY What? I'm just trying to establish the facts.

RAYMOND *has picked up* ELENA*'s bag and handed it back to her. Some items that have spilled out on the floor are being collected by* MOSSY. HAROLD *lifts his headphones again.*

HAROLD What's happened now?

EDITH We're not sure.

GERRY Sex pest in the carriage. Operates in the dark.

ELENA *has checked through her bag.*

ELENA My purse has gone . . .

RAYMOND Are you sure?

ELENA Yes, it was in here, I just had it. It's gone.

GERRY Strike that. Sex pest and thief.

EDITH Stop saying that word.

GERRY What word? 'Sex pest'?

EDITH Yes!

RAYMOND Sit down, please. I've got this.

GERRY *and* EDITH *sit.* RAYMOND *turns to* MOSSY.

RAYMOND *(cont'd)* OK, empty your pockets, young man.

MOSSY What?

RAYMOND Empty your pockets. This lady has had her purse stolen.

MOSSY What's that got to do with me?

RAYMOND I don't know yet.

MOSSY So why am I being singled out?

RAYMOND Well, I don't mean to be insensitive, but you are the one begging for money here.

MOSSY That doesn't mean I'm a thief.

RAYMOND Empty your pockets, then.

MOSSY No!

GERRY And she had her breast pinched.

EDITH Gerald!

ELENA No one did that.

GERRY Poor woman's already blotted it out. Coping mechanism.

RAYMOND Will you be quiet, please?

GERRY Sorry.

MOSSY Honestly, sir, I didn't do anything.

CLEO He doesn't have to empty his pockets for you. You're not the police.

FINN Maybe he is. They put them on the trains undercover, I've seen it.

RAYMOND Look, the thief was definitely someone in this carriage. In the absence of the law, I just want to check. I'm only trying to help this lady.

GERRY I think that's reasonable enough.

WILMA Absolutely it is! And if he needs strip-searching, I've got some vaseline and latex gloves in my fanny pack.

MOSSY But she just gave me two pounds. Why would I rob off her?

GERRY Oldest trick in the book.

MOSSY What is?

GERRY You remember what happened with Sting's accountant? Thought they were friends, scammed him for six million . . .

EDITH It's hardly the same thing, Gerry.

GERRY They always start small.

HAROLD *pipes up.*

HAROLD I don't mind showing you my bags.

RAYMOND *takes the cooperation where he can get it, and goes over to* HAROLD.

RAYMOND There, you see? Thank you, sir. It's all perfectly fine. Nothing to hide if you've nothing to hide.

HAROLD *holds open his bags.* RAYMOND *rummages through. He very quickly has second thoughts as it dawns on him the bags are just full of rubbish: empty cans, crisp wrappers, crumpled-up tissues. It's pretty disgusting. After the first bag,* RAYMOND *doesn't want to inspect any further.*

RAYMOND That's great. Thank you.

HAROLD I do have more.

HAROLD *offers up another bag and* RAYMOND *recoils at the smell.*

RAYMOND That's . . . fine.

HAROLD *(to* ELENA*)* Don't you want to check them?

ELENA No, I trust you.

FINN I wouldn't if I were you, miss.

FINN *taps the side of his head, indicating* HAROLD*'s headphones.*

FINN *(mouthing)* Not plugged in.

ELENA *looks and sees the end of the wire. The headphones are not plugged in to anything.* HAROLD *smiles, puts on his headphones and nods along to his imaginary beat.*

GERRY We're happy to be searched, aren't we Edith?

EDITH Well, yes, but . . .

GERRY To rule ourselves out.

EDITH We've just been to the theatre; we enjoy Gilbert and Sullivan. We're not hoodlums.

ELENA Honestly, you don't have to. It's fine.

FINN Did you have much money in it?

ELENA Not much, no. But there were all my cards . . .

FINN Don't use cards – why will no one listen to me?

ELENA . . . Err, and a photo of my father. I wouldn't want to lose that.

ELENA *becomes upset.* GERRY *turns out his pockets to* RAYMOND.

GERRY Well, look, I'm happy to comply and show that I haven't got it. Edie?

EDITH *seems annoyed, but goes along with it.*

EDITH This is just a car coat, it doesn't have pockets. But there's nothing in my handbag . . .

EDITH *opens her handbag.* RAYMOND *turns to* MOSSY.

RAYMOND See? That's what honest, decent citizens do. Now are you going to let me check your pockets?

MOSSY *feels all eyes on him. He slowly raises his hands, and* RAYMOND *steps in to frisk him, checking all his pockets. It's humiliating for* MOSSY. EDITH *looks away.*

RAYMOND *doesn't find anything.*

RAYMOND Thank you. Wasn't hard, was it?

WILMA Speak for yourself, dear. I found it quite erotic.

RAYMOND Don't be so childish.

WILMA Well, I bet you've never tried to keep a tuck with a semi on.

MOSSY Should I go and speak to the driver, tell him there's been an incident?

GERRY Good idea. Proper authorities.

MOSSY *walks down through the carriage and out of the door.*

CLEO What about your pockets, chief inspector? Can we look in them?

RAYMOND Of course. See?

RAYMOND *empties his pockets.*

RAYMOND *(cont'd)* None of us are above the law. We can't just do what we want without consequences.

EDITH That's true. I snipped our neighbours' hydrangeas back and they planted bamboo out of spite. The drive's ruined, isn't it, Gerry?

GERRY I'm afraid so. It was an act of madness, and now we live with the encroachment. Shafts of it, poking through the tarmac like hydra's teeth.

ELENA Have you tried boiling water?

GERRY Of course we have! It can't stopped! Sorry.

FINN *(to* RAYMOND*)* Who are you working for?

RAYMOND Highton Grammar. I'm a physics teacher.

FINN I don't trust him. He's been spying on us the whole time.

RAYMOND Don't be ridiculous.

FINN *picks up* RAYMOND*'s newspaper.*

FINN He's been writing things down about us in code.

RAYMOND That's a Polygon.

FINN See? 'Actor', 'fake', 'task force' . . .

RAYMOND It's a puzzle. You have to make as many words as possible using the given letters.

WILMA Oh I'm good at that, let me see.

WILMA *takes the newspaper.*

FINN You're collating. I see you collating.

RAYMOND Collating what?

FINN Data. For them.

FINN *points at the CCTV camera.*

FINN *(cont'd)* There's a bigger picture, yeah? We're all monitored. You must know that.

HAROLD *blurts out.*

HAROLD Yes! It's aliens. I've seen them too. They experimented on me at a bus stop in Preston. They put an R2-D2 in my bottom.

This is met with silence. HAROLD *clarifies.*

HAROLD *(cont'd)* To scale, obviously.

RAYMOND He's not kidding.

CLEO How do you know?

RAYMOND He's got it in that bag.

ELENA Oh dear God.

RAYMOND *turns his attention to* FINN*, who has been cradling his backpack.*

RAYMOND Speaking of bags, can we see inside yours?

FINN Definitely not. It's private property.

RAYMOND Everybody else has . . .

FINN I said no!

RAYMOND Why, what have you got to hide?

RAYMOND *reaches for the bag.*

FINN Fuck off!

FINN *moves away. A tense silence follows.* ELENA *becomes upset.*

ELENA I'm so sorry, I didn't mean to cause all this upset.

EDITH Don't worry, it's not your fault.

ELENA I'm just a bit shaken. I've never had anything stolen before.

EDITH I'm sure the police can sort it all out. We'll give a statement, won't we, Gerry?

GERRY Yes, of course.

CLEO I'm sorry, but I'm not saying shit to the police. I wouldn't trust them as far as I can throw them.

RAYMOND That's hardly surprising, is it?

CLEO Why'd you say that?

RAYMOND No reason.

CLEO No, go on. If you've got something to say, then say it.

RAYMOND I've been a teacher for twenty-five years. I've seen the erosion of respect for authority. There was a time I would walk into a classroom and thirty students would stand up immediately.

CLEO Oh, is that what you want? 'Good morning, sir!'

RAYMOND This lady is a nurse. It wasn't that long ago we were standing in the street applauding their efforts. Or maybe you never bothered?

CLEO No, maybe I never did. Do you have a list of everyone who banged a pan?

FINN The government do! They see everything!

GERRY Well, we were out there at least three times, weren't we Edith? Although that Le Creuset was bloody heavy.

HAROLD *starts to sing.*

HAROLD As someday it may happen that a victim must be found / I've got a little list – I've got a little list / Of society offenders who might well be underground / And who never would be missed – who never would be missed!

WILMA Frig me, it's like *Hamilton* for hobos.

HAROLD *(still singing)* There's the pestilential nuisances who write for autographs . . .

EDITH It's from *The Mikado.*

HAROLD *(cont'd)* All people who have flabby hands and irritating laughs . . .

WILMA Thank you, we'll let you know!

HAROLD *(cont'd)* All children who are up in dates and floor you with 'em flat . . .

RAYMOND *(to* FINN*)* Alright, we've played silly buggers for long enough. Open your bag.

FINN No.

HAROLD *(cont'd)* All persons who in shaking hands, shake hands with you like that . . .

RAYMOND I'm afraid I'm going to have to insist. You were sitting right next to her when the incident happened.

HAROLD *(cont'd)* And all third persons who on spoiling tête-à-têtes insist . . .

FINN Stay the fuck away from me!

HAROLD *(cont'd)* They'd none of them be missed, they'd none of them be missed!

EDITH If I can make a suggestion? Let's take a vote. See what the general feeling is.

GERRY Yes – very good, Edie. Democracy manifest.

EDITH Everyone who thinks . . . Sorry, I didn't catch your name?

FINN I didn't tell you it.

GERRY We could vote on whether he should?

ELENA He doesn't have to tell us his name, it's fine.

HAROLD Harold! My name's Harold.

EDITH Oh, hello, Harold. I'm Edith and this is my husband, Gerry.

GERRY Helloo!

RAYMOND Binks. Raymond Binks.

ELENA I'm Elena. Nice to meet you all.

WILMA My boy name is Jonathan – urgh, gives me the ick! – but my drag name is Wilma Dickshow.

GERRY Wilma . . . ?

WILMA Dickshow. I do a bottomless brunch the first Thursday of every month at the Purple Sock. I know, I'll put you all on the guest list . . . Gerry and Edith, Elena . . . *(To* FINN*)* . . . What was your name again?

FINN I'm not giving my name, alright?

WILMA Dammit! Thought I was going to Columbo him then.

CLEO *(to* RAYMOND*)* He doesn't have to give you his name. He doesn't have to do anything – just because you assume authority like the fascist prick that you are.

RAYMOND Well, when the police become involved, we'll all have to give our names, won't we?

CLEO I won't.

WILMA You tell him, Cleo! Oh, bum-cheeks.

RAYMOND Look, we're wasting time. Is there anybody here who thinks I shouldn't look inside this young man's bag, by force if necessary?

CLEO Yes!

CLEO *puts up her hand. She turns to* WILMA.

CLEO *(cont'd)* Come on!

WILMA Well, someone's nicked her purse, and it isn't me!

EDITH *is unsure. She goes to raise her hand, but* GERRY *quietly stops her.* RAYMOND *looks to* ELENA*, but she just looks down.* HAROLD *seems oblivious.*

RAYMOND There you are, you see. Hand it over.

RAYMOND *moves towards* FINN, *who clutches his bag tighter and backs away.*

FINN Is no one going to stand up to him?

RAYMOND Give it to me . . .

RAYMOND *takes the bag, but* FINN *won't let it go. They struggle, and* RAYMOND *grabs* FINN *by the throat. He seems overcome with rage.*

CLEO Someone help him!

Nobody moves. Suddenly, the rear door opens and MOSSY *steps back in.* RAYMOND *releases* FINN.

The DRIVER *comes back on the tannoy.*

DRIVER *(O.S.)* Me again, folks. Sorry about the continuing loss of power; we should be on our way fairly shortly. We are aware there's been an incident in one of the carriages, and the proper authorities have been informed. Once again, I apologise for any inconvenience caused.

FINN *stares defiantly at* RAYMOND. RAYMOND *backs off and goes to retrieve his newspaper from* WILMA.

RAYMOND Can I have my newspaper, please?

WILMA *hands it back to him.*

WILMA I got 'frock', unsurprisingly. And 'fork'. I wanted 'cock', but there's only one 'c'.

RAYMOND *sits on his own, away from* FINN.

GERRY Did you know Meryl Streep is an anagram of 'Try eel sperm'? It's always tickled me.

MOSSY *returns and walks past* FINN *and* RAYMOND *to sit next to* ELENA.

ELENA What did the driver say?

MOSSY He said there's a replacement service on the way. Shouldn't be long now.

ELENA *checks her watch.*

ELENA Looks as though I'm going to be late for work.

MOSSY I'd love to be late for work. My job's 24/7.

ELENA Your job?

MOSSY *rattles his cup.*

MOSSY Surviving.

ELENA Do you get much money going up and down?

MOSSY No. People are just embarrassed. I get it. I'm asking for generosity, and it puts them in the position of deciding to be kind or not.

ELENA Do you think people are not kind?

MOSSY I think most people don't believe me when I tell them I've got nothing. They think it's a con and I'm just lying.

ELENA At the hospital, I see the opposite. Lots of frightened people trying to make sense of what's happening to them. They want to believe everything will be alright. Sometimes they can't accept the truth.

MOSSY Here. You can have your two pounds back.

ELENA No, it's fine – you keep it.

MOSSY Are you sure?

ELENA Yes. I hope it brings you luck.

ELENA *hugs* MOSSY. *He's moved.*

GERRY *and* EDITH *sit at their end of the carriage.* GERRY *looks at the theatre programme.*

GERRY Says here they're doing *Salad Days* for their Christmas show. Shall we book for that? Edie? Boxing Day treat?

EDITH Hmm?

GERRY Shall we book to see *Salad Days* for Christmas?

EDITH No, I don't want to see *Salad Days.*

GERRY What's the matter?

EDITH I think that man's a bully.

GERRY Who?

EDITH The teacher. Why do we always let people like him boss us around? We're people in our own right, aren't we? We have our own opinions?

GERRY Of course we do. But we don't have to blurt them out to every Tom, Dick and Harry, do we?

EDITH I don't know. I think we've just sunk into ourselves. Anything for a quiet life.

GERRY There's nothing wrong with that, is there?

EDITH What happened to you, Gerry? You used to be such a firebrand. When you had that trouble at work, you were the first one to lead your team out on strike. Standing there with your whistle and your megaphone . . .

GERRY That was a long time ago, Edie.

EDITH I came and brought you all soup, do you remember? In a big pot with a ladle. And we all sang that song from *Oliver!*, 'Food, Glorious Food'.

GERRY What is it, love? What's the matter?

EDITH I want more, Gerry. I want more.

EDITH *looks across at* HAROLD, *who is staring at her, smiling. He nods knowingly with his headphones on.* EDITH *smiles back.*

CLEO *sits with her arms folded.* WILMA *offers up an earbud.*

WILMA Here, it's your favourite. 'All Too Well (10 Minute Version) (Taylor's Version) (From the Vault).'

CLEO *doesn't react.*

WILMA What? You're not going to throw an eppy because I didn't put my hand up, are you?

CLEO I can't believe you'd let him get away with that.

WILMA Oh, Cleo, come down off your frigging high horse – it's exhausting!

CLEO He assaulted those two young men.

WILMA Yes, and we had front row seats – lucky us! It's not every day you get a free sex show on your train ride home, is it? We should have filmed it for OnlyFans: 'The Teacher, the Tramp and the Terrorist'.

CLEO He's not a terrorist. Why is he a terrorist?

WILMA He was clinging on to that bag tighter than Judy Finnegan to a wine glass. And he was wearing a hoodie to hide his face from the cameras.

CLEO Not everyone with a hoodie and a rucksack is a terrorist, Wilma.

WILMA Yeah, and not everyone who tapes their knob to their arsehole is a drag queen but, ya know!

RAYMOND I think they could be right.

WILMA Did he just use my pronouns?

RAYMOND *(to* FINN*)* Where are you heading to?

FINN None of your business.

RAYMOND You didn't seem to know the area, that's all.

FINN Look, I'm not explaining myself to you. I'm not at school and I'm not on trial. I've done nothing wrong!

GERRY The lady doth protest too much, methinks.

ELENA They're sending someone to help us. Maybe we should just wait . . .

MOSSY Well, I believe him.

GERRY Thank you!

MOSSY Not you! Him!

He points to FINN.

RAYMOND That's not a particularly glowing endorsement, coming from a common thief.

MOSSY I'm not a thief.

RAYMOND Crawling up and down the train all day long, begging for change. You work your fingers to the bone, year in, year out . . .

MOSSY Shut your mouth!

MOSSY *gets up and joins* FINN.

MOSSY *(cont'd)* I'm with you. Someone's got to stand up to the man.

CLEO *gets up and joins them too.*

CLEO Exactly. He's been lording it over us this whole time like he's better than us - well, you're not! The rest of you can just sit there and do nothing, but I'm taking affirmative action.

RAYMOND There's still more of us than there are of you.

EDITH No there isn't.

EDITH *gets up and passes* RAYMOND.

EDITH *(cont'd)* Excuse me.

She joins FINN, MOSSY *and* CLEO *at the other end of the carriage.* GERRY *gets up.*

GERRY Edith, what are you doing?

EDITH *(to* RAYMOND*)* I think you're a bully, and I don't think it's fair what you've been doing.

FINN I want another vote. If the majority of passengers want to see in my bag, then you can. I won't stop you.

RAYMOND *raises his hand.*

RAYMOND Good, because I do. I intend to squash this little rebellion and prove that I'm right. Gerald?

GERRY *raises his hand.*

GERRY I agree.

RAYMOND Elena?

ELENA *meekly raises her hand and stands by* RAYMOND.

RAYMOND *(to* HAROLD*)* And this . . . gentleman?

HAROLD *raises his hand, smiling.*

WILMA Oh my gosh, it's all down to me. It's like *Kramer vs. Kramer.* Let me see . . . Ickle ockle, chocolate bottle, ickle ockle out, turn the dirty dishcloth inside out . . .

CLEO Everything's just a big fucking joke to you isn't it, Jonathan?

WILMA Erm, pretty much, yes.

CLEO You can't see through all those fake lashes and mascara that here in the real world, there's injustice happening everywhere you look. If you thought about anyone but yourself for at least thirty seconds, you'd realise that.

WILMA Oh, I know all about the real world, Cleopatra darling. I've been laughed at, beaten up, had dog shit pushed through my letter box – you don't have to tell me about injustice. And if I want to paint my face and lip-sync to Lady Gaga, that's just my way of coping with it, alright? Just like yours is rebelling against your posh-as-fuck upbringing by getting a nose ring and trotting after me like the ghastly little fag hag that you are. *(To* RAYMOND*)* I'm with you, Daddy.

WILMA *raises her hand and stands with* RAYMOND. CLEO*'s eyes well with tears.*

CLEO When did you get so mean?

HAROLD *stands.*

HAROLD Blessed are the mean, for they will inherit the earth.

Suddenly the train starts to move off again through the tunnel.

HAROLD *(cont'd)* Blessed are those who hunger and thirst for righteousness, for they will be killed.

FINN Here, you can look inside now.

FINN *throws his backpack across to* RAYMOND.

HAROLD Blessed are the merciful, for they will be shown no mercy.

A baffled RAYMOND *opens up the backpack to reveal a number of small gas masks inside.*

RAYMOND What is this?

HAROLD Blessed are the pure in heart for they will see . . . God.

The train pulls into the station.

EDITH *looks out of the window and is shocked to see three passengers standing quietly and blank-faced on the platform.*

These are NEW EDITH, NEW CLEO *and* NEW MOSSY.

EDITH *looks on in horror as her own subservient doppelgänger stares straight ahead.* MOSSY *looks confused.* CLEO *puts her hand to her mouth.*

CLEO What the fuck . . . ?

EDITH Gerry . . . ?

GERRY *doesn't look surprised.*

FINN Put them on. You've got about twenty seconds.

RAYMOND *hands masks to* ELENA *and* WILMA *and they put them on, as does* FINN.

RAYMOND *offers one to* HAROLD *who just smiles.*

GERRY We don't need them; it's alright.

EDITH Gerry, what's happening?

GERRY Don't worry, Edie. It doesn't hurt.

EDITH *looks back out at the blank-faced* NEW EDITH.

Suddenly, an invisible gas starts to fill the tube carriage from small nozzles in the ceiling. It quickly fills the space, choking and subduing EDITH, CLEO *and* MOSSY.

MOSSY *tries to prise the door open, but it's locked shut.* NEW MOSSY *watches impassively as* MOSSY *is overcome by the gas.*

CLEO *bangs on the windows as* NEW CLEO *watches from the platform.*

ELENA, WILMA *and* RAYMOND *look on in horror as the other passengers fall to the floor, gasping for breath.*

GERRY *simply closes his eyes.* HAROLD *seems as oblivious as ever.*

Eventually, the gas stops. FINN *checks his watch, then removes his mask.*

FINN *reaches into his pocket to reveal* ELENA*'s purse.*

FINN Here. Sorry about the inconvenience; your purse was just the inciting incident. You can take this off now.

The others remove their masks. FINN *shakes hands with* RAYMOND.

FINN No hard feelings, eh?

RAYMOND What . . . what's going on?

FINN We implement this action from time to time. Swap out disruptors, the ones who challenge the status quo. You have nothing to worry about.

WILMA *looks around at the gassed bodies.*

WILMA What do you mean?

FINN *offers up a small electronic device.*

FINN Sign here. It confirms that you took no part in today's events, as they never actually happened.

In a daze WILMA *signs the device, followed by* RAYMOND *and* ELENA.

FINN *(cont'd)* Tick the box if you'd be interested in helping us in the future. We need people like you, Elena. People that don't get involved.

ELENA What about these people?

She indicates the bodies of her fellow passengers.

FINN You can see them – they're right here.

FINN *indicates the doppelgängers on the platform.*

FINN *(cont'd)* But now, like you, they wouldn't say boo to a goose. Isn't that right, Gerry?

GERRY *nods.*

GERRY Yes, that's right, sir.

The doors to the train open and FINN *gets off the train and goes to speak to an* OFFICIAL *in a hazmat suit.*

DRIVER *(O.S.)* We do apologise for the delay in your replacement service today. This was due to earlier disruption on the line, which has now been rectified. We do hope you have a safe onwards journey.

ELENA *watches* GERRY *and* WILMA *get off and approach* NEW CLEO *and* NEW EDITH. NEW CLEO *smiles at* WILMA *and they head off, arm in arm.*

On the platform, GERRY *takes* NEW EDITH*'s hand.*

GERRY Alright, love?

NEW EDITH Yes.

GERRY So, what do you think? When we get home, shall we book to see *Salad Days*?

NEW EDITH Yes, I think we should.

GERRY *and* EDITH *walk off together, ignoring* MOSSY, *who sits quietly on the platform.*

ELENA *is shocked as two* OFFICIALS *in hazmat suits start to carry out the original* EDITH.

ANNOUNCEMENT *(V.O.)* If you see something that doesn't look right, speak to staff or text British Transport Police on 61016, and we'll sort it. See it. Say it. Sorted.

THE END

Episode 2

THE TROLLEY PROBLEM

CAST LIST

Blake – Steve Pemberton

Drew – Reece Shearsmith

Ellie – Eleanor Kirby

Robbie – Ethan Joseph-Robert

EXT. FARMHOUSE. NIGHT.

A dark, stormy night, windy and rainswept. An isolated farmhouse surrounded by moorland. A plaque bearing the house number hangs from a wall bracket, blowing in the wind: number 9.

TITLE: *'The Trolley Problem'*

INT. FARMHOUSE. NIGHT.

A kettle boils and clicks off. Hot water is poured into a teapot by BLAKE.

We are in a spacious farmhouse kitchen-diner. A fire crackles in the grate. The space is comfortable but ordered, perhaps a little masculine. Leather armchairs, nice wooden table and chairs.

BLAKE I'll just let it stew for a minute. Nothing worse than a weak tea, is there?

DREW *sits at the table, looking damp and somewhat downtrodden.*

DREW Well, there are a few things worse, but I know what you mean.

BLAKE Do you take sugar?

DREW No thanks.

BLAKE I'll put one in anyway, it's good for shock. And you're sure you don't want a tot of whisky or anything?

DREW I don't drink.

BLAKE Very wise. Is there anyone you want me to call?

DREW No. Thank you.

BLAKE *pours the milk into the teacups.*

DREW I don't want to put you to any trouble.

BLAKE It's only a cup of tea. Is cow's milk alright?

DREW As opposed to what?

BLAKE *smiles, brings the tea things over to the table.*

BLAKE Can I ask how long you were out there?

DREW I'm not sure. A couple of hours.

BLAKE And nobody stopped?

DREW Why would they? I suppose I was just a man standing on a bridge, looking at the view. Must have been twenty, thirty people walked by.

BLAKE It's the Bystander Effect. The more people there are, the less likely any of them are to help.

DREW So why did you stop?

BLAKE I thought you looked like a bit of a lost soul.

DREW *doesn't respond.*

BLAKE *(cont'd)* Anyway – don't feel like you have to say anything. I'm happy just to sit with you, give you some space.

DREW Thanks. I will just sit for a minute.

BLAKE Of course. I've got some stuff to do, anyway.

BLAKE *opens up a laptop and checks his emails.*

DREW *notices a picture of* BLAKE *with his teenage son,* ROBBIE. *Next to that on the sideboard is a phrenology head statue and a framed diploma displaying the name 'BLAKE CHAMBERS' followed by a string of letters.*

DREW You went to Cambridge?

BLAKE McCambridge. It's an online college.

DREW You should have got a bigger frame. Looks like it says Cambridge.

BLAKE Mmm.

DREW Are you a doctor?

BLAKE I'm a therapist. Don't worry, I'm not charging my hourly rate.

DREW Is there much call for that round here?

BLAKE Oh yes, you'd be surprised. I'm fairly new to this area, but I've already got a full client list.

DREW I suppose people go mad in the countryside, don't they? You're always hearing about farmers blowing their brains out.

BLAKE The isolation doesn't help. But yes, that's why I decided to come out here. Act as a listening post. This is a neutral space where people can feel able to say whatever they want to say.

DREW Like Free Parking.

BLAKE Sorry?

DREW Free Parking, in *Monopoly*. It's a neutral space.

BLAKE Exactly. I'm Free Parking. You can rest your boot here as long as you like!

DREW They don't have the boot any more. They changed it to a penguin in 2017. The bird, not the biscuit.

BLAKE Oh. I'm not a big fan of games.

DREW I am.

BLAKE *pours the tea from the pot.*

BLAKE Can I ask, have you ever talked to anyone about your . . . situation?

DREW What situation?

BLAKE Well, whatever it is that led to you standing on the bridge tonight, contemplating whatever you were contemplating.

DREW No, I haven't. I can't even get through to my doctor. You have to phone by eight, and it's engaged for forty-five minutes, and then they offer you a Zoom, and I haven't got strong enough Wi-Fi. It's all just totally fucked.

BLAKE You're right, yeah, it is fucked. The system is under a lot of pressure. I like to try and see clients face to face. I can get a better read that way.

DREW What do people talk about?

BLAKE That's up to them.

DREW And what if people don't want to talk?

BLAKE That's also up to them. There's no one way of doing things. I offer various mindfulness classes, sort of a cognitive detox.

DREW What kind of classes?

BLAKE CBT, hypnotherapy, laughter yoga . . .

DREW Laughter yoga?

BLAKE Mmm, it's a fairly recent practice, popularised in the mid-nineties by Dr Madan Kataria. He conjectures that you don't need comedy or funny stories to trick the body into the benefits of laughter. So, with these exercises, you can just start laughing - hee hee hee - and before you know it - ha ha ha - you can feel yourself - ha ha ha - really benefitting. Hee hee hee, ha ha ha . . .

DREW *watches throughout this, slightly bemused at first, but eventually finds it funny and joins in.*

DREW Ha ha. I don't know if I'm laughing at you or with you!

BLAKE It doesn't matter. As long as you're laughing. And then you can take some mental floss - ha ha ha - and just clear out your brain - ha ha ha! Try it!

BLAKE *mimes flossing out the bad thoughts while still laughing.* **DREW** *joins in the action, laughing more and more. His laughter becomes more and more manic, and is no longer pleasant or funny.*

BLAKE *stops.*

BLAKE OK . . .

DREW HA HA HA! HA HA HA! HAAAAA!

BLAKE And let's leave it there . . .

DREW HA HA HA . . .

DREW*'s laughter turns into sobbing.* BLAKE *goes over and rubs him on the back.*

BLAKE That's good. That's good. Let it out.

BLAKE *looks down and notices that there is a gun tucked into the back of* DREW*'s trousers. He freezes for a moment, then regains his composure.*

BLAKE *calmly reaches for a box of tissues.*

BLAKE Here you are – these are the main tools of my trade.

DREW Thank you.

DREW *blows his nose.*

DREW *(cont'd)* I'm sorry.

BLAKE No need, it's fine. I've seen a lot a worse, I promise you. Do you want to talk about it? Sometimes just saying a problem out loud can reduce how insurmountable it seems. You know we all have things we blow out of proportion . . .

DREW I think I might have killed somebody.

BLAKE *is silent for a moment.*

BLAKE You think?

DREW Yeah. I'm not sure.

BLAKE OK. Erm, do you feel able to share any more . . . ?

DREW Look, I didn't ask you to drag me off that bridge and bring me back here, did I?

BLAKE No.

DREW No. So I don't want to be fucking analysed, alright? Have a night off!

This outburst hangs in the air. DREW *calms down a bit.*

BLAKE Sorry.

DREW Can I use your bathroom, please?

BLAKE Sure – it's just through there.

DREW *goes out to the bathroom.* BLAKE *looks concerned.*

BLAKE *goes over to a drawer and gets out a packet of capsules. He looks towards the bathroom before popping three capsules from the foil.*

BLAKE *then pulls apart the capsules, carefully tipping the powder into* DREW*'s cup.*

INT. BATHROOM. NIGHT.

DREW *looks around the bathroom. He sees a pencil drawing on the wall of a pair of trainers.*

He reaches into his pocket and pulls out a bottle of pills. He shakes out a small handful into his hand. He looks at himself in the mirror.

INT. FARMHOUSE KITCHEN. NIGHT.

BLAKE *dries the teaspoon and places it back on the table. He waits nervously for* DREW *to return. He calls through.*

BLAKE Everything OK?

BLAKE *moves towards the hallway.*

BLAKE *(cont'd)* Hello?

BLAKE *hears a toilet flush. He hurries back to where he was standing.* DREW *appears.*

DREW Sorry for shouting.

BLAKE No problem. Please, sit down.

DREW Did you do the drawing in the bathroom?

BLAKE Oh no, that's my son, Robbie. He's doing art A level.

DREW It's good.

BLAKE Yeah, he's very talented. I'm proud of him.

DREW I used to like drawing when I was at school.

BLAKE A lot of people find it very therapeutic. Robbie's quite a shy kid, so it suits him. His teacher says it really brings him out of himself. What kind of things did you like to draw?

DREW Anything, really. Landscapes, portraits. I wasn't very good.

BLAKE You'll have to let me be the judge of that. If you fancy it.

BLAKE *gets up and goes over to a drawer, where he collects some coloured pencils and a sketch pad.*

While BLAKE *is gathering the paper and pencils,* DREW *puts the tablets in* BLAKE*'s tea and stirs it quickly.*

DREW Is this 'art therapy?'

BLAKE It's whatever you want it to be. Just express yourself.

BLAKE *offers up the art materials and* DREW *takes them.*

DREW I might draw you, then.

BLAKE Of course. Make sure you get my best side. I'm joking – I don't think I have one.

BLAKE *sits. He takes a sip of his tea.* DREW *notices this.* DREW *takes a drink of his tea.* BLAKE *notices this.*

They both seem satisfied.

DREW *starts to draw on the sketch pad.*

BLAKE Sorry, I don't even know your name.

DREW Drew.

BLAKE Drew! Funny. Past tense of 'to draw'.

DREW I don't like to think of myself in the past tense.

BLAKE No, sorry, that was . . . insensitive. I'm Blake, as you probably saw on my diploma. Do you work, Drew?

DREW *continues sketching.*

DREW I did. About a year ago, I was an assistant in an estate agent's. Just a high-street branch. It was fine. Didn't feel like it was something I'd do for ever, but I was happy enough. One afternoon, I was due to show a potential client around a rented property, short-lease six-month contract, and I arrived as usual, and this girl was waiting for me outside. Have you got . . . Oh no, it's OK. I wanted a brown.

DREW *finds a brown pencil and carries on drawing. He sips tea.* BLAKE *takes a sip from his cup as well.*

DREW *(cont'd)* Anyway, I introduced myself and we went inside. I could tell straight away that there was something not right with her. She'd definitely been crying, and she was jumpy and distracted. Anyway, I showed her round. Didn't take long – it was tiny. She was on her phone the entire time, barely looked up, and then she left. I thought, what a waste of time, and went back to the office. Didn't think of it again. But the next day at work, a police car pulls up and I'm arrested. Arm up the back, cuffs on, head down, driven away.

Apparently, the girl had made a complaint against me, saying I had been inappropriate with her and at one point grabbed her and pushed her against a wall.

BLAKE Oh no. And you hadn't, presumably?

DREW No, of course not. I was just horrified. Totally shocked. Next thing, my phone is taken off me, my shoes are removed and I'm put in a cell overnight.

BLAKE Oh, for God's sake.

DREW Anyway – the long and short is, I'm accused of attacking this woman, I'm served a restraining order, and the burden is on me to prove I didn't do it. It's her word against mine, and I've been fighting her for a year. I've had to stand in a court room and give evidence. Everyone looking at me like I'm already guilty.

BLAKE That's awful.

DREW It's cost me everything. My friends, my job. My family.

DREW *is starting to look heavy-lidded. As is* BLAKE.

BLAKE I'm so sorry to hear all this, Drew. The psychological damage of wrongful arrest can be enormous.

DREW Yeah . . .

BLAKE There should have been, um, safeguarding in place to prevent all of this.

DREW What do you mean?

BLAKE *gets up, a little unsteadily.*

BLAKE Look, Drew, do you want to gimme the gun?

DREW What gun?

BLAKE I seen it . . .

BLAKE *stumbles forward.* DREW *hauls himself from his chair.*

DREW Ge'off me . . .

BLAKE Let's just talk about this . . .

DREW No!

They trade limp punches, swinging and missing. BLAKE *tries feebly to take the gun, but* DREW *stops him.*

DREW What you doing? Assaulting me . . .

BLAKE Am gonna phone police . . .

DREW No . . .

BLAKE *staggers towards the phone,* DREW *alongside him. Like a race in slow motion.*

DREW *shoves* BLAKE *into the table, and the pencils fall to the floor.* BLAKE *tries to pick them up and put them back in the jar.*

DREW *picks up the phrenology head to hit* BLAKE *with, but it feels too heavy for him and makes his arm bend back with the weight, sending him falling to the floor.*

BLAKE *heads for the phone again, but* DREW *catches hold of his foot and drags him down. The pair slowly crawl along the floor towards the phone.* BLAKE *reaches it and pushes the '9' button once, then twice . . .*

DREW *has grabbed a cushion and holds it over* BLAKE*'s face. The pair grapple slowly once more.*

Finally, they end up passing out.

EXT. FARMHOUSE. NIGHT.

The farmhouse is silhouetted against the bleak moorland.

INT. FARMHOUSE. NIGHT.

BLAKE *wakes up groggily. His hand is tied to the Aga. He looks up to see* DREW *standing in front of him, now holding the gun.* DREW *throws a glass of water in his face.*

BLAKE Jesus . . .

DREW Why did you drug me?

BLAKE I could ask you the same thing.

DREW Are you in the habit of doping people you bring back here?

BLAKE Of course not. You were acting unpredictably, you have a gun, you said you'd killed somebody . . .

DREW I said I *might* have killed somebody.

BLAKE It was a precautionary measure. Anyway, are you in the habit of doping people who save your life?

DREW You didn't save my life. I was waiting for you on that bridge; I knew you'd be along at that time. I've been watching you for a while now.

BLAKE Why? Look, if you're going to rob me, just take what you want and go.

DREW That's not a very nice assumption, you know. You shouldn't put negative thoughts in my head. I'm in a very fragile state of mind.

DREW *points the gun at his own head. He's pacing round the room.*

BLAKE I can see that.

DREW I'm starting to wonder how good a therapist you actually are.

BLAKE You should know my son Robbie is on his way back; he'll be here any minute. He's been on a night out with his friends.

DREW I don't think so.

BLAKE It's true, I promise you. Let me go, please. I know you're facing some difficulties, but you can turn this around, Drew.

DREW Oh, can I? Thank you so much, Blake. Using your first name to establish trust.

BLAKE Look, I don't want to upset you, but please, just tell me what you want.

DREW I want you to know what it's like to be me.

BLAKE OK, that's understandable. A great man once said, 'Before you judge someone, walk a mile in his shoes. After that, who cares? He's a mile away, and you've got his shoes.'

DREW Is that from one of your therapy books?

BLAKE No, it's from a Billy Connolly video. What did you mean when you said you want me to know what it's like to be you?

DREW *is looking at the books on* BLAKE*'s shelf.*

DREW Have you read all these books?

BLAKE Yes.

DREW Really? They're not just there to make people think you're clever?

BLAKE No. I don't care what people think of me.

DREW *sees a framed set of eight black-and-white photographs of disturbing-looking people.*

DREW Who are these? Close family relatives?

BLAKE No, they're psychiatric patients. It's the Szondi test. It's designed to reveal your innermost traits. The parts of yourself you've pushed down into your subconscious.

DREW What?

BLAKE You're supposed to choose the person you find the most unsettling or scary. Who would you least like to meet in a dark alleyway?

DREW *points to a picture of a woman.*

DREW This one. Number six.

BLAKE She's the depressive. It suggests that you're repressing feelings of self-loathing and guilt. You have a predisposition to negative emotions and inadequacy.

DREW Not a wise thing to say to someone with a gun in their hand. Number one looks like you. What's his trait?

BLAKE He's the sadist.

DREW Really?

BLAKE It's been discredited for decades. It's just up there as a talking point.

DREW Alright, let me give you a talking point, then. You might know this one. There's a runaway train thundering down a railway track, and looking ahead, you see there are five people tied to the line. You are standing by a lever, which will send the train down a different route. However, you notice there is a single person standing on this side track.

BLAKE Yes, the Trolley Problem: do you pull the lever and kill one person, or do nothing and five people die?

DREW Exactly. So what would you do?

BLAKE Well, it's just an exercise to engineer a moral debate, isn't it? Utilitarianism versus deontology . . .

DREW In English?

BLAKE Do you focus on the best outcome or the most moral one? Pulling the lever is essentially choosing to murder. Clearly not the moral choice, but saves the most people. It's the difference between killing and letting die.

DREW So what would you do?

BLAKE It's all hypothetical. But sometimes the right choice is not to do anything.

DREW I thought you'd say that. Alright, what if there was a third option? You can throw yourself on to the line, stopping the train and saving everyone. All six people. Would you do that?

BLAKE So the dilemma becomes a trilemma. Well, in that case, it depends who the people are. You know, if it's Shakespeare, Gandhi, Galileo, Einstein and . . . Mary Berry . . .

DREW Mary Berry?

BLAKE Come on, she's a national treasure. Then yes, I probably would. But if it's Genghis Khan, Hitler and Gregg Wallace, then maybe not.

DREW I don't think you're taking this seriously, Blake.

BLAKE Then why don't you tell me what this is all about?

DREW *comes and takes a seat opposite* BLAKE.

DREW What do you remember about Ellie Dawson?

BLAKE Who's Ellie Dawson?

DREW She was a former patient of yours.

BLAKE In that case, even if I could remember her, which I can't, I wouldn't be permitted to discuss it with you. Doctor–patient confidentiality and all that.

DREW You're not a doctor.

BLAKE Well, therapist then.

DREW But anyone can call themselves a fucking therapist! Boo-hoo, my kids have grown up, what am I going to do with the rest of my life? I know I'll enroll at McDonald's University and do a psychotherapy course, print my own diploma from home.

BLAKE McCambridge Online is a well-respected educational hub, and . . . Anyway, I don't have to justify myself to you!

DREW Am I a therapist because I'm talking to you now?

BLAKE No.

DREW Why, what's the difference?

BLAKE Because I don't tie my patients up and make them listen to my rantings.

DREW No, you're far more sly than that, aren't you?

BLAKE What do you mean?

DREW Ellie Dawson. She came to you with low mood, depression, abandonment issues. You put her on a course of anti-psych drugs, the ones I just gave to you. Then what happened?

BLAKE I honestly don't know who you're talking about.

DREW Let's jog your memory, then.

DREW *takes out his phone.*

DREW *(cont'd)* Luckily, she recorded some of your meetings on her phone. Like you say, you've got to have safeguarding measures in place . . .

BLAKE I didn't consent to these recordings. This is a violation of my privacy.

DREW Shut the fuck up!

DREW *places the phone on the table and presses 'play' on an audio file.* BLAKE *and* DREW *listen.*

BLAKE *(V.O.)* And how does that manifest itself?

ELLIE *(V.O.)* What?

BLAKE *(V.O.)* The negativity you're talking about.

ELLIE *(V.O.)* Erm . . . I have fights with my mum. I drink. A lot.

BLAKE *(V.O.)* That's fairly common for a girl of your age. What are you, 18, 19?

ELLIE *(V.O.)* 22.

BLAKE *(V.O.)* You look younger.

ELLIE *(V.O.)* I cut myself.

BLAKE *(V.O.)* Where?

ELLIE *(V.O.)* My arms . . . and my legs.

BLAKE *(V.O.)* Do you want to show me? Just so I have an idea of how severe it is.

We hear some clothing being removed. BLAKE *and* DREW *stare at each other.*

BLAKE *(V.O.)* That's not too bad. I've seen far worse. What are these, a couple of weeks old? Does it hurt when you touch them?

ELLIE *(V.O.)* Erm, a bit.

BLAKE *(V.O.)* May I?

BLAKE Alright, turn it off.

DREW Listen!

BLAKE *(V.O.)* Do you want to take your jeans off so I can see the legs?

ELLIE *(V.O.)* Do I have to?

BLAKE *(V.O.)* Er no, not if you don't feel comfortable. You can send me some pictures, if you like . . .

BLAKE Please, you can turn it off.

BLAKE *(V.O.)* Let me give you my private email address . . .

DREW *stops the recording.*

BLAKE I remember Ellie; of course I do. She was a client, briefly, then we became romantically involved. It was unethical, yes, but wasn't illegal.

DREW So why did you take out a restraining order on her?

BLAKE She was young and delusional, she became obsessed with me. She was estranged from her father, and she saw me as . . . oh Christ, it's you isn't it? You're Ellie's dad.

DREW I was. She's dead.

BLAKE *closes his eyes.*

BLAKE I'm so sorry.

DREW I know I was partly responsible for what happened, I drove Ellie away. I was too strict, too mean about her mother. I could see she was becoming withdrawn, so I put some money in her account. 'Go see a therapist,' I said. I failed my daughter. I made the wrong choice.

BLAKE Is that what you meant when you said you thought you'd killed someone?

DREW I want you to confess to everything you did to her.

BLAKE What?

DREW Everything. You got her hooked on drugs, used her, abused her, then dumped her when she became an inconvenience.

BLAKE I cared for her. But as I said to the police at the time, she had all those problems when she came to me. I was not in any way responsible for her death.

DREW Really? So you didn't go to see her in her room at the Metropole Hotel on the fifteenth of October, breaking your own restraining order?

BLAKE No.

DREW *takes out a jotter pad from his coat and refers to scribbled notes.*

DREW The coroner's report stated that she would have taken the overdose at approximately 3 a.m., and that it would have taken about three hours for her to die. A man matching your description was seen leaving the hotel at around ten minutes past four.

BLAKE Seen by who?

DREW Never mind. Whoever that was could have seen that she'd OD'd and could have saved her if they'd raised the alarm. But no. I suppose it's the difference between killing and letting die.

BLAKE I didn't do anything.

DREW Exactly.

DREW *and* BLAKE *look into each other's eyes.* DREW *holds the gun to* BLAKE*'s head.*

DREW *places a pen down in front of* BLAKE.

DREW Write it all down. A full confession. Sacrifice your job, this cosy little life you've built up. And admit that you were there and you were directly responsible for her death. Then my Ellie can rest in peace.

BLAKE *considers for a moment, then nods.*

BLAKE OK, I'll do it. I'll throw myself in front of the train. But I'll need to . . .

BLAKE *indicates his tied-up hand.* DREW *goes to untie him.*

BLAKE So the whole estate agent story was made up?

DREW An innocent man ruined by a crazy woman. I knew it'd get you onside.

BLAKE Clever. But one thing to bear in mind, Drew. If you're going to coerce someone with a spud gun . . . make sure the barrel doesn't smell of potato.

DREW *sniffs the gun's barrel.* BLAKE *stabs him in the leg with the pen.*

DREW *screams and falls down on to the sofa.* BLAKE *kicks* DREW, *then runs away.*

EXT. FARMHOUSE. NIGHT.

Stormy night outside the house.

BLAKE *runs out of the front door and hides behind his car.*

He pulls out his phone and is about to dial a number when he stops. He thinks for a minute, then puts the phone away.

INT. FARMHOUSE. NIGHT.

DREW *is tying a piece of cloth from the sofa around the wound on his leg. He gets unsteadily to his feet and crosses to the table. He writes something on a slip of paper and puts it into his jacket pocket, which is on the back of the chair.*

Suddenly, all the lights go out in the room. DREW *looks around in the dark.*

DREW Hello?

DREW *hears the sound of a window being smashed. He hobbles to the door to investigate.*

INT. HALLWAY. NIGHT.

DREW *comes into the hallway and hears another crash.* BLAKE *is ahead with a torch and a crowbar. He pulls open a drawer from the dresser and empties the contents on to the floor.*

BLAKE This is one of the problems with being in the countryside. You're an easy target for burglars. I came back home after a night out to find my house being robbed and was viciously attacked. He had a gun – at least, I thought it was a gun – and so I hit him. Hard. I didn't mean to kill him. It was self-defence, officer.

DREW Is this how you make all your problems go away?

BLAKE What choice do I have? I've got my reputation to consider. I can't have all that business with Ellie dredged up again.

DREW So you moved out here, where no one knows what you really are.

BLAKE Look, your daughter was the one that was hounding me. She made me feel unsafe. I had my son to think about. Now, get on your knees.

DREW Please, Mr Chambers . . .

BLAKE On your knees.

DREW *slowly sinks to his knees.* BLAKE *raises the crowbar.* DREW *looks at him.*

DREW If you kill me here, now, there'll still be a police investigation.

BLAKE *considers this.*

BLAKE I should have let you jump off that bridge when I had the chance. Actually . . . That's it.

He lowers the crowbar.

DREW What?

BLAKE You said yourself, twenty or thirty people saw you there tonight, looking longingly into the river. I can take you back there. Me bringing you here is the side track. I should have just let the train take its course.

DREW So what, you're going to throw me into the water?

BLAKE That's up to you. You can go willingly or otherwise. But I do think it's the best solution.

DREW *considers his lot for a moment. He seems resigned.*

DREW Alright. I have nothing left to live for. Talking to you tonight hasn't brought my daughter back. I suppose it was never going to. But you can still do the right thing, Mr Chambers. Father to father, I'm begging you.

BLAKE Which is what?

DREW Confess to what you did to Ellie. Don't let me die not knowing. Please.

BLAKE As I said before, I didn't do anything.

DREW OK.

BLAKE *drags an acquiescent* DREW *out of the front door.*

EXT. FARMHOUSE. NIGHT.

BLAKE *drags* DREW *towards the car and unlocks it.*

BLAKE Get in.

DREW I've left my coat.

BLAKE For God's sake.

BLAKE *looks back to the house.*

DREW I won't go anywhere.

BLAKE Don't you move.

BLAKE *heads back into the house, leaving* DREW *by the car.*

DREW Mr Chambers . . . When you get my coat, you should look in the right-hand pocket.

BLAKE Why?

DREW You'll see.

INT. FARMHOUSE. NIGHT.

BLAKE *goes to get* DREW*'s jacket from the back of a chair. He spies the sketch pad that* DREW *was drawing in earlier. Curious to see the picture,* BLAKE *flips it open to look inside.*

There is a portrait of BLAKE *as if drawn by a court artist.* BLAKE *is in the dock, looking sombre in a dark suit. We see a judge in the background.*

BLAKE *rips the sketch from the pad and crosses to the fireplace. He throws the sketch into the fire and watches it burn.*

BLAKE *looks inside the right-hand pocket of* DREW*'s jacket and finds a slip of paper. He looks at the paper and frowns.*

BLAKE *looks out of the window. He sees* DREW *still outside by* BLAKE*'s car.*

BLAKE *pulls out his phone. We see that there is a phone number written on the paper. He enters the number into his phone. It rings a few times before being answered.*

ROBBIE *(V.O.)* Hello?

BLAKE Robbie? Is that you?

ROBBIE *(V.O.)* Dad, Dad, please, I can't breathe, you've got to help me.

BLAKE What? Calm down. Where are you?

ROBBIE *(V.O.)* I don't know where I am, it's dark. I'm in a box . . .

BLAKE What do you mean, a box?

ROBBIE *(V.O.)* I think he's buried me somewhere. Dad, please, just get me out.

BLAKE Robbie, try and calm down. Just tell me what happened.

ROBBIE *(V.O.)* He said you'd come for me. He said it'd be alright. He said you'd do the right thing . . .

BLAKE *looks back out of the window to see* **DREW** *has taken a can of petrol from the car boot and is pouring it over himself.*

BLAKE Oh God.

ROBBIE *(V.O.)* Dad, please . . .

BLAKE OK, don't worry, I'm going to find you.

BLAKE *runs back towards the front door.*

EXT. FARMHOUSE. NIGHT.

BLAKE *emerges from the front door.*

DREW *lowers the petrol can.*

BLAKE Tell me where he is.

ROBBIE *(V.O.)* Dad?

BLAKE I beg you, Drew, don't do this. Tell me where he is. I'll do anything.

DREW You made your choice. Now we're the same, you and I.

DREW *takes out a lighter from his pocket.*

ROBBIE *(V.O.)* Dad, are you there?

BLAKE If you do this, you're killing my son.

DREW I didn't kill him. You let him die.

DREW *sparks up the flame.* **BLAKE** *looks on in horror.*

BLAKE No!

ROBBIE Dad? Help me . . .

We hear a whoosh of flames, and see **BLAKE***'s face light up, the fire reflected in his glasses.*

He falls to his knees.

THE END

Episode 3

MULBERRY CLOSE

CAST LIST

DAMON – Reece Shearsmith

VAL – Vinette Robinson

LARRY – Adrian Scarborough

KENNY – Steve Pemberton

SHEILA – Dorothy Atkinson

POLICE OFFICERS – Stephanie Booty & Tyler Cameron

with the voice of

Michael Ball

EXT. DRIVEWAY. NIGHT 1.

The story is told through the lens of a doorbell camera, which shows a driveway, street and the houses opposite on a suburban close.

After a few moments of the quiet street, the front door opens and DAMON *comes out with a recycling bag full of mostly wine and beer bottles. He noisily empties it into the green recycling bin. We can faintly hear the TV playing within.*

He pulls the wheelie bin and a food recycling caddy to the end of the drive, which has a car parked on it. We can see the bin has a number '9' sticker on it.

DAMON *goes back inside.*

TITLE: *'Mulberry Close'*

EXT. DRIVEWAY. NIGHT 1.

Later that night, a fox is nosing around the food caddy. It manages to knock it over and open the lid. It starts to eat the contents.

EXT. DRIVEWAY. DAY 2.

The next morning, we see lots of waste food detritus scattered across the drive. VAL *comes out in her coat with some empty cardboard boxes and sees the mess.*

VAL Bloody hell.

VAL *gingerly starts to put the items back in the food bin. We hear her neighbour,* LARRY.

LARRY *(O.S.)* Morning!

VAL Oh, hiya Larry.

LARRY *(O.S.)* Foxes, is it?

VAL Yeah, that or Damon's had the midnight munchies. I might put some poison down, that'd soon stop them.

LARRY *(O.S.)* Best to use a brick.

VAL A brick?

LARRY *(O.S.)* Yeah, that's what I do.

VAL I'm not sure the animal cruelty people would be happy with that.

LARRY *(O.S.)* No, I mean to put on top of the bin, so they can't knock it over.

LARRY *comes into view with his dog on a lead.*

LARRY *(cont'd)* You settling in alright?

VAL Yes, not bad. We're still living out of boxes, but we're getting there.

The dog pulls towards the food.

LARRY Popcorn, get down! He's a beggar for food.

VAL Fill your boots, Popcorn. Saves me picking it all up.

LARRY Anyway, as I say, anything I can do, let me know.

VAL Thanks, Larry.

LARRY See you later. Come on, boy . . .

LARRY *heads off and* VAL *gets into her car.*

EXT. DRIVEWAY. NIGHT 2.

The street is quiet. A food-delivery DRIVER *pulls up on a scooter and takes a couple of takeaway bags from his top box. He approaches and presses the doorbell.*

DAMON *answers.*

DRIVER Hi – for Damon?

DAMON *(O.S.)* Yeah.

DRIVER And there's your wine – was it three bottles?

DAMON *(O.S.)* Yeah, yeah, thanks.

DRIVER Do you have a code for me, please?

DAMON *(O.S.)* Oh yeah, one sec . . . Val? Val, have you got the code?

VAL *(O.S.)* What do you mean, code?

DAMON *(O.S.)* For the food.

DAMON *runs up the stairs to get the code. The* DRIVER *waits. He farts.* DAMON *returns.*

DAMON *(O.S.)* It's 72.

DRIVER Great, thank you. Enjoy.

The DRIVER *hands over the food.* DAMON *closes the door and the* DRIVER *gets back on his scooter.*

EXT. DRIVEWAY. DAY 3.

We see a learner driver vehicle on the other side of the road kangaroo-jumping as they try to pull away. The car stops and tries again. More kangaroo jumps.

EXT. DRIVEWAY. DAY 3.

We see a couple emerge from one of the houses on the other side of the road and make their way over. They are KENNY *and* SHEILA.

SHEILA *is carrying a large Tupperware box.* KENNY *rings the bell and* DAMON *answers the door.*

KENNY Hi there! We just thought we'd come over and introduce ourselves – Kenny and Sheila, we're from number 11.

DAMON *(O.S.)* Oh, hi. Damon.

They shake hands.

KENNY Damian?

DAMON *(O.S.)* No, Damon.

KENNY Oh, *Damon*. Like, like the jam.

SHEILA That's damson, you dozy sod. Ignore him. How are you settling in?

DAMON *(O.S.)* Good thanks. Still living out of boxes, you know.

SHEILA Yes, we'd noticed a lot of takeaway bikes coming round. I said to Ken, 'She's probably not got her kitchen up together yet!' Anyway, there's a cauliflower quiche in there for you.

SHEILA *hands over the Tupperware box.*

SHEILA *(cont'd)* Probably healthier than all those curries and whatnot!

DAMON *(O.S.)* Thank you, that's very kind.

SHEILA Is it Valerie, your wife?

DAMON *(O.S.)* Val, yes, she's at work at the moment.

SHEILA Yes, we've seen her driving off every morning, but we've not had chance to say hello yet.

KENNY How do you find the Peugeot? I've heard mixed reports.

DAMON *(O.S.)* Er, yeah, it's fine as a runaround, but we've been looking into getting an electric next.

KENNY *winces.*

KENNY Oooh, good luck. Tricky customers if they break down, I believe.

SHEILA They run off an iPad, don't they? I'm just learning at the moment, but Ken won't take me out in our car.

KENNY We've got a Volvo estate, can you blame me?

SHEILA How am I supposed to practise, then?! Anyway, tell Val to pop over for a cuppa any time she likes, and once you're all settled in we'll have to have you over for some supper . . . Oh, and a little tip: I saw you left some boxes out with your recycling, but you have to break them down and put them in the bin with the lid fully closed, or they won't take them.

DAMON Oh, OK. They did actually take them, so . . .

SHEILA Yes, but for future reference. Bring the Tupperware back any time, no need to wash it.

DAMON *(O.S.)* That's really kind of you, thanks Sheila. Nice to meet you.

KENNY You too. See you!

The door closes. KENNY *and* SHEILA *head back across the street.*

SHEILA Were those pyjama bottoms?

KENNY I don't know.

SHEILA He looked a right state.

EXT. DRIVEWAY. NIGHT 3.

Inside the house, loud music plays and raised voices can be heard arguing. The music is turned down and then back up again. A spider crawls across the lens of the doorbell camera.

EXT. DRIVEWAY. DAY 4.

DAMON *is setting up a model skeleton in the front garden. A carved pumpkin sits on the drive.*

VAL *comes out with some fake spiderweb cotton fibre.*

VAL Help me with this, will you?

DAMON Just a sec . . .

DAMON *finishes securing the skeleton and switches it on. The skeleton model laughs demonically.*

SKELETON *(V.O.)* Happy Halloween!

VAL *and* DAMON *start to dress the front hedge with the spider's web.*

From across the road, we see SHEILA *approach.*

VAL Here she comes, I told you . . .

DAMON It's alright. She's probably just lost her broomstick.

VAL *smiles.*

VAL Hiya, Sheila!

SHEILA Hello! My goodness, you're a pair of busy bees, aren't you?

DAMON Yeah, we love Halloween. We always make a big thing of it.

SHEILA So I see. You won't be doing any more than this, though, will you?

VAL How do you mean?

SHEILA Well, we don't want to attract all the mischief-makers from the estate, do we?

VAL They're only kids, Sheila.

SHEILA Yes, I know, but as you can see, nobody else really indulges it in the close.

DAMON Well if you can grin and bear it for a couple of days. It doesn't last long and it's only a bit of fun.

SHEILA Of course, I'm not saying that. Kenny and I like fun – we love fun. We went to crazy golf at the weekend!

VAL Nice.

SHEILA No, I'm only thinking of you, Val. I don't want you attracting undesirables!

DAMON Don't worry, Humphrey'll scare them off.

SHEILA Humphrey?

DAMON Humphrey Bone-gart.

DAMON *sets off the motion sensor.*

SKELETON *(V.O.)* Happy Halloween!

VAL Will we see you and Kenny at the Stag later? They're having a fancy-dress do.

SHEILA I don't think so. It's Michael Ball's *Who Do You Think You Are?* tonight, and we've been looking forward to it. We once met him on a cruise, and we've been following his career ever since. But I hope you enjoy it – all three of you!

DAMON Oh, Humphrey's not coming. He's got no-*body* to go with.

SHEILA *smiles.*

SHEILA I see. Well, have a pleasant evening.

DAMON And you.

SHEILA *walks back to her house.* DAMON *and* VAL *suppress their giggles.*

VAL Michael Ball. Fucking hell.

DAMON *laughs.*

EXT. DRIVEWAY. NIGHT 4.

A small group of dressed-up children come to the door and ring the bell. The door opens.

CHILDREN Trick or treat.

VAL *(O.S.)* Oh wow, you look wonderful. Here you go.

VAL *proffers a bowl of sweets and the* CHILDREN *take some each.*

CHILDREN Thank you.

VAL Hey, if you go over to the house opposite, the lady there has some lovely sweets for you.

The CHILDREN *run off and head for* KENNY *and* SHEILA*'s house.*

SHEILA *answers. We see her have a brief exchange with the children, then close the door.* VAL *laughs.*

EXT. DRIVEWAY. NIGHT 4.

It's late at night and the street is quiet. After a few beats, a figure can be seen slowly approaching. They wear a rubber horror mask and a hoodie. The skeleton is triggered.

SKELETON *(V.O.)* Happy Halloween!

The figure approaches the house and stands by the front door, breathing heavily.

The scary figure hammers on the front door. No response. The figure looks directly into the doorbell cam and presses. VAL*'s voice comes through the intercom.*

VAL *(O.S.)* What?

The figure lifts his mask and we can see that it is DAMON. *He looks a little the worse for wear.*

DAMON Can you let me in?

VAL *(O.S.)* Where's your key?

DAMON Dunno. I think it's in my other jacket.

VAL *(O.S.)* You're a fucking joke, Damon, do you know that?

DAMON Yeah.

VAL *hangs up the intercom. After a few beats, the door opens and* DAMON *lurches inside.*

EXT. DRIVEWAY. NIGHT 4.

A milk float is parked opposite, and the MILKMAN *is delivering milk to one of the houses.*

From within the house, we hear an indistinct row going on between DAMON *and* VAL. *It's very heated. We hear a bang, a scream, then the sound of someone falling down the stairs.*

The milk float drives off into the night.

EXT. DRIVEWAY. DAY 5.

We see SHEILA *in the learner car opposite doing a slow three-point turn. The car edges back and forth in a badly executed manoeuvre.*

Inside the house, we suddenly hear the whine of an electric saw. As the car is turning, the saw continues to come on and off.

EXT. DRIVEWAY. DAY 6.

The Halloween decorations have gone.

LARRY *stands at the front door with his dog, Popcorn. He rings the bell and waits. He rings again.*

KENNY *from opposite is walking past with a newspaper.*

KENNY Hiya, Larry.

LARRY Oh hi, Kenny, you alright?

LARRY *joins* KENNY *at the foot of the drive.*

KENNY Yeah, not bad. Sheila's costing me an arm and a leg with these bloody driving lessons.

LARRY When's the test?

KENNY Oh, it won't be for ages yet. She's failed it twice!

LARRY Hey, have you heard any funny noises coming from in there?

KENNY What do you mean?

LARRY They've been banging about doing DIY and God knows what at all hours.

KENNY Oh, that's not on. Have you said something?

LARRY I've just tried, but they're not in.

KENNY Try and speak to the wife; she seems like the reasonable one. He's always half-cut.

LARRY I will.

KENNY Oh well, good luck. See you later, pal.

LARRY Yeah, see you Kenny.

They depart.

EXT. DRIVEWAY. NIGHT 6.

We see DAMON *lugging a large, heavy suitcase out of the house and dragging it to the car in the drive. He opens the boot of the car and hauls the case into it, then goes back to the house.*

In the house opposite, an upstairs light comes on, revealing the silhouette of SHEILA *watching from the window.* KENNY *walks into the room and* SHEILA *quickly turns and motions for the light to be turned off again.*

DAMON *comes back out with a heavy laundry bag. The bedroom light opposite is turned off.* DAMON *drags the second bag into the boot of the car.*

EXT. DRIVEWAY. DAY 7.

KENNY *is jogging past. He stops to examine something on the driveway of* DAMON *and* VAL*'s house. A few drops of red, though we can't clearly make it out. He looks up at the house, then jogs off again.*

EXT. DRIVEWAY. DAY 7.

A delivery van pulls up and the COURIER *gets out quickly and brings a box to the front door. He rings the doorbell, and we see the word 'FRAGILE' clearly printed on the tape sealing the box.*

The COURIER *seems impatient.*

COURIER Come on, come on, come on . . .

There is no reply.

COURIER Fuck's sake.

The COURIER *drops the package to the ground and starts to write a card. He looks round to his right.*

COURIER Oh, excuse me, will you take this package for me?

LARRY *(O.S.)* Eh?

COURIER Will you take this package for your neighbours? I'll say I've left it with you – are you number seven?

The COURIER *takes the package to give it to* LARRY.

LARRY *(O.S.)* What is it?

COURIER *(O.S.)* I dunno, carpet cleaner or some shit. Thanks sir, I'll leave him a note . . .

The COURIER *comes back into view to post the note through the letter box.*

COURIER Get in!

The COURIER *goes back to his van, singing.*

EXT. DRIVEWAY. DAY 8.

SHEILA *crosses the road and approaches the house, pausing to examine the stain on the driveway. She comes and rings the bell.* DAMON *answers.*

SHEILA Oh, I'm sorry, did I wake you?

DAMON *(O.S.)* No, I just had a late night. What can I do for you?

SHEILA Sorry to ask, only I wondered if you'd finished with my Tupperware?

DAMON *(O.S.)* What Tupperware?

SHEILA You remember I brought you the quiche round after you'd just moved in? I know I said bring it back in your own time, but it's been a few weeks now and I do like to bake for the old folks in the home up the road.

DAMON *(O.S.)* I don't know where it is.

SHEILA Oh. Well, maybe Valerie knows . . . Is she in?

SHEILA *cranes her head to see inside.*

DAMON *(O.S.)* Not at the moment.

SHEILA We haven't seen her for a while. How is she?

DAMON *(O.S.)* She's fine.

SHEILA Oh good. Do give her my best wishes. If you like, I could just bob in and have a rootle round myself, I'd probably have a good idea where she's put it . . .

DAMON *(O.S.)* I'm just in the middle of something at the moment, so it's not convenient. But if I find it, I'll bring it round.

SHEILA Lovely. Just pop it in the porch if we're not in. Alright, then. Toodle-pip. Love to Val!

DAMON *(O.S.)* Yeah.

DAMON *closes the door.* SHEILA *steps back and looks to the windows, then turns to go back to her house.*

EXT. DRIVEWAY. NIGHT 8.

DAMON *emerges from the house and gets into his car. He pulls out of the drive and exits.*

Almost immediately, we see KENNY *and* SHEILA *emerge from their house and hurry across.*

LARRY *comes from his house and joins them. They whisper.*

KENNY Have you got the key?

LARRY Yes. Are you sure we should be doing this, though?

KENNY You said yourself something fishy's going on, all that banging and shouting. Bloody footprints on the drive.

LARRY It doesn't mean he's murdered her.

SHEILA And it doesn't mean he hasn't! What's the point of having a Neighbourhood Watch if we're not watching out for each other? Now, everyone, get your gloves on.

SHEILA *starts to put on some Marigolds.* KENNY *wears driving gloves.* LARRY *has fingerless mittens.*

SHEILA Larry! What are they supposed to be?

LARRY It's all I've got.

SHEILA You can stay here and keep watch, then.

KENNY Give me the key.

LARRY *hands the key to* KENNY. KENNY *goes to open the door.*

KENNY It's not working. Are you sure it's the right one?

LARRY Yes! The Bensons gave it me. I've had it years. I used to go in and feed their cat.

SHEILA Let me have a go.

SHEILA *tries to gain entry.*

SHEILA *(cont'd)* No, it won't even go in. They must have changed the locks. Blither!

KENNY Let's see if we can see anything through the windows.

LARRY What are we looking for, exactly?

SHEILA Anything out of the ordinary. Signs of a struggle.

KENNY In my mind, he's chopped her up in the bath and put her in them suitcases.

LARRY They seemed like such a nice couple as well.

SHEILA Look, up there! Bedroom window's open. Kenny, go and fetch the ladder.

KENNY You're joking, it's right at the back of the shed.

SHEILA Just do it! She could be lying there half-conscious for all we know!

KENNY *runs back to his house.*

SHEILA I've got it all logged, you know. All his comings and goings. I've been keeping notes.

LARRY What for?

SHEILA Well, if this turns out to be real and he has actually murdered her, we'll have to turn it over, won't we?

LARRY What, to the police?

SHEILA No, to Netflix. They might do one of their documentaries on it.

LARRY Do you think so?

SHEILA Well, why not? *The Mulberry Close Murders.*

LARRY Murders? Has he done more than one?

SHEILA We don't know, do we? People get up to all sorts. I'd have my face pixelated, I think – I don't want people pointing at me in Waitrose.

LARRY Can I be me in it?

SHEILA Yes, I don't see why not.

SHEILA *looks at the keys.*

SHEILA *(cont'd)* What's this other one?

LARRY That's the back door. Maybe they didn't change that one.

SHEILA You stay here and keep a lookout; I'll go and check.

SHEILA *disappears round the side of the house. We hear a dog bark off-screen.* LARRY *looks round.*

LARRY It's alright, Popcorn, I'll be back in a minute.

SHEILA *(O.S.)* It worked! I'm going in!

LARRY OK, roger that!

LARRY *waits. We hear the dog barking again.*

LARRY Popcorn, be quiet! You'll wake up the whole bloody close!

More barking. LARRY *disappears off back to his house.*

A few beats. We see DAMON*'s car approach and park back in the drive.*

DAMON *gets out of the car and lets himself in.*

A few more beats. From the top of the screen, we see SHEILA*'s legs dangling down. She can't reach the floor.*

SHEILA *(O.S.)* Larry! Larry, where are you?

LARRY *re-enters the screen.*

LARRY I'm here. Popcorn was barking.

SHEILA *(O.S.)* He's come back!

LARRY Oh, sugar!

SHEILA *(O.S.)* Drag that bin over!

LARRY *goes to pull the wheelie bin across.* SHEILA *slowly lowers her legs and is about to stand on it when the door opens again and* DAMON *comes out.* SHEILA *quickly pulls her legs up again.* LARRY *stands there with the wheelie bin.*

LARRY Oh! Hello, Damon!

DAMON *(O.S.)* What are you doing, Larry?

LARRY Er, you'll know this – is it the recycling this week or next? I can never remember.

DAMON *(O.S.)* It's next Monday.

LARRY That's right, yes. I'll put this back for you, then. Just trying to be neighbourly.

DAMON *comes out of the house and closes the door. From across the road,* KENNY *runs over with a ladder.*

DAMON Kenny?

KENNY Hiya, Damon. Hiya, Larry. I just wondered if you wanted your gutters clearing? I've just done mine, and I thought, while I've got the ladder out . . .

LARRY You can do mine if you like.

DAMON It's nearly midnight, why would I want my . . .

DAMON *starts to turn to look at his gutters.*

KENNY Don't turn round! It's just there's a massive spider dangling above your head . . . Keep still . . . That's it, she's gone, you can look now if you want. Are you off out?

DAMON I was just going to fill the car up, but I forgot my wallet. If it's any business of yours.

KENNY Drive carefully then, Damon.

LARRY Yeah, have a good night.

DAMON You too.

DAMON *gets into the car and drives off again.* KENNY *and* LARRY *wave him off.*

SHEILA *tiptoes round from the side of the house to join* KENNY *and* LARRY.

KENNY I think we got away with that.

EXT. DRIVEWAY. DAY 9.

DAMON *stands on the drive, smoking a cigarette. He has his phone to his ear.*

DAMON Hi, Val, it's me . . . I've not heard from you in a couple of days. I'm just checking if you're still coming back tomorrow. I'm sorry about what happened the other night; I know it was a stupid thing to do. I overreacted. Anyway, it's all cleaned up now, so I look forward to seeing you later.

DAMON *seems to be looking straight into the doorbell camera.*

DAMON *(cont'd)* There's still some of that horrible cauliflower quiche in the freezer if you fancy that? Anyway. See you soon. Love you.

DAMON *hangs up, glances again at the camera, then goes back inside.*

EXT. DRIVEWAY. DAY 9.

DAMON *is in the drive, vacuuming the boot and back seat areas of the car.*

EXT. DRIVEWAY. DAY 10.

KENNY *stands in his garden, raking up leaves.*

DAMON *drives into his driveway and gets out of the car, then shouts across to* KENNY.

DAMON I'm glad that you're taking such an interest in my every movement, Kenny – thanks for that!

KENNY Eh?

DAMON *approaches* KENNY*'s house.*

DAMON You know what I'm talking about! I've just had a visit from a community police officer at my place of work . . .

KENNY What's that got to do with me?

DAMON Don't play the innocent, I know full well it was you. And I'm here you tell you it stops now.

KENNY *backs away from* DAMON. DAMON *tips* KENNY*'s wheelbarrow over.* SHEILA *comes out to see what's going on.*

KENNY Give over, what you playing at?

DAMON *starts to march back again. They follow him into the street.*

SHEILA Excuse me, Damon, you don't get to speak to my husband like that! He's got a pacemaker.

DAMON Oh, has he?

SHEILA Yes, and he can't be round any stressful situations.

DAMON Well, keep your nose out of my business then!

KENNY Come away, Sheila.

DAMON You're always making up excuses to come round and spy on us. 'Do you have a recipe for banana bread?' 'Can we check the water pressure in your bathroom?'

KENNY I just wanted to compare; we only get a dribble!

DAMON And I know you've been creeping round every time I go out!

SHEILA I beg your pardon!

DAMON I've got divots in my back garden from your heels, Sheila! It should be me calling the police on you.

LARRY *appears with Popcorn on a lead.*

LARRY What's with this shouting? Everything alright?

KENNY He's going round the twist, accusing us of all sorts here! Says we've been spying on him.

LARRY Well, I haven't!

DAMON Don't bother, Larry. I know you're their third wheel. They don't know where I work – you do.

SHEILA Where's Valerie in all this, Damon? We'd like to hear her side of the story.

DAMON She's up my arse, second shelf on the right.

SHEILA Disgusting. There's no need for crude language. I knew you'd be trouble the second you moved in . . . Those gnomes showing their bottoms, that was enough.

DAMON Oh, fuck off.

DAMON *heads back to his house. Popcorn starts to bark.*

KENNY Eh! Come on, we're not savages.

SHEILA Leave him, Ken, he's not worth it.

DAMON Just stick to your own side of the street from now on.

SHEILA Don't worry, we will.

LARRY We're just concerned, that's all. Val's such a lovely lady, it's not like her to disappear like that without a trace.

DAMON It's none of your fucking business. And you make any more accusations, and I promise you'll regret it, Larry – do you hear me?

DAMON *goes inside and slams the door closed.* LARRY, KENNY *and* SHEILA *stare, dumbfounded.*

EXT. DRIVEWAY. NIGHT 10.

All is quiet in the street. DAMON*'s car isn't on the drive. The recycling bins are out.*

Opposite, the door opens and SHEILA *steps out. She looks across at* DAMON*'s house.*

EXT. DRIVEWAY. DAY 11.

After a few beats, we hear LARRY *calling for Popcorn.*

LARRY *(O.S.)* Popcorn! Popcorn! Come on, boy, where are you?

LARRY *wanders into shot, carrying a lead. He looks around, bewildered.*

LARRY *(cont'd)* Popcorn!

LARRY *wanders back to his house.*

EXT. DRIVEWAY. NIGHT 11.

The quiet street at night. We hear a noise approach, and then see VAL *come into shot wheeling a suitcase. She comes up the drive and fishes her key from her handbag, then lets herself into the house.*

LARRY *wanders into shot, looking perplexed. He hovers outside the house.* VAL *comes back out, carrying some empty wine bottles and food waste.*

VAL Oh, hiya Larry! You're up late.

LARRY I've been looking for Popcorn. So you're back, then?

VAL Yeah – I'm away a week and the place is a tip!

LARRY Where've you been?

VAL Oh, I've just been at my sister's in Halifax. Damon and I had a stupid row about a futon.

LARRY A futon?

VAL Yeah. He was pissed and spilled red wine all over it. Then he pushed it down the stairs and it broke. Dickhead ended up chopping it up with a chainsaw.

LARRY Oh. We thought . . .

VAL What?

LARRY Nothing.

VAL *removes the brick from the food caddy lid and puts the food waste in the caddy.*

VAL So what's happened to Popcorn?

LARRY Oh, he's run off. He's found a way to get out the garden through the hedge, but he usually comes back. I'm getting a bit worried now.

VAL I'm sure he'll show up.

LARRY I hope so.

LARRY *nods to the food caddy.* VAL *has the bottles in her hand.*

LARRY You've had no more problems with foxes, then?

VAL No, fingers crossed. Open that up for me, would you, please?

LARRY *lifts the lid of the recycling bin.* VAL *looks inside. She gasps.*

VAL Oh my God, what . . . ? Oh, Larry, don't look.

LARRY *looks inside the bin.*

LARRY Popcorn . . . ?

VAL What's happened? What's he doing in there?

LARRY It was you . . . You poisoned him.

VAL What? No, I'd never do that.

LARRY You said you would. Poisoned him and dumped him in the dustbin.

VAL Of course I didn't! Let me go and phone Damon . . .

VAL *goes back into the house.*

LARRY *stares inside the bin. He looks to the food caddy and slowly takes the brick from the top.* LARRY *moves towards the house and disappears inside.*

VAL *(O.S.)* Larry, wait outside, would you love? Larry, what . . . ? No!

VAL *screams as we hear a struggle inside. We hear a thud, followed by a couple more.* VAL *is silent.*

LARRY *emerges in a daze. He turns to close the door, then heads back to the recycling bin. He takes the dead body of Popcorn from the bin and goes back home.*

EXT. DRIVEWAY. DAY 12.

It's the next morning, and we are suddenly seeing the events through a police body-cam worn by POLICE OFFICER 1.

There is an ambulance and a police car outside the house. A body in a black body bag is being lifted into the back of the ambulance.

DAMON *is led out of the house by a pair of* DETECTIVES. *He is handcuffed. They lead him down to the police car.* DAMON *sees* SHEILA, KENNY *and* LARRY *on their drive with* POLICE OFFICER 2.

DAMON Are you getting all this? Are you happy now? *(To* DETECTIVES*)* I didn't do it!

The DETECTIVES *push* DAMON *into the police car and it drives away.* POLICE OFFICER 1 *heads towards* SHEILA*'s house, still wearing the body-cam, and we pick up the statement they are giving to* POLICE OFFICER 2.

SHEILA To be honest, we were suspicious of him as soon as they moved in, weren't we Ken?

KENNY Oh, yeah. They were into satanism, witchcraft, all that type of thing. Wouldn't surprise me if they were devil-worshippers.

SHEILA They used to hang skeletons and whatnot in the garden and light candles.

KENNY Although to be fair, that was just at Halloween.

SHEILA Still, no smoke without fire.

LARRY And you saw him dragging her body out and putting it in the boot of his car, didn't you?

SHEILA Yes. Granted, this was a week before he actually killed her, but we think it was a trial run, don't we?

KENNY Yeah.

POLICE OFFICER 2 You've been very helpful, thanks.

SHEILA Can I just ask, do you think they might do a Netflix on it? *The Mulberry Close Murders.*

POLICE OFFICER 1 *and* POLICE OFFICER 2 *approach* DAMON *and* VAL*'s house.*

SHEILA *(O.S.) (cont'd)* I think it would be a good three-parter. And if they need anyone to do the voice-over, we do know Michael Ball a little bit . . .

POLICE OFFICER 1 *has almost entered the house when he steps back and we see the doorbell camera for the first time. He points at it.*

POLICE OFFICER 1 Do we know if anybody's checked the door-cam footage yet?

EXT. DRIVEWAY. NIGHT 10.

The street at night. DAMON*'s car isn't on the drive. The recycling bins are out. We wait; nothing happens. The tape fast-forwards a little.*

Opposite, the door opens and SHEILA *steps out. She looks across at* DAMON*'s house.*

We can hear Popcorn barking.

SHEILA *gets into* KENNY*'s car and haltingly drives off the drive. She reverses out of shot, and we hear a yelp. The barking stops. We hear the car door open and* SHEILA *get out.*

SHEILA *(O.S.)* Oh, for God's sake . . .

SHEILA *comes into shot. She is carrying the dead body of Popcorn, which she puts into* DAMON*'s wheelie bin. The image freeze-frames.*

MICHAEL BALL *(V.O.)* And it was at this point that detectives knew they'd blown the case wide open. I'm Michael Ball, and this . . . is *The Mulberry Close Murders.*

THE END

Episode 4

CTRL/ALT/ESC

CAST LIST

DOUG – Reece Shearsmith

JASON – Steve Pemberton

MILLIE – Kalli Tant

LYNNE – Katherine Kelly

AMY – Maddie Evans

DOCTOR DEATH – Angus Wright

INT. CCTV MONITOR. DAY.

Close on a grainy CCTV monitor showing a high angle of a doorway. The door opens, and we see DOUG *enter, followed by* JASON, LYNNE *and teenage children* MILLIE *(18) and* AMY *(15).*

There is a piece of card taped to the top of the monitor that says, 'Room 9'.

TITLE: *'CTRL/ALT/ESC'*

INT. ESCAPE ROOM. DAY.

The action takes place in an escape room. It is dimly lit and decked out like a serial killer's lair, with an eerie soundtrack playing in the background. The door through which they entered has a flickering Exit sign above it.

A plastic-sheeted area in one corner contains a padlocked filing cabinet. There is a bed with a bloodstained mattress and sheet, and a wooden desk with an old PC and a scrapbook on it.

A pile of discarded shoes is in one corner, and there are torture implements on the walls, as well as a map with pins in it and some newspaper articles. A butcher's sink with a mirror above it; all very grubby and sinister.

DOUG *wears a T-shirt and gilet. He carries a clipboard.*

DOUG Right, are we all ensconced? Excellent. So, have any of you done an escape room before?

JASON Yes, we all have.

MILLIE We've all been forced to do one, you mean.

LYNNE Jason's a big fan, aren't you, darling?

JASON I wouldn't say that, but we've done a lot of the local ones, most recently *The Haunted Submarine* at Endgame in Chester.

DOUG Yes, I've heard they're pretty decent. Did the props all work?

MILLIE No.

JASON Yes. Most of them did.

LYNNE There was a remote control that needed new batteries.

DOUG That doesn't surprise me; they're known for cutting corners. Anyway, you'll know the basics then. You've got sixty minutes to find your way out of the room, solving puzzles and unlocking things as you go. There's no need to force anything; if it's meant to move, it'll move, so please don't yank the smoke alarm off the ceiling as one group of ladies did the other week – stag and hen groups, the worst! But I assume you're a family team, so you'll know all about the C-word?

LYNNE Yes, I've been married to him for twenty years.

AMY Mum!

JASON It's alright, Amy, she's only joking – I hope! He means . . . 'cooperation'!

The others join in half-heartedly.

DOUG Exactly; you'll need to work together if you're going to escape in time. Now . . .

DOUG *attempts to create a spooky atmosphere.*

DOUG *(cont'd)* You've probably heard on the news about the serial killer known as Doctor Death.

MILLIE That's original.

LYNNE Shhhh!

DOUG So-called because he likes to experiment on his victims . . .

AMY This is too freaky. I don't like it!

MILLIE Oh for God's sakes, he's just an out-of-work actor, Amy. It's not real.

LYNNE Millie, don't be so rude! I'm sorry about that.

DOUG Well, I'm not technically out of work. And I did recently have an availability check for a three-man *Much Ado* touring schools in Germany so . . . fingers crossed.

MILLIE Sounds amazing.

DOUG If you could all line up for me against the bed . . .

JASON Absolutely. Come on, fall in.

They line up by the bed.

DOUG Now, you were on your way to a local beauty spot when you stopped at this cabin to ask directions. The friendly man offered you some iced tea, and the next thing you know, you're trapped down here in his basement. Oop, excuse me . . .

DOUG *drops his pen and bends down to get it.*

AMY Dad, I'm scared.

JASON It's alright Amy, we're going to get out.

MILLIE This is so lame.

We hear a click and see that DOUG *has chained* JASON*'s ankle to the bed.*

DOUG Looks like you're going to need to find a key for that.

JASON Oh no! Why's it always me?

MILLIE 'Cos you're the most competitive.

JASON Excuse me, wanting to succeed at something isn't the same as being competitive.

LYNNE No, but making your daughter cry because she couldn't guess '*Squid Game*' at charades comes pretty high on the list.

JASON There's no such thing as 'Octopus Tennis'.

AMY It's alright, Dad. I forgive you.

AMY *squeezes* JASON*'s hand.*

DOUG There's a walkie-talkie on the table, so if you get stuck or want a hint, I'll be there to guide you – but use them wisely, as you only get three clues per game. Good luck.

DOUG *hands* JASON *the clipboard and heads to the door.*

DOUG *(cont'd)* Oh, and if you hear this door open at any stage, then I'd hide if I were you. It's probably Doctor Death . . .

DOUG *exits.*

LYNNE I think he's one of the ones that's a bit too much into his job, don't you?

JASON Come on you lot, you know the drill. Start looking . . . Mark out your territory and shout if you find anything. We'll use this desk as HQ.

MILLIE *shakes her head and slopes off. They start searching the room.*

MILLIE You're not in the army now, Dad. You got invalided out, remember?

JASON So, we've got tools on the wall, shoes in the corner, looks like there's a hidden object in this pipe here. Can you get your hand in, Ames . . . ?

AMY *reaches into a half-drainpipe on the wall by the sink.*

LYNNE It would help if we knew what we were looking for.

JASON A key for this lock would be a good start. *(To* AMY*)* Can you get in?

AMY No.

MILLIE *is looking at the tools on the wall.*

MILLIE I've found something.

MILLIE *produces a plastic bloodstained knife. She wields it* Psycho*-style, and* AMY *screams.*

MILLIE Fucking hell, Amy. It's only red paint, he's not going to actually murder us!

LYNNE Millie, enough of the attitude, please. We're trying to do a nice thing for Dad.

MILLIE Oh yeah, really nice. A windowless room with a piss-stained mattress.

JASON Look on the bright side – it'll help you get used to your university digs!

MILLIE Ha ha.

JASON Anyway, this isn't just for me. It's for all of us, to spend some quality time together as a family.

MILLIE I bet that's what Mr Fritzl said.

JASON Millie!

AMY Who's Mr Fritzl?

JASON Come on, please. We're not going to have the chance to do things like this soon. Amy's growing up, you're going off to uni . . .

MILLIE Dad, the only way you can get us to spend time together is to lock us up in a basement and chain yourself to a bed – doesn't that tell you something?

LYNNE *is exploring the corner with a plastic curtain. It looks like there may be someone behind it.* LYNNE *pulls back the curtain to reveal a dressmaker's dummy wearing a mask of human skin.*

LYNNE Jesus.

LYNNE *spots a large filing cabinet with a locked bottom drawer.*

LYNNE OK, I've found a filing cabinet with a padlock on it, and there's four names . . . Jeannie, Bella Rose, Sammie and Georgina. Maybe they're all his victims?

JASON OK, and we're off.

JASON *writes down the names down on a clipboard.*

AMY *finds a scrapbook under the cabinet by the sink.*

AMY Dad, look – there's a scrapbook. There might be something in here . . .

JASON Clever girl, Ames, good thinking.

AMY *looks in the scrapbook.*

JASON I went to school with someone called Georgina. My first girlfriend. Bit of a tubby lass.

AMY Dad!

JASON Georgie Porgie, we called her.

AMY You can't say that.

JASON Alright, don't cancel me!

MILLIE *finds a wallet in a coat hanging on the door. Inside is a Polaroid of a girl in a bedroom. Written underneath is the word 'Sammie'.*

MILLIE I've found Sammie.

JASON OK, good, and what do you see . . . ?

MILLIE A girl.

JASON Anything else?

MILLIE A dead girl.

JASON If you *reflect* on it . . . ?

MILLIE *looks at the photo. The girl has a mirror behind her, and in it we can see the back of her T-shirt, which bears a number seven.*

MILLIE Oh, a seven. *(To* LYNNE*)* Sammie is number seven.

LYNNE Well done, Millie.

LYNNE *twists the numbers on the padlock.* JASON *looks in the mirror above the sink.*

JASON Always pays to check the mirrors . . . Sometimes they're two-way.

JASON *breathes on the mirror and wipes it.*

JASON *(cont'd)* I keep getting the feeling someone could be looking in on us.

AMY Dad! There's a newspaper report about a Jeannie Grey. It says she was found with an ear missing – ew. Could that be a one, for one ear?

JASON That's a bit of a stretch – let me have a look . . . ?

JASON *looks at the article with* AMY. MILLIE *joins* LYNNE, *who is looking at a letter she found crumpled in the toilet.*

MILLIE So, are you jealous about Dad and his fat girlfriend?

LYNNE No, of course not, don't be stupid. Anyway, your dad and I don't have any secrets from each other.

MILLIE *(knowingly)* Really?

LYNNE Yes.

MILLIE So he knows what's happening later?

LYNNE That's different.

MILLIE Is it?

LYNNE I'm not having this discussion in front of Dad, OK?

MILLIE OK, fine, let's just keep on playing happy families. But you're the one who's going to have to live with it.

LYNNE *looks concerned.*

JASON I've got it! It's eight. First letter of each line, look. 'Earlier today . . . Idaho . . . Grey', etc. E-I-G-H-T.

We see the acrostic showing the word 'eight' spelled down the left-hand side.

AMY That's amazing! How did you see that?

JASON The headline. Look: '*Initial* Clues Lead to Discovery'.

AMY You're so clever, Dad.

MILLIE *lifts a dirty towel which is hanging on the wall to reveal a 'Missing' poster.*

MILLIE There's a missing person poster here for Bella.

AMY *goes to look at the poster.*

MILLIE *(cont'd)* 'Last seen wearing a pink dress and bright green stilettos'.

JASON Shoes . . .

JASON *goes to look at the pile of shoes, but the chain prevents him from reaching them.*

JASON Dammit! I hate not being able to do anything.

LYNNE I'll do it.

JASON You're looking for a green stiletto.

LYNNE Yes, I'm not an idiot, Jason.

JASON I didn't say you were!

LYNNE *goes to look through the pile of shoes in the corner.*

JASON *(cont'd)* What was all that about?

LYNNE What?

JASON With Millie? I heard you whispering in the corner.

LYNNE Nothing.

JASON I don't like being excluded from these conversations, OK?

LYNNE OK!

LYNNE *has found the shoe.*

LYNNE Green stiletto, size six.

JASON *writes this down and looks through the scrapbook.* LYNNE *watches him.*

JASON Right, so that's eight, six, seven . . .

LYNNE I've never wanted to be with anybody else, you know. Even . . .

JASON Sorry?

LYNNE It's been a really hard couple of years. I just need you to know that . . . I still love you.

JASON What are you talking about? You're not leaving me, are you?

LYNNE *kisses* JASON.

AMY Ugh, will you two get a room, please?

LYNNE What's the matter? Don't you like seeing your parents do a bit of bondage?

LYNNE *refers to* JASON*'s chain.*

MILLIE Necrophilia, more like.

LYNNE Oh, Millie!

MILLIE *heads for the walkie-talkie.*

MILLIE I'm getting a clue.

JASON No, hang on, we've only been here ten minutes!

MILLIE So?

LYNNE Your dad's right, we can't be calling for back-up yet.

MILLIE *(to* LYNNE*)* I thought you told me never to be afraid to ask for help. 'If you ever need to speak to someone, Millie, there's no shame is seeing a therapist!' That's what you said.

JASON *(to* LYNNE*)* Did you?

AMY Is something wrong with Millie?

LYNNE No! I just wanted you to have someone to talk to, that's all.

MILLIE Instead of my parents, you mean?

DOUG *(O.S.)* Hello? Are you needing a hint?

MILLIE Yes. We need the number for Georgina.

DOUG *(O.S.)* OK. Well, I believe Doctor Death used to stalk his victims. Perhaps he was following her on the day she was abducted?

MILLIE Oh, for fuck's sake, can't you just tell us the number so we can get out of here?

DOUG *(O.S.)* Try and *map* her movements. You've got two clues left.

AMY The map!

AMY *points to the map on the wall through the plastic sheeting.*

LYNNE Come on, let's take a look at it then . . .

AMY Dad?

JASON I can't, can I? I'm hobbled.

LYNNE *and* AMY *go to the map. There are several pins in it. One of them has a red thread hanging from it.* LYNNE *reads the first location.*

LYNNE OK, Argyll Hotel, that sounds familiar. Oh, it's in the letter, down there, I found it earlier!

AMY *passes the letter to* LYNNE *and she reads.*

LYNNE That's where he first saw her. So, he followed her to County Hall, then the post office . . .

AMY *finds the pins and pulls the red thread along to join them.*

AMY Hang on, hang on . . . I think we've got to pull this along here . . .

MILLIE How many places are there?

JASON Let Amy do it!

LYNNE The Midway Diner . . .

MILLIE It's going to be a five.

LYNNE Doctor's surgery . . . And finally, Briar Park.

MILLIE So the numbers are eight, six, seven, five.

MILLIE *goes over to the filing cabinet and starts to enter the numbers.* AMY *completes the pattern.*

AMY Look, it's a five, Mum.

LYNNE Yay, well done, Ames!

MILLIE I said that half an hour ago.

MILLIE *removes the padlock and pulls opens the filing cabinet . . . to reveal a passageway leading to a dark tunnel.*

AMY Wow!

JASON What's happening?

AMY It's not a filing cabinet, it's a passageway!

LYNNE Go on, then, do you want to go through?

AMY I'm scared. You go first.

LYNNE OK, wish me luck . . .

LYNNE *starts to crawl through into the next room and* AMY *follows.*

JASON Hang on! Don't leave me, we need to find the key to this first!

JASON *refers to his ankle chain.*

MILLIE It might be through there, genius.

JASON We probably should have found it by now. Check under the tables.

MILLIE I should go with them.

JASON Please, Millie. I can't do it by myself.

MILLIE *is frustrated but starts to look around the room.* JASON *watches her.*

JASON Is there something going on between you and Mum? You can tell me, you know.

MILLIE I have been! You just don't listen.

JASON I do listen; I've heard everything you've said, I promise. Look, I know that you're angry with me and you feel I haven't been there for you . . .

MILLIE Dad, I don't want to have a 'big talk' now, OK? It's too late for that.

JASON The thing is, you're about to go away and have this whole new life at university, and I'm going to lose you. I want this time to count.

MILLIE So you've locked us in a serial killer's basement, thanks. Great parenting.

JASON Millie, you can't go through life being this furious at everything. Things happen and you need to find a way to deal with them, find some resilience.

MILLIE You don't have to worry about me. I'm not going to do anything stupid.

JASON But I do worry; I lie awake at night worrying about you. You've been around for eighteen years and then suddenly you're not going to be there. What am I meant to do?

MILLIE I won't go then.

JASON I don't want you to go! Honestly, I don't. You're my firstborn; it's going to kill me. But I want you to do it for yourself. Show everyone how strong and capable you are. I'm so proud of you. I just wish you could hear that.

MILLIE *is half-heartedly searching the room. She looks in a small box.*

MILLIE I remember when we went ice-skating one Christmas time, I must have been about seven or eight. And I was just clinging on to the barrier, sliding my way round.

JASON Yes, I remember.

MILLIE And you said I had to let go of the sides and dare to do it by myself. I was so scared I'd fall over.

JASON You did fall over.

MILLIE I know. And when you came to help me up, I dragged you down with me. I was terrified that someone would chop my fingers off with their skates.

JASON You can't not do something just because you're scared of getting hurt.

MILLIE Are you sure about that?

MILLIE *tips the box on to the desk, and a series of plastic severed fingers tumble out. They laugh.*

JASON Crikey. Looks like Doctor Death likes going ice-skating. Come here . . .

MILLIE *goes to hug* JASON. *Suddenly the voice of* LYNNE *can be heard in the room over a tannoy.*

LYNNE *(O.S.)* Hello? Hello, can you hear us?

JASON Yes, yes, we can hear you! Whe–

LYNNE *(O.S.)* Hello . . . Jason?

JASON Yes, where are you? What's happening?

LYNNE *(O.S.)* If you can hear us, we've found a key but we need Millie. It takes three people to get it. Can you come?

JASON Go on, you go.

MILLIE *(sarcastically)* What, let go of the sides, you mean?

JASON Yes, I'll be fine.

MILLIE OK. Hope Doctor Death doesn't come for you.

JASON I can take him.

MILLIE *smiles and goes through the filing cabinet tunnel.* JASON *is left alone.*

JASON Lynne, can you hear me? Millie's coming to join you.

Just a crackle from the speaker, no response.

JASON *(cont'd)* Lynne?

JASON *looks around, seeing how far his chain will allow him to move.*

He searches through the drawers of the desk. In one, there is some fishing tackle, and JASON *takes out some fishing line, which is attached to a magnet.*

JASON OK, where do we use this . . . ? A-ha!

JASON *remembers the narrow pipe in the corner by the bed, which is big enough for the magnet to be lowered down.*

He goes over and puts the magnet down the pipe, and it attaches to something. He pulls it up to reveal a small torch. JASON *turns it on and it shines a UV light.*

JASON Bingo. Now we're talking. Let there be light . . .

JASON *sees that he can just about reach the light switch for the room, and he turns the light off to plunge the room into near darkness.*

JASON *scans the room with the UV light and notices handprints on the door. He follows a trail of handprints across the wall to a picture of a sleeping child.* JASON *removes the picture from the wall and shines the torch so he can see the message on the wall behind it.*

There is another handprint and the words: 'NO ESCAPE'. JASON *places his hand on the painted hand, and it matches exactly.*

Just then the door starts to open. JASON *hurries back to the bed and lies in it, pulling the sheet over his head. As he lies under the sheet, he can hear the door open and close, followed by footsteps and laboured breathing.*

JASON *dares to peek out from the side of the sheet. He can see a pair of large, booted feet walk past. The figure wears mucky scrubs and a white coat, flecked with blood and dirt.*

*The figure (*DOCTOR DEATH*) crosses past the bed and takes something from the wall. We see the axe come down into shot. It is noisily dragged along the wooden floor as the figure heads towards the filing cabinet.*

JASON *is confused. He dares to look above the sheet and he sees, silhouetted in the corner of the room by the plastic sheeting, the imposing figure of* DOCTOR DEATH. *With an axe.*

JASON Hello?

DOCTOR DEATH *turns round. He wears a surgical mask and cap, and a powerful head lamp, which shines in* JASON*'s face.* JASON *shields his eyes.*

DOUG *(O.S.)* Only me . . .

JASON *turns to see* DOUG *coming into the room.* DOUG *turns the main lights back on.*

DOUG Sorry, but there's been a bit of a technical glitch.

JASON *looks back round to the filing cabinet, but the figure is no longer there. Just the dressmaker's dummy.*

DOUG *(cont'd)* I need to do an emergency assist.

JASON What is it?

DOUG It's annoying, the desktop PC should have come on when they found the tannoy downstairs. Sometimes if it's in sleep mode too long, it goes dormant and needs a manual reboot.

DOUG *goes to sit at the computer and holds down the keys to reboot.*

DOUG *(cont'd)* Control, alt, escape. How are you finding the difficulty level? Harder than Chester?

JASON It's OK. The acrostic in the scrapbook was a nice touch.

DOUG It's a good room. We do pride ourselves on being very authentic. Your daughters seem to be coping with it – either that, or they're putting on a brave face.

JASON A bit of both, I think. They're indulging me. I know none of them want to be here really, but it's nice to have something to do together while we can.

DOUG Oh yeah, they are going to do fine, I can tell. Right, there we go, we're back on. So this . . . is what you should have seen earlier.

The screen now shows a smaller room, where LYNNE, MILLIE *and* AMY *are working on a puzzle, the two girls turning separate handles to lift a screen.*

DOUG *(cont'd)* They can talk to you using the intercom, but you're going to need to find a way to communicate with them.

JASON OK, I'll work it out.

DOUG I'll be watching!

DOUG *exits and* JASON *goes to watch his family on the screen.*

INT. ANNEXE. DAY.

JASON *can see* LYNNE, AMY *and* MILLIE *in an adjacent room. In an alcove, there are shelves of medical jars containing body parts. There is a screen which allows access to the shelves, and wheels each side which operate it.*

INT. ESCAPE ROOM/ANNEXE. DAY

JASON *looks around the desk. There is an old dial phone. When* JASON *lifts the receiver, the whole unit comes away, revealing a button and red light underneath.*

JASON *presses the button, and light in the annexe dips on and off.*

JASON Hello? Ah . . .

LYNNE *goes to the intercom on the wall and we can see her speak.*

LYNNE Jason, is that you doing that? Flash twice if that's you.

JASON *presses twice.*

LYNNE Right, we can see the key in one of these jars, but there's a padlock on it. Millie and Amy can lift the screen, but I need a four-letter word to open the lock. Can you see us?

JASON *presses the button twice.*

AMY Tell him about the Morse code.

LYNNE Yes; there's a Morse code alphabet here, so you'll need to find something your end and tell us the word.

AMY You can do it, Daddy!

JASON *looks around the room.*

JASON OK, four-letter word. Book, lamp . . . Could be anything. Sod it.

JASON *picks up the walkie-talkie.*

JASON Hello, over?

DOUG *(O.S.)* Yes?

JASON We need another hint, please. The four-letter word to get the key, over.

DOUG *(O.S.)* Have you tried looking at their room from a different angle?

JASON No, how do I do that? Over.

DOUG *(O.S.)* Well, there's lots of space in that room. You could almost fit a bar in.

JASON Sorry, what's that? Over.

DOUG *(O.S.)* There's space for a bar . . . Space bar. You hit space bar on the computer.

JASON OK, thank you. Over and out.

DOUG *(O.S.)* One clue left!

JASON *returns to the desk and hits the space bar on the keyboard, which shows him a different angle of the annexe room. He presses it again and sees a high angle, showing the whole room.*

In the top corner of the screen, sitting on top of a shelf near the camera (unseen by the rest of the family), there is a large picture of a star.

JASON Star, OK . . .

JASON *presses dot-dot-dot.*

On the monitor, LYNNE *sees the lights.*

LYNNE Oh, wait! Dot-dot-dot, that's an 'S'.

The lights flash: 'dash'.

LYNNE *(cont'd)* 'T'.

The lights flash: Dot-dash.

LYNNE *(cont'd)* Er . . . 'A'.

The lights flash: Dot-dash-dot.

LYNNE (cont'd) 'R'. Star. Brilliant, well done, Jase!

MILLIE *enters the code, and she and* AMY *go to pull the rope pulleys, which open the screen.* LYNNE *goes to unlock the padlock.* JASON *watches on his screen.*

LYNNE *opens the jar and gets out the key. She waves it in the air. The girls lower the screen.*

JASON Yes, finally!

Suddenly, we see a secret door open in the annexe, and an imposing DOCTOR DEATH *stands there, holding the axe.*

JASON What the hell . . .? Lynne! Lynne!

We see the girls scream and back away as DOCTOR DEATH *approaches.*

JASON *scrolls through the screen options, and we see* DOCTOR DEATH *grab* MILLIE *as* LYNNE *tries to fight him off.*

AMY *presses the intercom.*

AMY Daddy please, help!

JASON Amy!

AMY Help us!

The screen crackles.

JASON Amy! I'm coming!

JASON *pulls on his chain, desperately trying to yank it off. He can't lift the bed.*

JASON Let me out! Please! Let me ouuuutttt!

JASON *grabs the walkie-talkie and presses the button. It hisses and crackles.*

JASON Hello, can you hear me? We need help in here, over . . . Hello? Help me, please . . . Why can't you hear me?

JASON *continues to shout, but we can no longer hear him, just the sound of a respirator.*

INT. HOSPITAL ROOM. DAY.

We see JASON *lying in a hospital bed in a gown. He is wired up to machines and a respirator, which is keeping him alive. The respirator sound is similar to the eerie soundtrack in the escape room.* JASON*'s eyes are taped closed. He is immobile.*

LYNNE, MILLIE *and* AMY *sit near by, red-eyed and weary.*

AMY What do you think he's thinking about?

LYNNE I don't think he can think anything at all, darling. It's only the machines that are keeping him going.

A tear runs down MILLIE*'s cheek.*

DOUG *enters, wearing blue nurse's scrubs.*

DOUG Only me. How are we?

LYNNE We're OK.

DOUG The doctor's just on his way. Here.

DOUG *offers a box of tissues and* MILLIE *takes one.*

DOUG *(cont'd)* I'm sure he'd be very proud of you.

MILLIE How the fuck do you know?

LYNNE Millie.

DOUG It's alright. I've just got to do one last check of his vitals.

DOUG *crosses to* JASON *and removes the tape from his eyes.* DOUG *lifts the eyelid and shines a torch in* JASON*'s eye.*

INT. ESCAPE ROOM. DAY.

JASON *reacts to a bright light in his face. We see* AMY *approach with a torch.*

AMY Dad!

AMY *runs towards* JASON *and embraces him.*

JASON Amy, it's alright. Where's Millie?

MILLIE I'm here . . .

MILLIE *is coming through the hatch. She runs towards him.*

JASON What's happening? Where's your mum?

MILLIE She's coming. It's not a game, Dad, it's real.

JASON I know, I know, I believe you. Have you got the key?

MILLIE Mum's got it.

AMY I don't want him to kill you . . .

JASON He's not going to kill me. I just need the key.

LYNNE Here . . .

LYNNE *comes in from the hatch area.*

LYNNE *(cont'd)* He's right behind me, Jason, you haven't got much time. I'm going to take the girls and go.

AMY I'm not leaving him!

JASON You've got to, Amy. I'll be fine, I promise. You can't stay here–

A terrifying growl comes from the passageway beyond the filing cabinet. LYNNE *presses the key into* JASON*'s hand and kisses him.*

LYNNE I love you.

JASON *looks down at the key in his hand. When he looks back up,* LYNNE *and the girls have disappeared. He is alone.* MILLIE*'s voice comes through the tannoy.*

MILLIE *(V.O.)* You've just got to get yourself out, Dad; you can do it. I know you can.

A low growl from the sheeted plastic alerts JASON *to the passageway. Over by the filing cabinet, a hand comes out and* DOCTOR DEATH *starts to emerge.*

JASON *takes the key and tries to unlock the padlock. He fumbles and drops the key.*

The plastic sheeting is pulled back, and the terrifying DOCTOR DEATH *stands staring at* JASON*, holding the axe.*

INT. HOSPITAL. DAY.

DOCTOR MORTON *enters. He's a tall man with an air of authority (same actor as* DOCTOR DEATH*).*

DOUG *is by the bed with* LYNNE*,* MILLIE *and* AMY*.*

DOCTOR MORTON Hello. How are you all doing?

LYNNE Alright. We're ready, I think.

DOUG *hands the notes to* DOCTOR MORTON *and he looks over them. All very medical and dignified.*

AMY *starts to sob.*

DOCTOR MORTON Very good. As I explained, we'll withdraw the feeding tube and the ventilator assistance, then administer a muscle relaxant to counter any agonal respirations. It'll be very peaceful.

LYNNE Sorry, what is that?

DOCTOR MORTON As the body shuts down, the breathing will become more laboured. But please don't be alarmed, we've run all the tests and we're as certain as we can be that Jason no longer has any brain function. All clear?

LYNNE *nods.*

DOCTOR MORTON *(cont'd)* And the children . . . ?

DOUG They want to stay.

DOCTOR MORTON Very good.

DOCTOR MORTON *nods to* DOUG, *and they begin the process of removing the feeding tube from* JASON. *Beside the bed, we see a photo of young* MILLIE *ice-skating in a star-shaped frame.*

MILLIE *looks on.*

INT. ESCAPE ROOM. DAY.

JASON *is fumbling with the key and manages to unlock the ankle chain just as* DOCTOR DEATH *approaches.*

DOCTOR DEATH *swings down the axe, but* JASON *manages to roll away just in time and the axe is buried in the wooden floor.*

JASON *scrambles over to the door marked 'EXIT' and tries to open it, but it is locked. He sees there is a keypad and he presses a couple of buttons in a panic, but just then* DOCTOR DEATH *spins him round, reaches round his throat and lifts him from the ground.*

JASON *struggles to breathe as he is choked by* DOCTOR DEATH.

INT. HOSPITAL. DAY.

DOUG *switches off the ventilator and it starts to slow down and stop.* JASON *makes a strange, guttural, gurgling sound.*

LYNNE *and the girls sadly watch on.*

MILLIE *(to herself)* Let go of the sides, Dad.

INT. ESCAPE ROOM. DAY.

JASON *is barely conscious; his eyes roll up into his head.*

DOCTOR DEATH *drops* JASON *to the ground and slowly goes over to the sink to prepare a large syringe.*

JASON *manages to get to his feet. He reaches for the walkie-talkie and presses it. He's facing the door marked 'EXIT'.*

DOUG *(O.S.)* Hello?

JASON I can't get out.

DOUG *(O.S.)* You need to enter a passcode, it's a single digit.

JASON Please . . . I need my last clue.

DOUG *(O.S.)* It's been staring you in the face all along.

JASON *turns to see* DOCTOR DEATH *approach with the syringe.*

He looks to the mirror opposite the door. He focuses in on the 'EXIT' sign. The 'E' and 'T' are no longer illuminated, and the 'XI' is flickering. But as seen in the mirror, it reads . . .

JASON Number nine.

We hear the click of the door and the light turns green.

INT. HOSPITAL. DAY.

LYNNE *puts her hand out.*

LYNNE Stop!

DOCTOR MORTON *is standing by the bed with a syringe.*

LYNNE *(cont'd)* Did he just say something?

They all look to JASON. *He opens his eyes.*

THE END

Episode 5

THE CURSE OF THE NINTH

CAST LIST

NATHANIEL - Eddie Marsan

THE CURSE - James Swanton

JONAH - Reece Shearsmith

DEVONSHIRE - Hayley Squires

LILLIAN - Natalie Dormer

DICKY - Steve Pemberton

INT. MUSIC ROOM. NIGHT.

It is 1912. NATHANIEL BURNHAM *sits at his desk in front of a large score manuscript. We see that it is 'Symphony No 9'.*

TITLE: *'The Curse of the Ninth'.*

NATHANIEL *pours himself a large glass of port and downs it in one. He steels himself and thumbs through a few pages of handwritten music before finding a clean sheet. He dips his pen in the ink, stares down at the blank page hesitantly, then writes the header 'IV Rondo'. He starts to fill the bars with notes.*

NATHANIEL *strikes through some notes and writes others. He seems feverish as he conducts the music in his head. He pours and drinks more port. The electric light starts to flicker and fizz before it pops and goes out completely, plunging the room into darkness.*

NATHANIEL *seems scared. He looks up to the window and sees a reflection of himself at the desk. But behind him, a dark* SINISTER FIGURE *is slowly reaching a hand towards him . . .*

NATHANIEL *cries out and turns sharply, but there is nobody there.*

NATHANIEL Leave me alone!

NATHANIEL *picks up and reviews what he's written, ripping out the page and examining it.*

NATHANIEL *looks up to see the handle of the door turning slowly. He drops the page, then hurries to the door, pushing it closed. He drags a large item of furniture in front of the door to stop it from opening.*

The door starts to rattle in its frame, someone or something pushing from outside. NATHANIEL *takes a small gun from the desk drawer and points it at the door, his hand shaking. As the music swells,* NATHANIEL *backs away, gripped by fear, slowly collapsing to the floor.*

The door is being pushed open bit by bit. NATHANIEL *covers his ears, terrified. He stares at the crack in the door.*

NATHANIEL*'s eyes widen in terror. The door opens.* NATHANIEL *puts the gun under his chin and pulls the trigger. The music stops abruptly.*

EXT. HOUSE. DAY.

A finger presses the doorbell. It is five years later. A large detached house with extensive gardens.

JONAH *stands on the doorstep with a workman's tool bag. The door opens and the formidable maid* DEVONSHIRE *stands in the doorway.* JONAH *hands her his card.*

JONAH Oh, hello. Jonah Quigley from Fletcher and Cadby. I've come to tune your piano.

DEVONSHIRE *steps aside and* JONAH *enters.*

INT. HALLWAY. DAY.

DEVONSHIRE *closes the door.*

DEVONSHIRE Where's your dog?

JONAH I don't have a dog.

DEVONSHIRE Last fella had a dog.

JONAH Ah, perhaps he was . . . unsighted. Many of my colleagues are. They have a heightened sense of hearing, which makes them ideal for the position.

DEVONSHIRE Relieved himself all up and down my lady's curtains, he did.

JONAH Really? Oh, you mean the dog! Well, I can assure you I won't be doing that!

DEVONSHIRE Follow me.

A stony-faced DEVONSHIRE *leads* JONAH *through the house, which is expensively furnished.*

INT. MUSIC ROOM. DAY.

DEVONSHIRE *shows* JONAH *into the music room, a bright room which leads on to the garden. An old baby grand piano in one corner. A white bust of* NATHANIEL BURNHAM *on the bureau with gramophone records and sheet music.*

JONAH Goodness, a Bechstein, if I'm not mistaken. They have one of these in Buckingham Palace, so I'm told. One of the sweetest-sounding instruments in Europe. May I?

JONAH *lifts the lid and tinkles the ivories, but the piano is woefully out of tune.*

LILLIAN *(O.S.)* She hasn't been fingered in a number of years.

JONAH *looks up to see* LILLIAN, *a glamorous-looking widow, in the doorway. She has a glass of champagne and a cigarette in a holder.*

LILLIAN *(cont'd)* I do hope you'll be able to tighten the strings. Devonshire, go and fetch a glass of gooseberry juice for Mr . . . ?

JONAH Quigley.

LILLIAN Mr Quigley, how quaint. Or would you prefer something stronger? I've just popped open a rather perky bottle of 'poo.

JONAH No thank you, water's fine for me. But no ice or lemon!

DEVONSHIRE Don't flatter yourself.

DEVONSHIRE *departs.* JONAH *gets out his tools and lifts the lid of the piano.*

LILLIAN You will have noticed that the Bechstein has seen better days. I really ought to have it replaced, but it's of sentimental value.

JONAH Do you play at all?

LILLIAN I'm afraid not. I don't have the patience. The instrument belonged to my late husband. After he passed, it rather went to seed. As did I.

JONAH I'm very sorry to hear that. About your husband, I mean, not your going to seed. Which, of course, you haven't – still most becoming . . . A fan of Burnham, was he?

LILLIAN Sorry?

JONAH Your husband, a fan of Nathaniel Burnham? I couldn't help but notice your bust.

LILLIAN *raises an eyebrow coquettishly.*

JONAH On the desk! And the sheet music. His 5th symphony was incredible.

LILLIAN If you like that sort of thing.

JONAH I was a keen student of his. The way he blends so many different styles and moods, brooding and violent one minute, romantic the next. I studied his symphonies at the Guildhall.

LILLIAN Did you really?

JONAH Yes. I had aspirations to compose myself at one point, but . . . life got in the way. Inspiration failed to strike. So now I do this. Satisfying in its own way.

DEVONSHIRE *returns with the water.*

DEVONSHIRE Glass of water, no lemon, no ice. Will there be anything else, Mrs Burnham?

LILLIAN No, that's fine for now. Thank you, Devonshire.

JONAH*'s eyes widen.* DEVONSHIRE *leaves.*

JONAH Mrs Burnham?

LILLIAN Nathaniel composed his 5th at that very piano, Mr Quigley. And you are quite correct; he could be romantic and brooding and, yes, violent. Especially when the muse deserted him. Which is why I wish to preserve his legacy. After all, there's many a good tune can be played on an old piano.

LILLIAN *downs the last of her champagne and sweeps out of the room, leaving* JONAH *gobsmacked, looking in awe at the piano he is tuning, laying his fingers on the hallowed keys.*

INT. MUSIC ROOM. DAY.

JONAH *is tuning one of the keys in the highest register, but it doesn't respond. He looks inside the workings of the piano to investigate. He can see that there is a tightly folded-up piece of paper jammed between the hammers.*

JONAH *pulls the yellowing paper from inside the piano and carefully unfolds it. It is a torn page of manuscript with handwritten musical notes. It is headed 'IV Rondo' (the same page* NATHANIEL *wrote five years previously).* JONAH *studies the notes closely.*

INT. DINING ROOM. DAY.

DICKY*, a dapper man, and* LILLIAN *sit at the table, finishing their lunch.*

DICKY That was delicious; thank you, Devonshire.

DICKY *reaches for his cigarettes as* DEVONSHIRE *starts to clear the plates.* JONAH *knocks and enters.*

JONAH Mrs Burnham, I– Oh, sorry, I didn't realise you had company.

LILLIAN Not at all. This is Dicky Van Aas, a dear friend of mine who was also Nathaniel's lawyer. He takes care of all my business affairs.

JONAH Of course. A pleasure to meet you, sir!

DICKY How de do.

LILLIAN Mr Quigley here is servicing the piano in the music room. Won't you join us?

JONAH Oh, well, I don't want to impose . . .

DEVONSHIRE *steps back to allow* JONAH *to sit.*

JONAH *(cont'd)* Thank you, Somerset.

DEVONSHIRE Devonshire.

JONAH Of course, sorry. The thing is, Mrs Burnham, I found this piece of manuscript paper jammed between the C4 and D4.

JONAH *shows the paper to* LILLIAN.

JONAH *(cont'd)* I wondered whether it might have been written by Mr Burnham? Only it looks to be part of a symphony, and it isn't anything I recognised . . .

LILLIAN *studies the paper, then hands it to* DICKY. *They exchange a knowing glance.*

DICKY It's his, alright. What a sharp-eyed fellow you are.

JONAH Does that give me leave to hope that there may be an unperformed piece? This could be a major discovery.

DEVONSHIRE *is busying herself while listening to the conversation, and* LILLIAN *clocks this.*

LILLIAN That will be all, Devonshire, thank you.

DEVONSHIRE Ma'am.

DEVONSHIRE *leaves.*

LILLIAN Are you familiar, Mr Quigley, with 'The Curse of the Ninth'?

JONAH Vaguely, yes. Isn't it a kind of superstition?

LILLIAN Exactly. It's the misguided belief that a composer is going to die after writing their 9th symphony. Mahler started it, it's all poppycock.

DICKY *lights his cigarette.*

DICKY It isn't poppycock, Flora. Ever since Ludwig, it's been a decisive landmark. Beethoven, Dvorak, Schubert, Bruckner – after the 9th, they all went from composing to decomposing. To embark upon symphony number 9 is considered a folly, Mr Quigley, a challenge to Fate.

DICKY *gets up and places a record on the gramophone: Mahler's 9th Symphony.*

DICKY *(cont'd)* Poor old Mahler, well, he was possessed by the idea. He tried to dodge the curse by refusing to number his 9th symphony, passing it off as a song cycle.

JONAH *Das Lied von der Erde.*

DICKY Exactly. But Death was not to be cheated. By the time he composed this, his true 9th, his daughter had died, his wife had begun an affair, and his health had started to fail. He didn't live long enough to hear it performed.

JONAH But Burnham, your husband, he only wrote eight symphonies, correct?

LILLIAN Technically, yes. He'd been very much affected by what had happened to Mahler . . .

INT. MUSIC ROOM. DAY.

NATHANIEL *sits at his desk, staring at a piece of blank manuscript paper. He seems troubled.*

LILLIAN *(V.O.)* Two months after attending the funeral in Vienna, Nathaniel announced he was going to start composing his next symphony in Gustav's honour. It would be his 9th.

LILLIAN *comes in and places a cup of tea on the desk. She lays a comforting hand on* NATHANIEL*'s shoulder and he brushes it off.*

INT. DINING ROOM. DAY.

We are back with JONAH, LILLIAN *and* DICKY.

LILLIAN He never found it easy to begin any new work, but this was . . .

DICKY It was torture. To begin with, we dismissed it as nothing more than writer's block, but I believe he'd been gripped by the fear of the curse.

LILLIAN The thought of actually finishing the symphony came to terrify him. Then, one night . . .

INT. HALLWAY. NIGHT.

LILLIAN *hears* NATHANIEL*'s cry coming from the music room.*

NATHANIEL *(O.S.)* Leave me alone!

She crosses to the door and turns the handle slowly, but the door is suddenly pushed closed.

LILLIAN *starts to push open the door, but something has barricaded it.*

LILLIAN Darling?

LILLIAN *pushes and pushes until she finally can squeeze herself inside. She hears the sound of a gunshot.*

INT. MUSIC ROOM. NIGHT.

LILLIAN *pushes open the door, only to find* NATHANIEL *dead, his brains blown out against the wall.*

INT. DINING ROOM. DAY.

DICKY *extinguishes his cigarette.*

DICKY We reported it as a heart attack, of course, but it appears he'd driven himself completely mad.

JONAH I'm so sorry.

LILLIAN He brought it upon himself.

JONAH So the work was left . . . unfinished?

LILLIAN *and* DICKY *look at each other.*

INT. HALLWAY. DAY.

DEVONSHIRE *is at the door, listening in.*

LILLIAN *(O.S.)* He'd just begun the final movement. It would have been his masterpiece.

INT. DINING ROOM. DAY.

JONAH *looks at the torn page.*

JONAH. And you think this rondo could be part of it?

DICKY So it would seem.

JONAH This is incredible; I've never heard mention of it before. I'm sure the Burnham Society would be . . .

DICKY Nathaniel made it clear to me that should he die before the 9th was complete, he wanted it buried with him.

LILLIAN So that's what we did. It's out there. Six feet under. Sad, really. To deprive the world of such genius.

She takes the sheet of music from JONAH *and locks it in a drawer. She looks out of the window, and we see* NATHANIEL*'s grave in the garden.*

LILLIAN *(cont'd)* But we had to respect his wishes.

INT. MUSIC ROOM. DAY.

JONAH *is packing up his tools.* DEVONSHIRE *appears. She starts dusting.*

DEVONSHIRE Private burial, it was. Just my ladyship, Mr Van Aas and a couple of other witnesses. All very cloak and dagger.

JONAH What are you getting at, Kent?

DEVONSHIRE Devonshire.

JONAH Devonshire, sorry.

DEVONSHIRE Just that he deserved more.

JONAH Well, lucky for us, his music lives on.

DEVONSHIRE Yes. Most of it.

JONAH To have another Burnham gifted to the world, you couldn't put a price on such a thing.

DEVONSHIRE *fishes a key from her pinny.*

DEVONSHIRE This is the key to the tradesman's entrance. I'm giving it to you now so you can make your own way out. Via the garden.

JONAH Oh, thank you.

DEVONSHIRE I don't want you disturbing Mrs Burnham; she usually retires early on a weekday. Nine o'clock, I should imagine. She'll be asleep by then.

JONAH Oh, no, I won't disturb her. I'm pretty much done now, actually . . .

DEVONSHIRE And Mr Quigley . . . Do be careful when leaving that you don't trip up over the gardener's spade. Which you'll find located in his shed by the pear tree.

JONAH I shan't trip up over it if it's tucked away in the shed, shall I . . .?

DEVONSHIRE *produces another key.*

DEVONSHIRE Here is the key to the shed.

JONAH But why . . .? Oh. I see. But I'm not sure that I can . . .

DEVONSHIRE Nine o'clock. We working people have to make our own opportunities, don't we?

JONAH Yes. I suppose we do.

DEVONSHIRE *leaves.* JONAH *takes the keys.*

INT. DINING ROOM. NIGHT.

LILLIAN *is engrossed in a jigsaw, which is nearing completion.* DEVONSHIRE *enters.*

DEVONSHIRE Just to let you know, I've turned down your bed and left your cocoa on your dressing table . . .

LILLIAN Bring it down here, would you, Devonshire? I'm determined to finish this sky . . .

DEVONSHIRE It's almost nine o'clock, ma'am . . .

We see JONAH *peeping in through the window.* DEVONSHIRE *clocks this.*

LILLIAN The picture isn't complete . . . until the last piece goes in . . .

DEVONSHIRE *waves* JONAH *into the garden, and he runs off.* LILLIAN *places the last piece of her jigsaw.*

LILLIAN *(cont'd)* There! Most gratifying. Glorious to see all the little details–

DEVONSHIRE *suddenly reaches in and gathers up the jigsaw, breaking it up into the box.* LILLIAN *looks displeased.*

DEVONSHIRE I'll tidy this away for you, ma'am. Don't want your cocoa getting cold.

LILLIAN Very well. Good night, Devonshire.

DEVONSHIRE Night, ma'am.

LILLIAN *leaves.* DEVONSHIRE *steals a glance into the garden.*

EXT. GARDEN. NIGHT.

JONAH *brushes the soil away from the coffin's nameplate: 'N BURNHAM'. He starts to prise open the top half of the lid to reveal . . . a mummified skeleton in a moth-eaten suit. The bones of the hands clutch a large leather-bound manuscript tightly to its chest.*

JONAH *is horrified. He slowly leans down to free the volume from the hands. He has to snap some of the finger bones to free it. He sits back, looking at the skull, which stares at him eyelessly.*

JONAH *closes the top half of the coffin lid again. He opens up the document and scans the yellowed pages.*

DEVONSHIRE You found it, then? Here, let me help you.

JONAH *hands* DEVONSHIRE *the manuscript and climbs out of the grave.*

DEVONSHIRE You're going to have to fill this back in.

JONAH Yes, I'm aware of that.

JONAH *takes the spade and starts to fill the earth back into the open grave.*

DEVONSHIRE I think it's better if we don't see each other for a while. I've got several people interested.

JONAH Interested in what?

DEVONSHIRE In buying this, of course. Like you said, it's priceless. We just need to find the highest bidder.

JONAH I didn't say it was priceless, I said you couldn't put a price on it! This is a work of art, it's not a piece of merchandise!

DEVONSHIRE What did you think we were going to do with it?

JONAH I want to study it, to hear it played. I could be the first person to conduct it!

DEVONSHIRE You need your head examining. Who's going to let you conduct this?

JONAH Why not me? I'm one of his biggest admirers. I studied his music for years.

DEVONSHIRE You remember your place, Mr Quigley. You're just staff, like me, a paid-by-the-hour lowlife piano tuner! This is our ticket out of here.

JONAH I'm not like you – don't you dare say that. This music is a miracle. A gift we can give back to the world. I'm not using it to line my own pockets.

DEVONSHIRE Well, I am.

DEVONSHIRE *turns and starts to walk away.*

JONAH Come back Derbyshire, please!

DEVONSHIRE *turns.*

DEVONSHIRE My name is Devonshire!

JONAH *swings the spade and hits her on the side of the head, knocking her to the ground.*

JONAH *is horrified at what he's just done. He spins* DEVONSHIRE*'s body and sees blood running down her face. His trembling fingers reach to feel for a pulse in her neck but can't find one. She is dead.*

JONAH *is panicked. He looks around at the house, then quickly starts to drag the body towards the open grave. He then rolls* DEVONSHIRE*'s body into it, and she lands with a thud.*

JONAH *grabs the spade and starts to hurriedly fill in the earth on top of* DEVONSHIRE*'s body. He's working on autopilot. As she is almost covered,* JONAH *is horrified to see* DEVONSHIRE*'s hand raise up slowly.*

JONAH *quickly continues his digging, shovelling more and more earth on to* DEVONSHIRE*'s slowly moving face and body. The earth muffles her cries.* JONAH *fills in more and more soil as the music intensifies.*

Finally, all the earth is replaced and JONAH *flattens it violently with several smacks of the spade. He steps back, breathing heavily, sweating. He picks up the manuscript and runs back towards the shed.*

EXT. HOUSE. DAY.

Establisher of the rear of the house and garden. All seems calm. The sound of a doorbell.

INT. HALLWAY. DAY.

LILLIAN *opens the door to find a rather dishevelled-looking* JONAH. *He seems tired and haunted.*

LILLIAN Mr Quigley, how nice to see you again. Do come in.

LILLIAN *admits* JONAH.

LILLIAN *(cont'd)* We've been trying to get hold of you all week. Your employers said something about a leave of absence?

JONAH Yes, I've not been in the best of health since I was last here.

LILLIAN Oh dear, I am sorry to hear that. I apologise for having to admit you myself, but I'm afraid Devonshire has rather disappeared.

JONAH Oh?

LILLIAN Yes, it's quite a mystery. She took off in the night without a by-your-leave. All her things left in her room, most perplexing.

JONAH Well perhaps she's just . . .

LILLIAN Gone to ground? Yes, that's what we thought. Come through.

LILLIAN *leads an anxious* JONAH *into the music room.*

INT. MUSIC ROOM. DAY.

DICKY *sits in the music room.*

LILLIAN You remember Dicky, don't you?

JONAH Yes, of course, hello.

DICKY How de do.

JONAH *(to* LILLIAN*)* What seems to be the problem?

LILLIAN Something seems a little off. A trifle flat, maybe. See what you think.

LILLIAN *pats the piano stool.* JONAH *sits.*

JONAH What would you like me to play?

DICKY How about this piece of Nathaniel's unfinished symphony that you unearthed?

DICKY *produces the folded piece of manuscript.* JONAH *seems agitated.*

JONAH I'm not very good at sight-reading . . .

LILLIAN Nonsense. As a student of my late husband's work, it's surely of some interest.

LILLIAN *puts the music on the stand.* JONAH *seems discomfited. He falteringly starts to play.* DICKY *smiles.* JONAH *nervously plays on.*

He looks up at DICKY *and is terrified to see a blood-and-dirt-covered* DEVONSHIRE *– not Lillian – standing behind him.*

JONAH *jumps up from the piano stool in fear.*

JONAH Aaaaghhhh!

LILLIAN Mr Quigley! Is everything alright?

When JONAH *looks at* DICKY *again, the spectre of* DEVONSHIRE *has gone.*

DICKY Perhaps he'd like a glass of water.

LILLIAN Of course. Devonsh– Oh, I forgot. She's not here. And she's not coming back, is she?

LILLIAN *departs.* JONAH *stares at* DICKY.

JONAH You know?

DICKY Sit down.

A shaking JONAH *sits.*

DICKY *(cont'd)* We knew Devonshire was greedy; we hoped she might encourage you to dig up the manuscript, but we didn't expect you to kill her. Still, gives us more leverage, I suppose.

JONAH What do you mean, leverage?

DICKY I've been auditing the accounts, and it seems that Lillian's been living beyond her means. To put it bluntly, she's broke. She needs a lot of money quickly, and the unexpected discovery of her late husband's final work would be just the ticket, as they say.

JONAH I'll give it back to you. I wanted to return it anyway; I think that's what's been making me ill . . .

JONAH *pulls the manuscript from his bag.*

DICKY Perhaps. That and guilt of murdering a defenceless young woman. The problem is, Mr Quigley, the symphony is unfinished.

LILLIAN *returns with the glass of water.*

LILLIAN And who better to complete it than my husband's greatest admirer? Water, no lemon no ice.

JONAH But I can't complete it . . . I'm not up to it . . .

LILLIAN Is it not good?

JONAH It's brilliant. The most beautiful score I ever set eyes on . . .

LILLIAN You said yourself you'd dabbled with composing. You have the allegro-sonata from the first movement, the andante, the scherzo. It should be possible for you to complete the final rondo.

JONAH But what about the curse? Surely whoever completes the 9th will bring it upon themselves?

LILLIAN The curse is a nonsense, as I've already told you. It's simply a state of mind, and you can choose not to succumb to it.

JONAH I'm already in its grip. I feel a darkness following me wherever I go, Death's hand on my shoulder.

DICKY Better than a policeman's hand on your shoulder.

JONAH I'm sorry, I can't. I won't.

LILLIAN If I'm not able to settle my accounts, the house and gardens will have to be sold, and who knows what discoveries will be made? Take all the time you wish. You can work here, have access to Nathaniel's archive, all his notes. I just need you to finish the symphony and then you'll be free.

DICKY Splendid, that's settled then. We look forward to hearing it.

JONAH *looks disturbed.*

INT. MUSIC ROOM. NIGHT.

JONAH *sits at the desk. He has the manuscript in front of him and he turns to the empty page. He unscrews his fountain pen lid and dips the pen in ink. He hesitates. The bust of* NATHANIEL BURNHAM *stares down at him.*

NATHANIEL *(O.S.)* What's the problem?

JONAH *looks at the bust of* NATHANIEL.

JONAH I don't know where to begin.

NATHANIEL *(O.S.)* You're not at the beginning, boy, you're at the end. It's the final movement, remember. Have you studied what's gone before?

It appears that the bust is addressing JONAH, *until we see that* NATHANIEL *is sitting behind him. He has a blackened gunshot wound under his chin, which dribbles odd spots of blood. The back of his head is matted with blood and brains from the exit wound.*

JONAH Of course I have.

NATHANIEL Then build upon it - a modified sonata form.

JONAH A false recapitulation?

NATHANIEL Exactly - but we must first consider the melody. What do you have?

JONAH *hums the melody he is looking for as he searches through his manuscript.*

JONAH Er . . . the second subject in the strings.

He finds what he is looking for.

JONAH *(cont'd)* A sequence resolved with a plagal cadence.

NATHANIEL Where's the risk? The final movement mustn't be timid! Fragmentation, inversion, imitation between the woodwinds. Use the diminished seventh to imply the secondary dominant.

JONAH And underneath, return to the drone in the brass as before, in the exposition. This is it, I can hear it.

NATHANIEL Satisfying, isn't it?

JONAH *writes in some notes. He turns to face* NATHANIEL.

JONAH Can I ask you a question?

NATHANIEL Of course.

JONAH Why are you helping me?

NATHANIEL It amuses me. I want to see how far you get before it grips you.

JONAH You mean the curse?

NATHANIEL Of course. You'll get so far, and then you'll find it impossible to put one note in front of the other. You'll be lost in a dark forest, not knowing which path to take. All roads leading back in on themselves . . .

JONAH That was your torment, not mine.

NATHANIEL I can already see the black shadow of doubt enveloping your every choice.

JONAH *turns back to the desk.*

JONAH Be quiet now.

NATHANIEL Why bother? You'll never match the heights of Beethoven or Mahler. Or indeed me. You never even tried. Why? Because 'inspiration failed to strike'? Piano-tuning is 'satisfying in its own way?' It's an act of courage to create anything and you, boy, are a coward.

JONAH I'm not listening to this. What you're talking about is self-doubt; it's not the same thing.

JONAH *has picked up* NATHANIEL*'s crumpled rondo, the piece of score he found in the piano.*

NATHANIEL Whoever completes my 9th symphony will end up like me – food for the Conqueror Worm.

JONAH I've been assured by your wife that the curse isn't real.

NATHANIEL Then why didn't she complete it herself?

JONAH *picks up the bust of* NATHANIEL *and carries it, past the real* NATHANIEL*, to a chest, where he puts it inside, out of sight.*

JONAH Thanks for your advice. But now I need you to be quiet.

When he returns to his desk, NATHANIEL *has disappeared.*

JONAH *takes a deep breath and begins to write with renewed vigour.*

EXT. HOUSE. DAY.

Dawn over the house and garden.

INT. MUSIC ROOM. DAY.

JONAH *is slumped on the desk, a pile of written manuscript papers in front of him.*

LILLIAN *enters with breakfast on a tray. She starts when she sees him; he looks dead.*

LILLIAN Mr Quigley?

LILLIAN *puts down the tray and approaches, lightly touching his arm. Suddenly he wakes and she jumps.*

LILLIAN *(cont'd)* Ah! You gave me quite a fright. I brought you some breakfast. Busy night, I see?

JONAH It's finished.

JONAH *hands her the manuscript and she looks through it.*

LILLIAN Glad to hear it. I don't believe in writer's block. Never did. Nathaniel just got trapped. As he reached the summit of his career, the oxygen of creativity grew thinner. He became convinced it was only ever going to be downhill.

JONAH Yes, you've been at great pains to tell me. Several times.

JONAH *crosses to the piano and picks up the missing piece of the symphony.*

JONAH *(cont'd)* I can't say it was easy, but after an initial block, it began to flow. Here . . .

JONAH *holds out the paper.*

LILLIAN Thank you.

JONAH The picture isn't complete until the last piece goes in.

LILLIAN Of course.

LILLIAN *takes it and inserts it into the body of the manuscript. Then she freezes. She looks down at the completed symphony.*

LILLIAN Oh . . .

JONAH Congratulations, Mrs Burnham. You just finished your husband's 9th symphony. Just as well you don't believe all that poppycock about a curse.

LILLIAN *looks a little put out, but steels herself.*

LILLIAN Indeed. In the absence of Devonshire, you can see yourself out, Mr Quigley. Nice doing business with you.

LILLIAN *leaves.* JONAH *starts to gather his things.*

INT. HALL. DAY.

LILLIAN *stands at the foot of the stairs with the manuscript in her hands. She seems discomfited. She looks round nervously.*

LILLIAN *has a terrible sense of foreboding. She starts to climb the stairs; they creak underfoot. Suddenly the chandelier flickers and the bulbs blow out.*

LILLIAN *stops when she hears a sound behind her. She looks around. We become aware of a* SINISTER FIGURE *reaching towards her. Startled, she turns and falls over the balcony.*

INT. MUSIC ROOM. DAY.

JONAH *is packing away his things when he hears a scream and a clatter. He runs out of the room.*

INT. STAIRWELL. DAY.

JONAH *runs up to find* LILLIAN *at the bottom of the stairs. The pages of the manuscript are strewn all over the stairs and floor. The carpet on the stairs is rucked.*

LILLIAN *lies crumpled on the floor, her limbs horrifically twisted. Her neck is broken, and her head seems to be facing the wrong way. Manuscript pages flutter down around her. Her face a rictus of terror. She is dead.*

FADE TO BLACK:

EXT. HOUSE. NIGHT.

Establisher. We hear a piano being played.

INT. MUSIC ROOM. DAY.

It is twenty years later. An older JONAH *sits in the music room as a girl,* CORA, *plays the piano.*

CORA A little like that, Mr Quigley?

JONAH Yes, very good. Perhaps exaggerate the pianissimo in the fourth bar, but yes, good progress. Thank you, my dear.

CORA *closes the manuscript book, which has '9th Symphony by Jonah Quigley' handwritten on the cover. She hands it over.*

CORA It's so good, Mr Quigley. I hope you don't mind me saying, but it reminds me of your first symphony. The one you dedicated to Burnham.

JONAH Yes, it does have echoes of that. I suppose we all recycle ideas in the end.

CORA Oh, I'm not saying that; I think it's wonderful. Is it true he used to live here?

JONAH Yes. I was always a great admirer of his. It's no wonder that my first symphony had Burnham's fingerprints all over it.

CORA And now you've surpassed him. This is your 9th, and Burnham only ever did eight.

JONAH Indeed.

CORA Anyway, I'll be back in the morning and hopefully we can finish it then.

JONAH *(to himself)* Yes. Hopefully you can.

CORA *opens the door. The light above her flickers.* CORA *feels a little uneasy.*

JONAH *(cont'd)* See you tomorrow.

JONAH *smiles.*

THE END

Episode 6

PLODDING ON

CAST LIST

THEMSELVES

Reece Shearsmith

Katherine Parkinson

Tim Key

Amanda Abbington

Robin Askwith

Steve Pemberton

Rosie Cavaliero

Nick Mohammed

Sian Gibson

with

Anne Reid

Jason Watkins

Emily Howlett

Mark Gatiss

Party Guests

Mark Benton

Kevin Bishop

Mark Bonnar

Asim Chaudhry

Kenneth Cranham

Phil Daniels

Adam Deacon

Monica Dolan

Michele Dotrice

Adrian Dunbar

Kevin Eldon

Gaby French

Tamsin Greig

Jessica Gunning

Julie Hesmondhalgh

Conleth Hill

Jim Howick

Paterson Joseph

Elsie Kelly

Denis Lawson

Europa Lepus

Rula Lenska

Ralf Little

Alice Lowe

Lyndsey Marshal

David Morrissey

Tamzin Outhwaite

Gemma Page

Bill Paterson

Maxine Peake

Sheila Reid

Julian Rhind-Tutt

Alexandra Roach

Debbie Rush

Poppy Rush

Claire Skinner

Alison Steadman

Sophie Thompson

Noah Valentine

Saskia Wakefield

Zoë Wanamaker

Gemma Whelan

Ben Willbond

Susan Wokoma

Jack Wolfe

EXT. #9 BAR. NIGHT.

An upmarket bar/club in Manchester called #9. A sign in the window reads 'Closed for a private event'.

TITLE: *'Plodding On'*

INT. TOILETS. NIGHT.

Inside the gender-neutral toilets, spacious and smart. A row of cubicles and a vanity unit of mirrored sinks with rolled towels and posh hand-wash.

KATHERINE *walks in, and we can hear the sounds of music and a party going on in the main bar. We may hear the dull thud of music throughout.*

KATHERINE *crosses to the sinks and checks her reflection. She washes her hands, then smells them. Liking the scent, she sets about pulling the hand wash from its bracket on the wall, yanking it out with some force. She wraps it in a towel and puts it in her bag.*

She hears a cough from one of the cubicles. She looks under one of the closed doors to see a pair of men's shoes. She taps on the door and we hear it being unlocked.

KATHERINE *pushes the door open to find* TIM *standing awkwardly inside.*

TIM Ooop. Hello.

KATHERINE Sorry, I got cornered by Anne Reid. Have you been here ages?

TIM No, it's been about twenty-five minutes. There's been three number ones and one number two, so . . . I haven't been bored.

KATHERINE Do you want to keep an eye out while I . . . ?

TIM Sure, sure.

KATHERINE *steps into the cubicle and* TIM *hovers in the doorway, keeping an eye out.* KATHERINE *cleans the top of the lavatory with toilet paper.*

TIM Is it busy out there?

KATHERINE Yeah, usual showbiz do, everyone looking over your shoulder to see if there's anyone more famous to talk to.

TIM I usually just do two circuits pretending I'm looking for someone and then leave. I never know what to say to people.

KATHERINE Well, this'll loosen you up a bit.

KATHERINE *takes a small bag of white powder from her bag and starts to prepare two lines of it on the cistern top.*

TIM You mean talking-wise? Because I have heard it can have a laxative effect.

KATHERINE No, it just gives you confidence, that's all. You've not had it before?

TIM No, never. I once tried to buy an E tablet from a dealer at Latitude, but he came back with a second-hand iPad, so . . . miscommunication. Have you seen Steve or Reece yet?

KATHERINE I saw Reece, surrounded by people blowing smoke up his arse. Not literally, Tim.

TIM No, I get that. Still, nine series, that's . . .

KATHERINE Oh no, it's good, fair play to them. But I think it's right for them to end it now, don't you? It has got a bit self-indulgent.

TIM Yeah, fuck 'em. I heard from Katherine Kelly that there was a bit of a drama on her episode. Apparently, Steve was rushed to hospital.

KATHERINE Really? Well, that doesn't surprise me, hardly the picture of health, is he? It won't be long before his face pops up on the BAFTA 'in memoriam' to Coldplay or some maudlin shite. Right, I think we're good to go . . .

The door opens and AMANDA *starts to enter.*

AMANDA Oh, hiya, Tim, how are you?

TIM Good, er, sorry, these loos are closed at the moment; there's been a blockage.

AMANDA Oh, OK. Erm, I'll have to hold it in for a bit.

TIM Yes. Keep your finger in the dike!

AMANDA . . . OK. See you out there.

TIM Sure.

AMANDA *disappears.*

KATHERINE Who was that?

TIM Katherine Parkinson.

KATHERINE *I'm* Katherine Parkinson.

TIM Oh, that's right, yes. It was the other one, then. So shall we . . . assume the position?

TIM *looks uncertain and steps into the cubicle.* KATHERINE *locks the door.*

KATHERINE Have you got any cash on you? I need a note, for the . . .

TIM No, sorry.

TIM *picks up a cardboard toilet tube.*

TIM *(cont'd)* That's probably too big, isn't it? Yeah. Maybe we should just forget this and get a couple of beers instead . . .

KATHERINE No, it's alright, I've got this Body Shop voucher – that'll do. I'll dust it off before I swap it for a Mango bath bomb.

KATHERINE *rolls the voucher into a tube.*

KATHERINE So have you been busy?

TIM Yeah, pretty busy, just developing a few things, you know. Irons in fires, poems . . .

KATHERINE Any paid work?

TIM No.

KATHERINE You must have auditioned for this *Divine Comedy* thing that Amazon are doing?

TIM Never heard of it.

KATHERINE You're kidding. Every cunt with an Equity card's been up for it; they want English actors, apparently. It's like a *Dungeons and Dragons* type of thing based on Dante's *Inferno*.

KATHERINE *sniffs a line of coke.*

KATHERINE *(cont'd)* Sounds dreadful, but they're paying people shitloads. You should get your agent on to it.

TIM I will. Thanks for the tip, Amanda.

KATHERINE Katherine!

KATHERINE *gives him a look, then hands the rolled-up voucher to* TIM.

KATHERINE Here.

TIM *hesitantly takes the voucher and holds it to his nose. He bends down and hovers above the cistern, cupping his nose with his other hand. He sniffs loudly, then comes back up.*

TIM Oh yeah, that's good shit. Thanks. Lovely.

KATHERINE Tim, you didn't have any.

TIM I did. I can feel the twinge.

KATHERINE It's still there.

TIM Oh. Well, I definitely smelled it. Maybe that's enough?

There's a tap on the door. They look at each other.

KATHERINE Hello?

ANNE *(V.O.)* Katherine, it's Anne Reid. Can you let me in?

KATHERINE *nervously opens the door to reveal* ANNE *standing before them.*

ANNE I hear you scored some good snow from the dummy-man on Deansgate. Any chance of a quick toot?

ANNE *holds up a rolled £20 note.*

KATHERINE Yes, you're in luck. We've got a spare line haven't we, Tim?

ANNE *steps in and closes the door*

INT. TOILETS. NIGHT.

REECE *enters and looks around. Again, we hear party noise from the adjacent bar.* REECE *checks out the stalls, which are empty.*

REECE Steve?

He checks his phone.

ROBIN *enters and approaches* REECE *for a hug. He's smartly dressed and wears tinted glasses.*

ROBIN Here he is, hello, my liege! How are we? Great to see you.

REECE Hi Robin.

ROBIN It's heaving out there, what a turn-out! I think I'm the only one I've never heard of.

ROBIN *unbuckles his belt and enters one of the stalls. He drops his trousers to the ground and starts to wee, chatting all the while.* REECE *doesn't know where to look.*

ROBIN *(cont'd)* I don't mind these gender-neutral toilets, do you? It's equality - and you get to queue up with all the lovely ladies!

REECE Yeah.

ROBIN So, what's next for you both? Have you got anything lined up?

REECE Yes, actually, we're writing a comedy-drama thing for the BBC, playing two detectives. It's called *Plodding On*.

ROBIN Oh. So you're really not doing any more *No. 9*s then?

REECE No. Well, they said they'd have us back to do specials if we wanted.

ROBIN Oh, that's good, because people are always coming up to me, talking about that bus episode, you know.

REECE Yeah, some of the fans were disappointed that we didn't actually do it.

ROBIN Exactly!

ROBIN *pulls up his trousers up and re-buckles his belt. He joins* **REECE** *at the sink to wash his hands.*

ROBIN *(cont'd)* Anyway, I've been thinking about it . . .

REECE What?

ROBIN The bus episode, *Hold on Tight.* What I thought we could do, you're the driver and Steve's the clippie . . .

REECE *(sceptical)* Yeah . . .

ROBIN And you're both at the depot when this dolly bird comes in with, like, the three-inch cleavage, you know, and she says 'I don't know what route I'm on today,' and Steve says, 'I'm sure we could give you a ride' – like, 'ride' as in 'sex' – and she says, 'What number bus are you on, then?' And *you* say '69, erm, number 9!' – like oral sex – and Steve says, 'Come up here, then, and I'll take you up the back passage . . .'

REECE Like anal sex.

ROBIN What? Oh yeah, I hadn't thought of that. Then I come in as Mr Cole, the posh geezer . . .

ROBIN *pulls out some handwritten pages of script from his pocket and hands them to* **REECE**.

REECE Oh right, there's a full script.

ROBIN Yeah, and you're showing her round the bus when I come in as Mr Cole, the posh geezer, and start reading a list of all the stops . . . Top of page four.

REECE *reads from the script.*

REECE 'Ere, this way darling. Come up to the cab and see my . . .'

ROBIN 'Nelson's Column!'

REECE '. . . my steering wheel. When I'm up here driving, I sometimes get bored, so I like to have a little . . .'

ROBIN 'Bank!'

REECE '. . . bite to eat. In fact, I'm starving now, I'd really love to chow down on your . . .'

ROBIN 'Shepherd's Bush.'

REECE 'Cheese and ham sandwich.'

ROBIN Then you look at her tits, and I'm like, 'St Paul's Cathedral.' So it's all clever wordplay like that. Sort of stuff David Renwick wrote for the Rons, you know.

REECE Right, you've obviously thought a lot about it. And is there a twist, or . . . ?

ROBIN Well, that's what you and Steve do, just fill in all the clever bits. Maybe they're all dead or ghosts or something – that's what you usually do, isn't it?

REECE Well, we've done that three times.

ROBIN I just think it'd be great, because I was never in an actual episode, was I?

REECE No, I suppose not. Well, I'll have a read.

ROBIN Thank you, my liege. So anyway, what happened on the latest series? I heard Steve ended up in hospital or something?

REECE Yeah, it was serious. We were filming this episode about an escape room and he just collapsed. Started having a seizure.

ROBIN Shit, is he alright?

REECE Yeah, he was fine; he was back the next morning. It was really scary, though.

ROBIN I'll bet it was. Actually, there's a joke on page seventeen about my missus having acute angina. I thought of Sue Holderness – she'd do it, she's a mate.

REECE Well, I'll talk to Steve and I'll get back to you.

ROBIN You are a gentleman, sir. Enjoy your night, you deserve it.

ROBIN *leaves.* **REECE** *looks at the script again and smiles.*

REECE 'Oi, sugar-tits, pass me that rag so I can wipe my dipstick, there's a good girl.'

As **REECE** *says this,* **AMANDA** *has entered. She looks shocked.*

REECE *(cont'd)* No, no, Amanda, wait!

AMANDA *leaves and* **REECE** *runs out after her.*

INT. TOILETS. NIGHT.

STEVE *vapes as he stares at himself in the mirror.*

He is casually dressed in T-shirt and jeans. A smart three-piece suit hangs on one of the cubicle doors, and there is a shoebox on the side.

STEVE 'My family has been wronged, Dante. Is this nothing? You call this nothing?'

The door opens and **ROSIE** *enters, carrying three cocktails.*

ROSIE Sorry, Steve, the queue at the bar is horrendous.

STEVE Yeah, well, we've worked with a lot of people.

ROSIE I didn't know whether to get you a Diddle Diddle Daiquiri or a Bloody Marily Marily, so I got you both.

STEVE Good call, thank you. What did you get?

ROSIE Riddle of the Aperol Spritz. It's nice.

ROSIE *puts down the drinks.*

ROSIE *(cont'd)* They also had a Mother's Ruin Martini, a Last Night of the Pimms and a Whisky Sourdekatriaphobia, although nobody was ordering that one because they couldn't pronounce it.

STEVE Did you see Reece?

ROSIE Yeah, he was outside putting Anne Reid in a taxi. I hope she's OK, she was really grinding her teeth. So go on, then, what's the gossip? Why are you avoiding him – have you fallen out?

STEVE *unzips his suit bag, takes out his shirt and starts to put it on.*

STEVE No, not really.

ROSIE So what's happened? I promise I won't tell anybody.

STEVE Yeah, right! Well, you must know about this *Divine Comedy* thing Amazon are doing?

ROSIE Oh God, yes, I did a self-tape for it, it was awful.

STEVE What part?

ROSIE One of the fucking maids, I don't know.

STEVE Well, I'd auditioned for the part of Virgil, who's obviously one of the main characters . . .

ROSIE Oh, you'd be so good at that.

STEVE Thank you . . . Anyway, weeks went by, I didn't hear anything and we'd started filming series nine, when I get a phone call saying the showrunner's in town and he wants to meet me. I said, I can't, I'm doing a scene with Reece . . .

ROSIE Here, let me help you.

STEVE *has been fiddling with his cufflinks, and* ROSIE *puts them in for him, then continues helping him to dress in his tie, waistcoat and jacket.*

STEVE Anyway, I thought, fuck it, you only live once, so I said yes to the audition, then I pretended to be ill and I got taken off set.

ROSIE What do you mean?

STEVE Well, first of all, I fainted, but then I thought . . .

ROSIE You hadn't gone far enough.

STEVE Exactly. So I started fitting as well.

ROSIE I wish I'd seen that, I bet you were brilliant.

STEVE Thank you. I mean, I'd filmed all my bits and there was only Reece's reverses to do, so they put my wig on the producer and he sat in for me.

ROSIE No?

STEVE Yeah. If you look closely, you can tell. Anyway, the audition went really well, and I just found out a couple of hours ago . . . I got the part.

ROSIE Oh my God, that's amazing! So hang on, where's it filming?

STEVE It's between LA and Canada, so I'm going to have to move. It's at least seven years' work, unbelievable money – like, unbelievable – relocation package for my family, everything.

ROSIE You so deserve it, Steve, you really do. Do you know who's playing the maid?

STEVE No, no. But if you have Monica Dolan's number, I think she'd be perfect.

ROSIE Yeah, she's . . . she's great. She's upstairs, actually, I saw her ten minutes back.

STEVE Great. Have you got my shoes?

ROSIE *goes to open the shoebox and screams when she looks inside it.*

STEVE Oh no, that's just a present from Jack Whitehall. It's not real.

ROSIE Jesus.

STEVE They're in my bag.

ROSIE *gets the shoes from* STEVE*'s suit bag and bends down to help him on with them.*

STEVE Anyway, the trouble is, in the meantime, Reece has come up with this stupid detective comedy-drama thing, which is BBC money, pathetic, and now I can't do it.

ROSIE He'll understand, surely. It's not like you go around using people, is it?

ROSIE *is lacing up* STEVE*'s shoes.*

STEVE Exactly. I've had twenty-five years working with him. I've got to put myself first for once, haven't I?

INT. TOILETS. NIGHT.

NICK *stands at the vanity units, speaking into a microphone that is attached to his smartphone. He presses 'record'.*

NICK Hello, pod-fans! This is Nick Mohammed with episode number 279 of *Mountain to Mohammed*, where each week I get to scale the heights of a famous personality – well, not always famous actually, we have done a nurse and stuff like that, but the numbers are never great – anyway, I start at the base camp of childhood – whether, like me, they were very badly bullied – and we work our way up to the summit to see what's next for them on the horizon. So this week's Mountain is writer and actor Steve Pemberton! Now I should explain I'm actually in the toilets at the wrap party for series nine of *Inside No. 9* . . .

STEVE *enters and waves at* NICK. NICK *carries on talking and waves back.*

NICK *(cont'd)* . . . where Steve and Reece have invited back a whole galaxy of stars from previous series, including little old me! So I thought it'd be a great way to grab him for my pod and he's just walked in – so Steve, hi, welcome to *Mountain to Mohammed*! How's it going out there?

STEVE It's great, yeah, so many old friends have turned up, and it's just lovely to celebrate the past ten years. It's like my whole life flashing before my eyes.

NICK Aw. Now, tell us a bit about your upbringing. Where were you born and where did you grow up?

STEVE Well, I was born in Blackburn in Lancashire . . .

NICK Oh, right, that's interesting, because I was born in Leeds, which is obviously the other side of the Pennines, and then I went to Durham to study English. So I don't know Blackpool that well . . .

STEVE Blackburn.

NICK Yes, Blackburn, that's right, so . . . Sorry, what was the question?

STEVE I think you asked me where I was born.

NICK Yes, and the answer was . . . remind me?

STEVE Blackburn.

NICK Yes, amazing. *(pause)* Have you ever considered double-glazing your windows?

STEVE Erm, well, they're–

NICK *holds up a finger.*

NICK Do you ever sit at home, listening to the sound of traffic going by?

STEVE *is confused.*

NICK *(cont'd)* Let White Seal Windows give you a free quote with up to 20 per cent discount, and give your ears the holiday they deserve. *(Very quickly)* Ts and Cs, participating stores only, for more information go to www.whiteseal.org, conditions apply.

NICK *covers the microphone.*

NICK *(cont'd)* I've got to do one every two minutes for the sponsors, it's so annoying . . . I'm back with Steve Pemberton. So, Steve, we've heard all about your childhood in Blackburn, let's move up the mountain now to explore the foothills of your early days in comedy. Because, like me, you started out at the Edinburgh Fringe, didn't you, in nineteen-ninety . . . ?

STEVE Six.

NICK That's right, because the last time I was there was 2018 with *Mr Swallow*, which was my twelfth show there. Was it my twelfth? Let me think. *Hello It's Mr Swallow, Oh No It's Mr Swallow, Mr Swallow Flies Again, Mr Swallow Houdini, Mr Swallow's Christmas Carol . . .*

STEVE *indicates to Nick that he has to go.*

STEVE Nick, I've got to . . .

NICK Of course, sorry . . . So, Steve, we've reached the summit of the mountain – what's next for you?

STEVE Well, it's only just been confirmed, actually, so hot off the press, but I've got a part, quite a big part, in a major new series for Amazon. So I'll be heading out to Los Angeles, and I'll be there for at least seven years.

NICK Oh, that's interesting, because I've already been to Los Angeles.

STEVE Have you?

NICK Yep. Now, that's a big commitment for you, isn't it, because I thought you and Reece were doing a new show for the BBC?

STEVE No, I won't be free to do that now – and anyway, I was never really . . .

Click. The door to one of the cubicles opens and REECE *comes out. He smiles at* NICK *with 'a don't mind me' gesture.* NICK *mimes 'Have you been doing a wee?' and* REECE *nods.*

STEVE *has to awkwardly carry on with the podcast.*

STEVE *(cont'd)* . . . sure that was the right project for us, but you know, never say never. There's always ways of communicating, emails and Zoom, so fingers crossed that we can keep developing ideas . . .

NICK Well, as luck would have it – we have been joined by your partner in crime, Reece Shearsmith. Reece, welcome to *Mountain to Mohammed.*

REECE Twin Peaks.

NICK What?

REECE You've got two mountains now, so – Twin Peaks.

NICK Oh yeah . . . Let me say that. Reece, welcome to *Mountain to Mohammed.* I've never had two mountains before; it's like Twin Peaks.

REECE Yes.

NICK What do you make of Steve's new job?

REECE It's great news. I haven't heard much about it; I can't wait for him to explain it all to me.

NICK *moves the microphone back to* STEVE *for him to respond.*

STEVE Well, there's nothing to explain. You just go for an audition, you don't know if you're going to get it, and in this instance I got it. It's just all whims, isn't it?

NICK It is all whims. When I auditioned for *Lasso* . . .

REECE *takes the microphone back.*

REECE But you don't audition for things when you've got your own project greenlit and ready to go.

STEVE Well it wasn't greenlit, was it? We were commissioned to write a script, which we'd barely started . . .

REECE Barely started? We've been talking about it for six months!

NICK Guys, guys. In a perfect world, we'd all have peace of mind, all the time.

REECE *and* STEVE *look at each other.*

NICK *(cont'd)* At Wills Unlimited, we can provide you with that peace of mind from as little as £42. Ts and Cs, subject to status, over-18s only, offer ends 31st March, conditions apply . . . Sorry.

REECE When did you go for the audition, anyway? You never told me.

STEVE I don't remember.

NICK I can tell you exactly when it was, because I saw you there, didn't I, Steve? We were laughing because he still had make-up on from filming. It was December 15th.

REECE The 15th. The afternoon of December 15th? So was this audition before or after you'd been rushed to hospital with a suspected brain aneurysm?

STEVE *looks down.* REECE *is quietly fuming.*

NICK So! So we're here tonight celebrating nine series of *Inside No. 9*. It's such an achievement, guys, you must both be over the moon. Can you put it into words?

Neither REECE *nor* STEVE *speak.* NICK *cottons on and gathers up his things.*

NICK *(cont'd)* Well, I've probably got enough; I can make it in the edit. So good to see you both. *(To* REECE*)* I hope you're not going to smash his head in with a BAFTA!

NICK *hurriedly leaves. A silence.*

REECE You lying fucking monster.

STEVE Are you actually saying that to me, or are you doing an *Inside No. 9* quote?

REECE Both.

STEVE Well, I'm sorry I lied to you, but I didn't think you'd understand.

REECE I don't understand. Explain it to me.

STEVE Look, we've come to the end of the road with this project, and I wanted to see what else is out there.

REECE This project? What am I, a science experiment?

STEVE No, but it's the perfect time for us to try and do new things, independent of each other. We're not joined at the hip, are we?

REECE I never said we were. But this is bigger than that; this feels like a statement.

STEVE I knew you'd make it difficult. Why can't you just be pleased for me? Everyone else is.

REECE I *am* pleased for you; I'm happy you're going to go off and work with exciting new people and earn lots and lots of money – well done. But at the end of the day, Steve, it's just a television programme. It'll be on, and then it won't be on. Like you've always said, it's just another line on your CV.

STEVE Alright, well, I don't want to spoil tonight . . .

REECE Oh, you don't want to spoil tonight? Well, that ship's already sailed.

STEVE OK, if you want to know the truth, I feel like you've been holding me back.

REECE What?

AMANDA *comes in.*

AMANDA Hi!

STEVE Not now, Amanda!

AMANDA Oh, for fuck's sake. I'm growing a monkey tail here!

AMANDA *leaves again.*

STEVE I just feel, as an actor, I haven't been free to give certain performances . . .

REECE That's rubbish.

STEVE I get overlooked for so many things because we come as a package; it's always 'the boys'. 'Steve and Reece.' I want to be me in something in my own right.

REECE You did *Death in Paradise.*

STEVE I'm not talking about fucking *Death in Paradise.* I mean big American things with a proper five-series character arc, not these little half-hour nothings. Every fourth one a dud.

REECE I told you I don't begrudge you that. I don't care about the actual job; I care about me and you, if you can imagine that. I'm not going to see you for seven years – that's all I'm thinking about. Who am I going to sit in a little office and have a laugh with? When I come in in the morning with two coffees and you're lying on the floor with a pen in your ear pretending to be dead, and we cry laughing for ten minutes – that's what I'm going to miss.

STEVE That joke hasn't been funny for years. Not since *Psychoville.*

REECE Alright, whatever. I'm just saying that I'm going to miss you. You're my best friend.

STEVE Are you quoting 'Merrily, Merrily' now?

REECE No, I mean it. I was so frightened when you collapsed, or pretended to collapse. I thought you were going to die and I'd lose you, and now I *am* going to lose you. I've barely got any real friends as it is.

STEVE Reece, we've been working together for so long now . . . I don't even know if we are friends any more.

REECE *looks hurt. A long silence. We become aware of a song being played in the bar next door.*

SIAN *comes in.*

SIAN Oh, there you are . . . Sorry, am I interrupting something?

REECE No, it doesn't matter.

SIAN Just to let you know they're showing the film now, if you want to . . .

STEVE Sure.

They all exit.

INT. #9 BAR. NIGHT.

STEVE, REECE *and* SIAN *join the crowd and linger at the back.* REECE *walks off to the side,* STEVE *heads towards the bar.*

A large screen shows a montage of clips from Inside No. 9. *The soundtrack is 'Time to Say Goodbye' by Sarah Brightman and Andrea Bocelli.*

The bar has been lightly themed for the Inside No. 9 *wrap party. There are some production stills on the walls. A purple balloon tied to a chair. Someone is dressed as the mascot from 'The Referee's a W***er'.*

The bar is busy with many old cast members from previous episodes with cocktails in hand, watching the montage.

SARAH BRIGHTMAN *(V.O.)* Time to say goodbye / *Paesi che non ho mai / Veduto e vissuto con te / Adesso si li vivro . . .*

The screen shows clips of STEVE *and* REECE *laughing from different episodes.*

STEVE *looks across at* REECE. REECE *just looks at the screen. We see a clip from 'The 12 Days of Christine'.*

STEVE *moves to the bar and stands next to* JASON, *who is going through his bill. The barmaid wears a 'Gorge' t-shirt from 'Thinking Out Loud'.*

A chalkboard menu on the wall behind JASON *advertises Spaghetti Bolognaise, Pot Noodle, Tangerines, Popcorn, Lotus biscuits, Granola (Granola).*

JASON Oh, this isn't right she's charged me for two Cokes. 'Scuse me! *(To* STEVE*)* Congratulations, by the way, about *Divine Comedy*. You must be thrilled.

STEVE Who told you about that?

JASON Rosie Cavaliero.

STEVE Yeah, I'm excited. New start and all that.

JASON The Yanks are so driven, you'll love it out there. You've got to pay for your own cars, but I know a clever little scheme where you can claim it back . . . Yes, hello, I thought with the voucher we got one drink free . . . ?

We see different cast members enjoying the montage on screen.

REECE *is by the buffet table, cutting a slice of cake. The cake is the same as the one from 'Nana's Party'.*

A series of Inside No. 9 *posters by Graham Humphreys adorn the wall behind* REECE *('The Harrowing', 'The Devil of Christmas', 'Private View', 'Tempting Fate', 'Nine Lives Kat', 'The Bones of St Nicholas').*

REECE *looks across at* STEVE, *who is talking with* JASON.

REECE *looks up to see a clip from 'Misdirection', which shows* REECE *guillotining* STEVE, *then another from 'The Stakeout', which shows* REECE *is about to stab* STEVE *in the neck. He looks down at the knife in his hand . . . before being tapped on the shoulder by* EMILY.

EMILY Hi!

REECE Hello!

REECE *puts down the knife and they hug.* REECE *glances at* STEVE *over her shoulder, but he doesn't look back.*

ANDREA BOCELLI *(V.O.)* Time to say goodbye / *Paesi che non ho mai . . .*

EMILY *spells out a word in BSL.*

EMILY *(BSL)* Cuntgrotalaions.

REECE *smiles.*

REECE *(BSL)* Thank you.

EMILY *(BSL)* So, what's next for you two?

REECE *(BSL)* Just *Plodding On.*

EMILY *(BSL)* Yeah, I bet you could do with a break.

REECE *(BSL)* No, that's what I'm doing next. It's called *Plodding On*, it's a detective thing.

EMILY *(BSL)* Oh right! Part in it for me?

REECE *(BSL)* Maybe. We've . . . I've got to write it first.

ANDREA BOCELLI *(V.O.) Con te partiro / Su navi per mari / Che, io lo so . . .*

STEVE *is watching the montage when he gets a phone call. He answers.*

STEVE Hello . . .? Say again . . . No, I can't hear you. Just a sec . . .

STEVE *heads out of the bar to take his phone call.*

REECE *is watching the montage, clips of* STEVE *and* REECE *dancing, from 'Death Be Not Proud', 'The Last Weekend', 'Bernie Clifton's Dressing Room'.*

STEVE *re-emerges into the bar and locks eyes with* REECE *on the other side of the room. There is a key change in the music . . .*

SARAH/ANDREA *(V.O.)* Con te partiro . . .

STEVE *starts to move towards* REECE, *but he's interrupted by another guest.* STEVE *embraces them and excuses himself, but when he looks back,* REECE *has gone.*

INT. TOILETS. NIGHT.

We hear REECE*'s voice from within a cubicle.*

REECE *(O.S.)* So it would be a different case each week, and we'd be playing the detectives . . .

INT. CUBICLE. NIGHT.

REECE *is holding his phone.*

REECE They've commissioned two scripts, so it's pretty much greenlit . . .

We cut to see MARK *on the screen on a FaceTime call. He is in his theatre dressing room.*

MARK Right. And why aren't you doing it with Steve?

REECE Well, I just feel like we've come to the end of the road with this project. We're not joined at the hip, are we?

MARK No, no. I'm just not sure I want to do another detective thing, having done, you know . . .

REECE *Midsomer Murders*?

MARK *Sherlock*.

REECE Oh yeah, of course. I just thought it'd be great to work on something together again, could be really fun.

MARK Definitely.

Awkward pause.

MARK *(cont'd)* Tell you what, why not send it to my agent, so it's all through the official channels, and then it's a lot easier for me to . . .

REECE Say no.

MARK Yeah. Anyway, I've got to go, I just heard my call. Great seeing you, Reece, enjoy your party.

REECE Yep, will do. Bye.

MARK *taps the screen but the call doesn't end. He moves out of shot.*

MARK *(O.S.)* Fucking hell, that was a close call . . .

REECE Mark, you didn't hang up properly. Mark . . .

Silence. A finger slowly moves into shot and terminates the call.

INT. TOILETS. NIGHT.

STEVE *enters the toilets. One of the stalls is occupied.*

STEVE Reece? Are you in there?

REECE *(O.S.)* I've taken some tablets.

STEVE Stop it. Are you coming out?

REECE *(O.S.)* No. My mum's ordered me a biryani.

STEVE Come out, I've got something to tell you. There's been a twist.

The stall is unlocked and REECE *steps out.*

REECE Has it been seeded?

STEVE I've just had a call from my agent . . . Apparently, if I still want the part, I've got to go back in and re-audition. Another actor's thrown his hat into the ring, and the director's really excited.

REECE Who?

STEVE Tim Key.

REECE Haha. He'll probably get it now. What are you going to do?

STEVE I don't know. I don't want to re-audition. The script was terrible. It was like a pig wrote it.

REECE Of course.

STEVE What would you do?

REECE Don't ask me. I'm just stuck doing my little nothings, aren't I?

STEVE *Plodding On*, double-d?

REECE Yeah. I don't know. I'm not even sure about that any more. It won't be the same doing it on my own.

A moment of silence.

STEVE *(singing)* 'If you're going to cry . . .'

REECE Don't.

STEVE Sorry. So what are we going to do, then?

REECE There is a third option.

STEVE What?

INT. STUDIO. DAY.

The bus depot set of Hold on Tight. *Audience applause and jaunty sitcom music. A caption reads 'You have been watching . . .'*

STEVE *as Wolfie (eating an onion like an apple). He stands by a bus with a IN9-3X3 number plate and wears a blue and white football scarf.*

REECE *as Clark, sitting in the driver's cab of the bus, mouthing off something we can't hear à la Felix Bowness.*

ROBIN *as Mr Cole stands on the bus, looking at his watch. Behind him, an advert for 'Summerland'.*

KATHERINE *as a canteen worker with a Farrah Fawcett hairdo and hair-removal cream on her upper lip. A Wise Owl poster on the noticeboard behind her instructs us to 'WASH YOUR HANDS!'.*

TIM *is a mechanic in a boiler suit and vest coming up from the pit. He is holding a dead white mouse by the tail.*

ROSIE *is a prim secretary in pointed glasses and a frumpy coat. The bust of Nathaniel Burnham stands on a table near her.*

NICK *is a passenger, a turbaned Sikh in a suit. He is reads a newspaper with the headline 'LONELY HEARTS KILLER!'.*

AMANDA *is a passenger standing among the parked buses in a catsuit and a Purdy wig. She's eating a carrot.*

SIAN *is a busty trainee clippie in a short skirt at the clocking-in machine, the Szondi test picture placed on top.*

The end credits whizz by.

THE END